TO THE SECRETARY

TO THE SECRETARY

---

*Leaked Embassy Cables and
America's Foreign Policy Disconnect*

MARY
THOMPSON-JONES

W. W. NORTON & COMPANY
Independent Publishers Since 1923
NEW YORK   LONDON

Copyright © 2016 by Mary Thompson-Jones

For information about permission to reproduce selections from this book, write to Permissions, W. W. Norton & Company, Inc., 500 Fifth Avenue, New York, NY 10110

For information about special discounts for bulk purchases, please contact W. W. Norton Special Sales at specialsales@wwnorton.com or 800-233-4830

Manufacturing by RR Donnelley, North Harrisonburg
Book design by Brian Mulligan
Production manager: Louise Mattarelliano

ISBN 978-0-393-24658-2

W. W. Norton & Company, Inc.
500 Fifth Avenue, New York, N.Y. 10110
www.wwnorton.com

W. W. Norton & Company Ltd.
Castle House, 75/76 Wells Street, London W1T 3QT

1 2 3 4 5 6 7 8 9 0

To my mother and father,
Mary and Chet Thompson

CONTENTS

- - - - - - - - - - - -

TO THE SECRETARY

PROLOGUE

- - - - - - - - - - - -

ONE MORNING IN THE AUTUMN OF 2010, I STOOD IN front of a group of university students, handling the by-now-easy routine of questions and answers that followed the information session "What Is It Like to Be an American Diplomat?" As the State Department's New England Diplomat in Residence, I was one of a group of senior diplomats spread across the country, trying to connect with prospective candidates and demystify the route to becoming a foreign service officer. Diplomats in Residence appear at career days, as guest lecturers in international relations classes, and on panel discussions. Equipped with everything from glossy pamphlets to tablecloths, our job is to animate the role of an American diplomat. Most of us draw on our own years of experience and explain how foreign policy initiatives in Washington play out in our day-to-day work in embassies and consulates.

I used each student's question at the end of my talk to make a point about the foreign service, the selection process, the lifestyle, or how one moves through the ranks. Then came the question I was dreading.

"I was wondering how you feel about the WikiLeaks cables? I mean, they are supposed to be classified and all that, but some of us have been following all these stories in the *New York Times* and we're really fascinated by the cables they are publishing. Are they for real? Do you really get to go to weddings in Dagestan?"

I thought wryly, why should my job today be any easier than that of my colleagues overseas, who were no doubt really scrambling? I was lucky—my audience was a group of genuinely curious graduate students; theirs was genuinely furious foreign ministers.

I tried to place the leaked cables in historical context. I told the students that historians and other researchers rely on the FRUS volumes, the Foreign Relations of the United States, in which the government publishes cables and other official documents after they have gone through the declassification process. That process takes a long time and is always several decades behind current events. What makes the leaked cables so unprecedented is that they are available in real time.

Another student looked worried. "Should we be reading them at all? I heard that someone at Columbia University asked about this and was told that if you admit you read them, it could bar you from getting your security clearance."

A discussion broke out. "But how can we not read them? They are right there in the *New York Times*. They tell us we have to prepare for the exam by reading daily newspapers and news magazines. It's a free country and I'm not going to stop reading the newspaper!"

Exactly.

A student shyly raised her hand. "I knew you were coming today, so I looked for your cables, and I see that there are several hundred with your name at the bottom. Would you be willing to discuss some of the cables you wrote?"

Now we really were getting into uncharted waters. Of course I had read the *Times*'s stories, but I had not thought about how the leaked cables would change the kinds of conversations I had with students. Would I suddenly be accountable for every leaked cable on the WikiLeaks website? Momentarily dodging the question, I took the easy way out, explaining that most of the cables that bore my signature reflected the tradition that chiefs of mission sign off on cables written by officers on their staff.

My adventures that morning pulled me into the controversy in ways I hadn't expected. As a Boston-based diplomat for my current assignment, I missed the chance to sit in the State Department cafeteria in the lumbering Harry S Truman building, more commonly called Main State (to distinguish it from the many annex buildings around Washington) to exchange views with my colleagues. Even more, I missed being at my last embassy in Prague where I could commiserate with fellow officers and think strategically with them about the unforeseen impact of what had just happened. As WikiLeaks quickly became the week's lead news story, those who did speak out were mostly retired diplomats, and their take was one of outrage. As they harrumphed through the nightly news, I realized they hadn't heard the teachable moment I had in the classroom, where one student had said somewhat wistfully, "But this stuff is so cool."

Five years later, the passage of time offers a calmer vantage point to assess what the leaked cables did and didn't do to the world of diplomacy. When the newspaper-reading world awoke November 28, 2010, to read about the 251,287 leaked State Department cables, the scandal epitomized a digital information age replete with societies of hactivists, leakers, and outlaws. Most of the published cables were written between 2006 and 2010 and dealt with modern issues and contemporary leaders, the majority of whom were still in office.

The media outlets handpicked by WikiLeaks founder Julian Assange quite naturally explained the cables from a journalist's perspective. They selected the most newsworthy cables—ones that would make headlines, raise eyebrows, and irritate foreign governments. As a result, cable excerpts that were gossipy, titillating, or sure to shock fueled WikiLeaks' 15 minutes of fame (the five weeks between late November and the end of 2010).

And shock they did. When the world got an unprecedented behind-the-scenes look at what American diplomats had written,

then–Italian foreign minister Franco Frattini, no doubt voicing
the thoughts of many, said ominously, "This will be the September
11th of world diplomacy." Even the journalists involved felt they
had crossed a Rubicon. *New York Times* Executive Editor Bill Keller
wrote in his introduction to *Open Secrets*, the *Times*'s book based on
the news stories, "By the end of the year, the story of this wholesale
security breach had outgrown the story of the actual contents of the
secret documents, and had generated much breathless speculation
that something—journalism, diplomacy, life as we knew it—had
profoundly changed forever."

The story of the leaked cables is really 251,287 separate stories,
many of which are routine, some of which are sensational. Under the
terms of access granted by Julian Assange, competing media institutions suddenly had to find ways to work together—and to do so
quickly. The newspapers were further challenged by the mercurial
and temperamental personality of Assange, who alternately trusted
and distrusted his chosen outlets and managed to get arrested on
unrelated charges in the midst of the transaction.

Assange and the media were not always on the same page.
WikiLeaks's culture draws on a profound anger against government
institutions, an assumption of wrongdoing, and an anarchic dedica-
tion to radical transparency. Newspapers, at least those handpicked
by Assange, have a more balanced approach. They share a sense of
duty about exposing wrongful acts, but most reporters and editors
at elite papers also take a professional pride in getting it right. They
spend years developing high-level contacts in government and the
diplomatic corps, something Assange and his followers did not have.

The establishment media were slowed by legal and ethical fears
of inadvertently revealing information about embassy sources that
could put them in harm's way. The *New York Times* went so far as to
inform the White House of its intent to publish the cables on Friday,
November 19, nine days before the release date, and within hours the
Obama administration assembled a 120-person task force. Keller

described a tense scene the following Tuesday, November 23, when three *New York Times* staffers met with an interagency group at the State Department. The goal of subsequent meetings and conference calls was to redact names and other identifying material that would endanger sources. In contrast to other leaks of this magnitude, the State Department was an active participant in the days before the November 28 publication, redacting names and identifying vulnerable individuals. It also focused on damage control, arguing (usually unpersuasively) that unflattering portraits of world leaders would strain diplomatic relations. While it could not avoid embarrassment, by working with the *Times* it would at least know the worst.

The tight deadline was an important element in the drama, creating a race against time to get the cables into print. Assange's collaboration with the London *Guardian* began in June 2010, with the release of military dispatches from Afghanistan and Iraq, published as the War Logs, beginning in July. *Guardian* editor Alan Rusbridger contacted Keller at the *Times* to propose a collaboration to share the enormous labor and to increase the impact. Assange later raised loud objections to any collaboration with the *New York Times* after it ran a frank and unflattering profile of him on October 24. He told the *Guardian* that he preferred the *Washington Post* but was overruled because the *Guardian* had by then established working relationships and shared expertise with the *Times*. Assange widened the media circle to include German news magazine *Der Spiegel*, French daily *Le Monde*, and Spanish *El Pais*. Adding more media increased the chance of leaks, and dissenters within the WikiLeaks organization had begun their own series of smaller rogue leaks to other media. Accounts by both Keller and Rusbridger of the weeks leading up to publication are stories not only of rare collegiality but of breakneck speed and stress.[1]

And therein lies the problem. Even the best newspapers are by nature not reflective. They get one chance to publish and move on. Once a story is out, it is rare for a news organization to go back for a second look to add context, research, or additional quotes. This was particularly difficult for the WikiLeaks stories. No currently serving diplomats were allowed to discuss them or comment on the reaction to them since the cables were still considered classified. As a result, the WikiLeaks operation had an air of both haste and unfinished business. Barely a month after the story broke, the newspapers left it for the next big event.

In some ways, the leaked cables did U.S. diplomats a favor. They brought to light the importance of their role and their descriptive powers and offered glimpses of the fascinating backdrop against which they work. The U.S. government may have been embarrassed by candid descriptions of world leaders, but the cables reveal diplomats who are eager to interpret people and developments on the world stage for bosses back in Washington. They contribute to the body of knowledge policymakers rely upon to make decisions. They also add pathos and drama to crises. Minutes after a major event they are out and about, describing the scene on the streets. They rival the best travel writers in their engaging descriptions of remote places. Some of their cables are very funny.

With a few exceptions, the majority of cables discussed in the following chapters were written between January 1, 2006, and February 28, 2010, reflecting the end date of the tranche of cables that Private Chelsea Manning uploaded while stationed in Iraq. The vast majority were *from* embassies and consulates *to* Washington, offering a rare chance to hear from the practitioners and implementers in the field. WikiLeaks established a website, www.wikileaks.org, which contains a searchable database where all the cables can be read. Readers can search by embassy or consulate, by date, or by keyword. This leaves an almost infinite number of research possibilities. One could search for human rights, human rights in China, or human rights in China in 2008.

The chapters offer nine glimpses into embassy reporting on issues, countries, and people of particular interest between 2006 and 2010.

They also reveal some disturbing disconnects between Washington and the field. One of the legacies of the leaked cables is the dissonance they reveal between diplomats in embassies and policymakers in Washington. In an era in which America's global stock was exceptionally low, diplomats sometimes found themselves communicating to a headquarters that could not hear them. While every institution must deal with bureaucracy, and a certain amount of tension between the field and headquarters is normal, the stakes from 2006 to 2010 were particularly high. A Washington bureaucracy shaken by virulent anti-Americanism was obsessed with countering it. The diplomats gamely tried but reported little long-term success and offered their own analysis of the underlying problems.

As the students I'd addressed that morning in 2010 learned, this is the first time in U.S. diplomatic history that the public has had access to nearly the entire contents of four years' worth of embassy and consular reporting in real time. It is also a rare chance to see the practice and conduct of American diplomacy through the eyes of those posted overseas.

The cables depict two worlds that did not always align. Despite the Italian foreign minister's cry that the leaked cables would mark the end of diplomacy, a better image might be a *Through the Looking-Glass* moment in which readers could see diplomatic activity as it unfolded, with all its challenges and frustrations, carried out by a competent diplomatic corps, many of whom excelled at descriptive writing. What follows is their story of how, from 2006 through 2010, foreign service officers patiently advanced multiple and complex sets of competing interests in American foreign policy and tried to explain the outcomes to an occasionally distracted audience in Washington.

Chapter 1

251,287
LEAKED CABLES:
Monday, November 29, 2010

This disclosure is not just an attack on America's foreign policy interests. It is an attack on the international community, the alliances and partnerships, the conversations and negotiations that safeguard global security and advance economic prosperity.

—*Secretary of State Hillary Clinton*
November 30, 2010

AT 6:30 A.M. ON MONDAY, NOVEMBER 29, 2010, THE political officer at the U.S. embassy in Prague spun the dial for the third time, frustration at a maximum. The clunky steel Mosler safe contained her computer hard drive, without which there would be no cable writing. The tech team had reset the combination lock and she struggled to remember the new sequence.

She was anxious to record her impressions from a recent reception. At this still-dark hour, no one else had yet arrived who might help. Writing a classified cable on her laptop and then transferring it onto the classified system was a security violation. So were several other workarounds she could think of.

To get to the safe, she had already passed several checkpoints, beginning at the chancery entrance and post one, where a friendly new marine waved her in. She crossed the cobblestoned courtyard, long since accustomed to the oddly spaced stairs, designed for horses centuries ago when the building served as a palace. She coded in the cypher lock and climbed the elegant carpeted staircase, feeling a blast of welcome heat. At the landing, she took out her cell phone, forbidden beyond this point, and slid it into a cubby opposite rows of photos, mostly black and white, of former ambassadors, among them the mysteriously named Outerbridge Horsey. She punched in the second-floor code, crossed the foyer, and entered a third code to open the door to the political-economic section. Still ahead of her were a series of log-ons and passwords, and she made a mental note to forward calls from her cell phone in the cubby so they would roll over to her desk phone. But she still needed to retrieve her hard drive.

She gave the safe an unproductive kick. The collection of scuff marks near the bottom attested to a long history of officers in a hurry. She looked blankly at the dial, hoping for inspiration.

This was the state of embassy security in late November 2010. Foreign service officers sat through mandatory security seminars in Washington before being dispatched to the field. Once they arrived at their embassy, they were briefed again by the regional security officer, given badges to be worn at all times, and granted access—or not, depending on clearance level— to other restricted-access areas such as the DIA and CIA offices and the all-important SCIF (Sensitive Compartmented Information Facility), a room within a room and site of country team meetings, where the ambassador meets with senior officers and section heads from the many different U.S. government agencies that constitute an embassy. Large embassies may house representatives of more than two dozen agencies in addition to the State Department. Officers filled out clearance updates every five years and routinely sat with diplomatic security agents popping in to ask the usual questions about a colleague from a previous post who was up for security clearance renewal. Any unusual behavior—drugs, alcohol, financial problems?

For years the milder security infractions had meant little, but by 2010 the State Department had changed. Woe betide the officer who left a classified document on his desk. Once the safes were locked for the night, officers flipped wooden in-boxes upside down and topped them with tent cards that read NO CLASSIFIED DOCUMENTS! Marine security guards, whose mission at embassies is to protect such documents, patrolled determinedly in the dead of night looking for security violations. Unlucky officers who left a classified document out overnight arrived the following morning to find a dreaded pink form. Absolution required a meeting with the deputy chief of mission (DCM) and a lot of contrition. The State Department was now noting violations on an officer's permanent record, and too many incidents might bar a promotion, a coveted DCM assignment, or even an ambassadorship.

The political officer stood back, looked at the ceiling, and tried to clear her mind. She gave the dial one last try, pulled the steel lever, and heard the heavy *ka-dunk* that sounds the same at every post. The drawer screeched open, and she grabbed the hard drive. At last, her day could begin.

But on that morning, she wouldn't write her cable. The WikiLeaks scandal had broken the day before, stunning not only Washington, DC, but embassies, consulates, and other U.S. diplomatic installations. The impact was so profound that foreign service officers the world over were wondering how they would ever write—or be allowed to write—cables again. Could they ensure that confidential information never fell into the wrong hands? How could they perform what they considered to be the most important part of their jobs—providing subtext, context, and details that Washington policymakers would have no other way of knowing? On that Monday morning, nothing was clear.

The irony was not lost on the officers. All the cypher locks, combinations, steel safes, and marines were not enough to prevent the theft from within of a staggering number of cables—251,287, to be exact. In one of the more surreal elements of the breach, officers were forbidden from clicking on the WikiLeaks website, because the U.S. government insisted that the material (which the officers themselves had written) was now stolen property and still classified. Protests that foreign journalists and governments were voraciously reading the cables made no difference.

That Monday, officers huddled at every embassy around the world, trying to make sense of what had happened, to assess the damage, and to think what to do next. A culture with deep respect for protecting data and sources had suddenly blown wide open, revealing for all the world the careful, sometimes humorous, sometimes shocking details written for the tiniest of audiences.

CABLE LORE

The stolen cables had a long pedigree. Letters, early telegrams, and cables run like a seam through more than 235 years of American diplomacy. In the external world of England's Whitehall, France's Quai d'Orsay, and scores of other foreign ministries, diplomats attend meetings, present their government's position, and carefully negotiate. In their internal world, they try to make sense of what they see and hear for themselves and convey it to Washington through the quieter and more introspective act of writing telegrams for the official record.

Telegrams are old-fashioned, but irresistible. They serve a well-worn function in literature, largely because they are reserved for life's most important events. In period dramas, the arrival of the telegraph boy on his bicycle triggers suspense. Will it be news of a death, announce a visitor's unexpected arrival, or provide the vital clue to a murder mystery? An actor has only to open the envelope to transport the audience.

When telegrams are clothed in diplomatic lore, they become the game changers in power plays and secret plots. Diplomatic dispatches, a phrase that summons images of the British Empire and frantic messages from colonial outposts, bespeak a time when communications were not instantaneous but perhaps more considered. Secrecy was an essential part of the process, and writing and reading were time-consuming chores involving ciphers, codes, and transcriptions. This secrecy feeds notions of diplomacy as a world of elegance on the surface—with subtlety and calculation swirling underneath.

American diplomats have been writing home since colonial times, starting with America's first diplomat, Benjamin Franklin, who spent nine years in France (1776–1785) before being succeeded by Thomas Jefferson. Their missions—to get military help against the British and to obtain recognition as an independent nation, respectively—were not so different from the upstart states of today. Franklin, who never planned to stay for nine years, performed the job remarkably, and with notoriously poor French. Jefferson, who served in Paris from 1784 to 1789, seemed to enjoy it more before returning home to become the first U.S. secretary of state in 1790. The correspondence of these two men, which predates the advent of the telegram, forms the bedrock of American diplomatic history.

American diplomats also have been known for *not* writing home. Jefferson, by then president, became exasperated with one of his uncommunicative diplomats, and in a famous line that leaves harried modern diplomats longing for the good old days, wrote, "We have not heard from our Ambassador in Spain for two years. If we do not hear from him this year, let us write him a letter."[1] Jefferson had cause for concern. He was caught up in the Louisiana Purchase and had need of Ambassador Charles Pinckney's help to secure the deal.

No one would be allowed to be so dilatory as Pinckney ever again. The advent of the telegraph had, by the 1860s, slowly transformed diplomacy, reducing communication time from weeks or months (or years, in Pinckney's case) to a single day, giving governments the opportunity to issue instructions and demand answers, seizing the reins from freewheeling ambassadors and quickening the pace of diplomacy. For envoys used to autonomy and leisurely reflection, the instantaneity was a rude awakening. Stories of their institutional resistance read like comedies of manners. Technology-averse diplomats dug in against typewriters in favor of quill pens and copperplate calligraphy; they argued about whether correspondence should be kept folded or flat for filing and conspired against the intrusion of telephones in their offices.[2]

In a historical sense, the WikiLeaks release is not unprecedented. The tradition of governmental control of post and telegraph offices meant virtually all diplomatic correspondence was routinely intercepted. Gentlemen were indeed reading one another's mail. Leaks have been around for a long time, as have frustrated diplomats who believe their point of view is not heard back home. The advent of the telegraph office, a logical extension of the post office, opened a new era in intelligence gathering, with resulting requirements for both encryption and code breaking. Every advance in encryption was countered by an equal leap in deciphering, to the point that diplomats reverted to human couriers as a means of subverting this new and seemingly uncontrollable technology of their era.

Sometimes the content of a diplomatic telegram was so momentous it changed the course of history. For impact, it's hard to beat the Zimmermann Telegram, written in 1917 by German foreign secretary Arthur Zimmermann and sent to the German ambassador in Washington, DC, who was to forward it to the German ambassador in Mexico. The telegram instructed the German ambassador to meet with the Mexican president and propose Mexico's entry into World War I on the side of Germany, in exchange for Germany's help in regaining Mexico's lost territories of Texas, New Mexico, and Arizona. The Germans were about to resume unrestricted submarine warfare and knew this action would likely bring an outraged United States into the war. The telegram was deciphered by the British and given to the Americans, who now had two reasons to be angry at Germany. Given their own expertise in telegraph decoding, the Germans should hardly have been surprised that the British were reading their messages.

Another telegram that made history was Consul General Archer Blood's cable sent from the U.S. consulate in Dhaka on April 6, 1971, famous for being "probably the most blistering denunciation of U.S. foreign policy ever sent by its own diplomats."[3] Blood and his staff described the slaughter of Bengalis by the Pakistan Army and denounced the U.S. policy that allowed Pakistan to continue this genocide unchallenged. The famous cable was part of a stream of urgent accounts of atrocities sent from the consulate, all of which were met with silence from Washington. The cables were leaked, by an unknown source, to the *New York Times* and to Senator Edward Kennedy, giving him ammunition against Richard Nixon and Henry Kissinger's foreign policy. The series of reports out of Dhaka culminated in what became known as the Blood Telegram, the famous dissent cable signed by twenty officials at the Dhaka consulate and endorsed by nine officers working on South Asian issues within the State Department.[4]

Dissension from U.S. foreign policy while serving as a diplomat is a long and protected tradition—at least in theory. The State Department has a dissent channel, although few officers use it to express policy disagreement. The reception of Blood's cables is telling. Upon receiving the April 6 message, Secretary of State William Rogers was alarmed enough to call National Security Advisor Kissinger. "The telegram was 'miserable,' 'terrible,' and 'inexcusable.' It was bad enough that they 'had bitched about our policies,' but the real problem was that 'they had given it lots of distribution so it will probably leak,' railed Rogers to Kissinger."[5] Blood was soon transferred, as were many of his colleagues.

But even Blood's courageous telegram has not had the enduring influence of George Kennan's Long Telegram, setting out the U.S.

containment strategy for the Cold War era. Several generations of American diplomats and scholars of diplomacy view Kennan's cable, written on seventeen single-spaced pages not counting corrections in February 1946, as an aspirational ideal. The cable was later revised and published as "The Sources of Soviet Conduct" in *Foreign Affairs* in July 1947 under the pseudonym X. Even today the impact and reach of Kennan's cable astounds. What lonely foreign service officer, sitting in some forgotten outpost, has not dreamed of setting out for Washington's benefit the next containment policy? But many officers do not realize that Kennan, serving then as deputy chief of mission in Moscow, wrote partly in frustration. He felt his viewpoint was not reaching policymakers in Washington. It appears the disconnect between the field and Washington is indeed an old story.

Alas, Kennan's Long Telegram is remarkable for its uniqueness. No diplomat today, however ambitious, will be making policy from overseas. Even those who serve in Washington find themselves seated around crowded interagency tables that include an expanding list of members of the foreign policymaking, intelligence, and defense communities. Kennan's time is long past, and the opportunities for a talented foreign service officer to make a similar impact are as historical as the containment policy Kennan authored. But that doesn't mean they've stopped writing.

THE DIPLOMATS: WHO THEY ARE AND WHY THEY WRITE

Everyone has fun defining diplomacy. Some see it as a politer version of espionage, making it the world's so-called second oldest profession. Other half-serious definitions dwell on duplicity, such as Sir Henry Wotton's: "An ambassador is an honest man sent abroad to lie for his country." Thomas Pickering, one of the highest-ranked American diplomats and a seven-time ambassador said, "In archaeol-

ogy you uncover the unknown. In diplomacy you cover the known."
Another famous quip, attributed to Caskie Stinnett, suggests that
there is something not so nice about diplomacy: "A diplomat is a
person who can tell you to go to hell in such a way that you actually
look forward to the trip." Like all aphorisms, these exist for a reason.
They attest to the art of subtlety.

American diplomats may or may not be guilty of all the traits
ascribed to them, but they most certainly are analysts and writers. The
arduous selection process, which can take up to two years, ensures that
most diplomats write well. The fallout from that morning in November marked a rise in their stature. WikiLeaks, if nothing else, earned
diplomats the respect of journalists, who often write about the same
countries and issues. At the *Guardian*, one reporter mused, "Who knew
American diplomats could write so well?" *New York Times* chief Washington correspondent David Sanger said the cables were "often eloquent
and occasionally entertaining," while his colleague Executive Editor Bill
Keller found them to be "written with wit, color, and an ear for dialogue."[6] They wowed *Slate*'s Christopher Beam, who thought they read
"like their own literary genre, with an identifiable sensibility and set
of conventions."[7] Fareed Zakaria, writing in *Time*, found they showed
"an American diplomatic establishment that is pretty good at analysis,"
and British scholar Timothy Garton Ash celebrated accounts "almost
worthy of Evelyn Waugh," with writing that he found to be astute.[8]

According to the most recent Agency Financial Report, the State
Department employed about 73,000 people worldwide in 2015. The
roughly 7,900 foreign service officers (FSOs) are only a small fraction
of the U.S. government's overseas workforce, which also includes
about 5,700 foreign service specialists and 49,000 locally employed
staff, along with others from affiliated agencies such as USAID and
the Departments of Commerce and Agriculture. The FSOs populate
the five traditional career fields: consular, administrative, political,
economic, and public diplomacy. The specialists cover twenty-two
functions ranging from office management to information technol-

ogy to medical fields. Locally employed staff are the backbone of any embassy, spanning drivers in the motor pool all the way up to economic and political analysts, some of whom have PhDs. Given the two- to three-year tours of most FSOs, the local staff provides invaluable continuity, contacts, and historical perspective.

At any given time, about a third of all foreign service officers are assigned to Washington, DC, meaning that nearly all the reporting for cables that later appeared in WikiLeaks was done by about 5,500 FSOs serving in some 270 diplomatic missions overseas.[9]

Foreign service officers tend to be older than one might think—the median age of a newly hired FSO is thirty-one, but many begin this career in their forties or later. Virtually all have bachelor's degrees; more than half have master's or professional degrees. Some are former Peace Corps volunteers; others have served in the military. Some come from academia, some from private industry, some are lawyers, some are linguists. An increasing number have significant overseas experience, running exchange programs, working with nongovernmental organizations (NGOs), or reporting for news media. Nearly all have held jobs in which writing was important. They join the foreign service to serve their country, out of a sense of adventure, and with a desire to observe other cultures. The relatively short tours for most posts mean that their observations are fresh and rarely become routine.

All foreign service officers write cables, although the ones that garnered the most attention in WikiLeaks tended to come from political officers. By convention, cables are signed on the last line by the ambassador, or in his/her absence, by the chargé d'affaires, the acting ambassador who covers the gap until a new ambassador arrives. In point of practice, very few ambassadors do the actual writing, apart from first-person official-informal (OI) cables. Most diplomats aspire to become ambassadors, and some 65 to 70 percent of ambassadors are career diplomats who rise through the ranks, garnering years of experience at embassies, consulates, and domestic tours in the State

Department and other agencies. The remaining 30 to 35 percent, usually sent to Western Europe or to countries of enormous significance, such as China or Mexico, are political appointee ambassadors.

Some political appointees are former elected officials or distinguished public servants, such as former senator Max Baucus, ambassador to China, but others have come under fire for having minimal qualifications beyond financial support of the winning presidential candidate, a factor that sometimes puts Washington and career officers at odds in a way that long predates WikiLeaks. One group of ambassadorial nominees that appeared before the Senate Foreign Relations Committee for confirmation hearings in January 2014 was apparently so underprepared that Senator John McCain began correcting their erroneous statements. Hollywood producer Colleen Bell, nominated to be ambassador to Hungary, stumbled badly trying to articulate U.S. strategic interests in that country. "Great answer," McCain said, his sarcasm readily apparent. At the end of an embarrassing hearing for Bell and two other political ambassadorial nominees, McCain looked disgusted. "I have no more questions for this incredibly highly qualified group of nominees." Career FSOs may have grimaced inwardly but held their tongues.

If writing cables is not a fast track to an ambassadorship, why do diplomats write? In part because it is irresistible. FSOs seek careers that will transport them far from home. But that distance can be confusing, and reconciling Washington's policies with truths on the ground is frustrating. Diplomats make meaning of their surroundings by writing about them. For many officers, the process helps them make sense of new experiences. They often write private journals or blogs in addition to their official writing duties. A few write books upon retirement, especially memoirs. But some also put great effort into making their observations part of the historical record. While there will never be another George Kennan, there are plenty of opportunities to recount a conversation, to describe a political development, a crisis unfolding, or even a trip to the hinterlands.

Diplomats jump at penning these tiny pieces of history that will be part of the official record.

THE ART OF DIPLOMATIC REPORTING

Every day hundreds of cables flood into the State Department from its missions around the world. Dozens of bureaus are filled with personnel assigned to read them and take action. Mandatory reporting requirements mean the number of cables continues to increase, but too often foreign service officers are writing for a distracted audience of one: an overtasked desk officer who spends the usual two years in the assignment, discouraged from bringing any but the most noteworthy telegrams to the attention of busy superiors.

Understanding the flow of diplomatic reporting to and from Washington is a story of both too much and too little, and often not at the right time. Too much, because the daily tranche of cables guarantees an overwhelming amount of data; too little, because it is impossible to know and report on everything. At the wrong time, because of the speed at which Washington decision makers must function. While yesterday's diplomats waited for mail packets to be shipped across the Atlantic and for telegrams to be deciphered, today's can barely be out of the office for an hour before an urgent communication might arrive.

Knowing by instinct when and what to communicate back home is what makes a good diplomat. Their reporting must walk a line between loyally carrying out assignments from Washington, while making essential, sometimes contradictory, points to a foreign policy establishment that does not always want to hear them. In a tragic example of this disconnect, Ambassador Prudence Bushnell famously wrangled with the State Department over the security deficit at Embassy Nairobi in the months before the 1998 bombing that destroyed it and several surrounding structures. She sent multiple cables and pleaded for assistance, but with the State Department budget cut to the bone, security was expensive and subject to lengthy congressional consultations. "When I returned to Washington on consultations in December of '97, I was told point-blank by the AF [Africa Bureau] Executive Office to stop sending cables because people were getting very irritated with me. That really pushed up my blood pressure." Bushnell had the grim satisfaction of being right, as she stood at attention, still injured herself, alongside the flag-draped coffins of her colleagues following the al-Qaeda bombing that had left 213 dead.[10]

Ironically, when long-delayed security upgrades resulted in a building boom of dozens of new embassy compounds situated far from urban areas, diplomats fruitlessly complained that they were now working in fortresses that kept them away from terrorists and contacts alike. Some saw the new fortress mentality as a challenge—just another security hurdle to be overcome in a world full of locked safes and doors. Then, fourteen years after Bushnell's Nairobi experience, Ambassador J. Christopher Stevens and three of his colleagues were killed in Benghazi, Libya, on September 11–12, 2012.

Stevens, part of a new generation of diplomats, was a prime exemplar of the "transformational diplomacy" both Secretaries Condoleezza Rice and Hillary Clinton advocated. He had lived and worked in the region for years, spoke fluent Arabic, and performed the job he'd been asked to do—reaching out to segments of Libyan society during a troubled transition after the overthrow of dictator Muammar Gaddafi. The question of how much the State Department knew about the deteriorating Libyan security situation would derail Susan Rice's ambition to follow Hillary Clinton as secretary of state and colored Clinton's last appearance before the Senate as she ended her tenure. The Benghazi tragedy illustrates the tension between the security demands for safety and diplomats' need to get out of fortresslike embassies and meet with local people.

The U.S. Congress has an abiding interest in American diplomacy, and its engagement with diplomats encompasses Senate confirmation hearings for ambassadorial nominees and senior State Department officials; embassy efforts to broker meaningful in-country visits for congressional delegations; and Congress's interest in diplomatic reporting. Many of the 133,887 unclassified cables in WikiLeaks demonstrate the enormous growth of congressionally mandated cables. This category includes reports written to a one-size-fits-all template. Some examples include the annual Human Rights Report, the Trafficking in Persons Report, the International Religious Freedom Report, and the International Narcotics Control Strategy Report. Others are specific to certain groups of countries, such as the Special 301 Report, which rates countries' compliance with intellectual property rights, and the President's Emergency Plan for AIDS Relief, or PEPFAR.

The main categories of secret, confidential, and unclassified are just the beginning. Official-informal cables are often written in the first person by ambassadors, such as Christopher Dell's now well-publicized assessment of Zimbabwean leader Robert Mugabe. Scene setters are required in advance of visiting American policymakers, ranging from congressional delegations and administration officials up to and including cabinet officers and the president; such visits are always followed by a cable describing the visit, cleared when possible by the delegation head. Embassies also craft and update biographic profiles of heads of state, cabinet ministers, and parliamentarians, along with high-profile leaders from civil society, with the idea that any abrupt change of government should not leave Washington starting from scratch.

Foreign service officers also file spot reports, meant to be quick updates on unexpected developments, and election reports before, during, and after foreign voters go to the polls. Many embassies also submit daily media reaction, in which staffers translate excerpts from editorials and op-eds that cover themes Washington has flagged in a weekly watch list. During a crisis, embassy officers file situation reports, or sitreps, meant to provide the State Department's operations center with daily—or even hourly—updates. In the aftermath of the Haitian earthquake of January 12, 2010, there were dozens of sitreps from the embassy in Port-au-Prince. (More were likely sent after February 28, beyond the end date of the WikiLeaks release.)

Sometimes the demand for embassy reporting becomes insatiable. The State Department inspector general's May 2012 report on Embassy Islamabad came down hard on Washington's "intense and at times intrusive involvement and voracious appetite for information on Pakistan . . . consuming extraordinary amounts of the mission's time and energy and adding significantly to the stresses at the already stressed post."[11]

But when all of the above is accomplished, diplomats carve out time to record their own impressions, unbidden by Washington. These cables, akin to feature stories in journalism, are slices of life, things that catch the eye or ear of a curious diplomat. They round out the routine reporting and are among the best of the WikiLeaks release. Some of the more widely publicized cables chronicled weddings in Dagestan and conversations in cafes or corridors of power. Reading them offers insight into why people would do this work, despite the hardships of unaccompanied tours in Iraq, Afghanistan, and Pakistan. They want to experience something no Washington cubicle can offer. The cables illustrate too that the real meaning of living in Laos won't be found sitting behind the embassy walls of Vientiane.

Of course, cables are not the only way, nor always the best way, to communicate. Diplomats also use phones, and the frequency of visitors from Washington, as well as chances to return to headquarters for consultations, offer ample opportunities for face-to-face conversations, none of which are part of WikiLeaks. The leaked cables have their limitations. The format and intended audience predispose writers to portray countries through a solidly American lens—not always the best way to uncover more subtle distinctions. Officers are trained from the outset to link their cables to Washington interests and to anticipate and answer the "so what?" question.

Globalization has made countries more similar—especially in capital cities. Foreign ministries tend to organize themselves and operate in recognizable ways. Outside their doors, brand-name clothing stores, fast food outlets, and international manufacturers are familiar. Often, it is only when diplomats leave the embassy behind and travel beyond the capitals and government districts that countries appear different. Sometimes writers let go of the American lens and describe a country, its people, or an event in its own right. Unsurprisingly, these are often the most interesting cables.

SECRECY VERSUS DIPLOMACY

WikiLeaks claimed the cable dump was "the largest set of confidential documents ever to be released into the public domain," a claim that needs examining. It makes the feat sound more sensational than it actually was. Only about 6 percent of the cables—some 15,652—are classified as secret. Those marked confidential number 101,748. That means that a little more than half, or 133,887, are unclassified. The reason for this is obvious. Much of diplomatic work is routine, and diplomats frequently write with a wide audience in mind.

Much of the initial reporting about WikiLeaks focused on the sheer volume of the release. But volume does not equate to insight or revelation. Size is also relative. In the period from 2006 to 2010, the U.S. government disseminated 2.4 million cables, ten times as many, through other systems.[12] Seen that way, the total amount of classified data held by the U.S. government makes the WikiLeaks release look almost small.

News articles about WikiLeaks didn't mention that the officer writing the cable decides its level of classification—and gives a date upon which the cable may be declassified. What makes a cable deserving of classified status? The need to protect sources, along with the need to protect the U.S. government. Officers are told to ask themselves how damaging the information would be to national security were it to be disclosed. The government requires that the classification "secret" be applied to information whose unauthorized disclosure could reasonably be expected to cause *serious* damage to national security. "Confidential" should be applied to information whose unauthorized disclosure could reasonably be expected to cause damage to the national security.

This very imprecise, almost theological distinction assumes all officers define national security the same way. It also assumes an officer sitting in a remote posting would be able to know precisely how much damage disclosure of the information would cause. Sometimes the classification is obvious; other times it is arguable. Officers tend to overclassify on the theory that a secret cable will get more attention in Washington than a confidential one, and a cable marked unclassified must not say anything of importance. Former secretary of state George Shultz makes the point, "The higher the classified level of secrecy, the quicker you will report it." Thus relative importance tends to creep upward as officers consider how to classify their writing. And although the WikiLeaks release was an embarrassment to the U.S. government, potential embarrassment is not a classification factor.

The WikiLeaks organization made its selection of cables sound calculated and intentional. In fact, the feat was the electronic equivalent of sticking your hand into a bag of candy and scooping up as much as possible. In this case, the grab covered the period from December 28, 1966, through February 28, 2010, although the bulk of the cables are from January 2006 through February 2010. They originated from 275 American embassies, consulates, and diplomatic missions.

WikiLeaks director Julian Assange told the media that the cables showed "the extent of U.S. spying on its allies and the UN; turning a blind eye to corruption and human rights abuses in 'client states';

backroom deals with supposedly neutral countries; lobbying for U.S. corporations; and the measures U.S. diplomats take to advance those who have access to them."[13]

That is one interpretation, and some of the cables published in the *New York Times*, the *Guardian*, and elsewhere lend that view some credence. But lost in all the controversy is the understanding that the leaked cables are only half of the equation—they reflect the view from the field, not the home office. Assange was shooting the messenger, who, the cables show, was making the best of instructions that were not always feasible.

Assange also castigated diplomats for lobbying for corporations. Indeed, that is a straightforward part of their mission, and one that Congress and the corporate world emphatically expect. Seeking a level playing field when U.S. corporations are bidding on lucrative tenders is a time-honored part of diplomatic work. And in a world where bribery, corruption, and lack of transparency are too frequently the norm, it is a necessary part of the job.

WikiLeaks misunderstands the purpose of diplomacy by confusing it with secrecy. Assange's overriding contempt for the American government blinded him to some subtle aspects of the practice of modern diplomacy. He was sure the cables showed "duplicity and mendacity in action." Journalists were largely unpersuaded, with Fareed Zakaria noting, "There is little deception." A more considered explanation is that the cables show the analytical value added of officers in the field and demonstrate the reason all countries have embassies. If Washington needed only facts, policymakers could read the *New York Times* and watch CNN. Diplomats are trained to provide far more. Like reporters, they rely heavily on sources, and for the same reasons they would not survive if they were, as Assange believed, duplicitous and mendacious.

Ambassadors enjoy enviable access and go where reporters often cannot. They are invited to the inner sanctums of presidents, ministers, and parliamentarians. Working-level diplomats seek out thinkers

behind ideas and causes that may or may not coincide with U.S. interests. Where it exists, they engage with civil society. With resources
unmatched by any but the wealthiest of NGOs, they go everywhere.
Diplomats stay in one country for only two or three years, but over
the course of a career they learn to find the right people, ask the right
questions, and make the most of their limited time. Timothy Garton
Ash noted the similarities between diplomats and foreign correspon-
dents, but he also drew a distinction. "There is a particular quality to
what a head of state or government—the king of Saudi Arabia or the
French president—says to the ambassador of a superpower—which,
of course, gives it a different quality. It's not just like talking to the
New York Times."[14]

Diplomats also deliver messages, but doing that well is a two-way
street. They are not only adept at writing *to* Washington but invaluable at helping foreign leaders decode messages *from* Washington.
While onetime presidential candidate Ross Perot famously said that
diplomats could be replaced by fax machines, he ignored the real art
in delivering a message that offers an opportunity for a conversation.
Diplomats listen for the reaction. In many cultures a diplomat has to
know when yes means no, or maybe, or we'll see. The most skillful
diplomats not only deliver messages but explore them with the recipients, test out scenarios, suggest ways of using the information, and
discuss the implications of the message. This is hard work. Assange's
rant falls far from the reality.

THE DIPLOMATIC FALLOUT

In Buenos Aires, the chargé told his colleagues, "We have two bad
choices: try to run and hide or go out and take a beating." He
chose to engage the press and defend diplomacy—with a dose of
humility.[15]

Half a world away, the political officer's cell phone rang out in the cubby, and the call rolled over to her desk phone. An old source, sounding more bemused than worried, wanted to know if he would be featured on WikiLeaks.

Throughout the week of November 29, 2010, American diplomats around the world were receiving similar phone calls and queries. At best, their contacts were unsettled. At worst they felt betrayed.

Obama administration officials were quick to deplore the leaks but almost equally quick to minimize them. Members of Congress were also out of sync. Some took a hard line, such as Senate Republican leader Mitch McConnell, who called Assange a "high-tech terrorist," and Senator Lindsey Graham, who said "People who do this are low on the food chain, as far as I'm concerned." On the other side of the question, if not the aisle, former Representative Ron Paul said the leaks had caused "no harm to any individual," and that "the hysterical reaction makes one wonder if this is not an example of killing the messenger."

Former Arkansas governor and presidential candidate Mike Huckabee said, "Anything less than execution is too kind a penalty" for the source of the leaks. Former senator Joe Lieberman offered an assessment worthy of a middle school principal with the underwhelming suggestion that the *New York Times* was guilty of "bad citizenship."

Every aspect of the circumstances surrounding the leak was contentious. Some Washington columnists pointed to the more gossipy bits of the cables as proof that the reporting should not be taken seriously; others used examples from the same cables to argue that it should be. One victim of the difficulty in striking the right tone was State Department spokesperson P. J. Crowley, who was forced to resign on March 13, 2011, after describing the conditions under which Private Chelsea Manning was being held as "ridiculous and counterproductive and stupid."

The diplomats in the field kept their own counsel, having been stunned twice. It was bad enough to deal with the publication of writings about sources they still saw on a daily basis, but now they were thrown off balance by the whipsaw PR offensive in Washington.

While most of those currently serving refrained from speaking, they counted on their retired colleagues to defend and explain their work. The retirees took a predictable line.

Former ambassador Ronald Neumann, president of the American Academy of Diplomacy, told NPR, "I'm amused by the fact that people are finding it surprising that cables are frank. . . . They think because we're not always frank in public that we can't be frank with each other." Speaking on the same program, former ambassador Christopher Hill, now dean of the Josef Korbel School of International Studies at the University of Denver, said WikiLeaks would have a chilling effect. "It's hard to have a senior official of a foreign government say things in front of a note taker just to begin with, and now to worry that those notes will be not only turned into a cable but that the cable will be turned into a newspaper article is worrisome."[16]

Former ambassador to NATO and Greece and current Harvard Kennedy School professor Nicholas Burns said the damage was enormous. "I think the leaking of these cables has been a travesty," Burns said. "He [Assange] has done great harm to our diplomacy, because it strikes at the heart of what diplomacy is: The building of trust between people and between governments. The leaks violate that trust and are going to make some people, not everyone or every government, but some people, much more reluctant to discuss their affairs with American diplomats."[17]

Stephen Hadley, former national security advisor, said on the PBS *NewsHour* that in the short run, "It's going to have some very deleterious effects . . . if we cannot keep the secrets and the confidences of other governments, they will be reluctant to share their innermost thoughts with us. It also is corrupting because our people in diplomatic posts overseas want to be able to give their candid assessments about people with whom they're dealing . . . It's important to inform the president, secretary of state. They will now be reluctant to be as candid in the reporting cables."[18]

Speaking on the same news show, former national security advisor

Zbigniew Brzezinski, also inclined to the long view, breezily described the leaks with a phrase he said dated back to the Austro-Hungarian Empire: "It's catastrophic, but not serious." Brzezinski also deprecated the impact of leaked biographic reporting: "Who cares if Berlusconi is described as a clown? Most Italians agree with that. Who cares if Putin is described as an alpha dog? He probably is flattered by it."

Secrecy is a troubling concept for the American body politic. John Campbell, writing in the Council on Foreign Relations' Expert Roundup, noted that WikiLeaks offends a fundamental American assumption about openness.[19] Taking that argument further, the idea of secret cables contradicts the Wilsonian view of diplomacy that has worked its way into the American consciousness as evinced in the first of Woodrow Wilson's Fourteen Points: "Open covenants of peace, openly arrived at, after which there shall be no private international understandings of any kind but diplomacy shall proceed always frankly and in the public view." Such ringing words sound great but reveal a naiveté about how modern diplomacy works.

This uniquely American belief that diplomacy should be transparent ran headlong into WikiLeaks, which seemed to show American diplomats as secretive. Politicians found it easy to use WikiLeaks to leverage the notion that diplomats are disloyal and unaccountable for the behind-the-scenes deals they make. This kind of thinking is compounded by the State Department's inability to articulate and create public support for its role. A comment by former Texas governor Rick Perry in a November 11, 2011, radio program with Fox News host Bill O'Reilly symbolized the depth of the problem. "I'm not sure our State Department serves us well. I'm not talking about the Secretary of State here. I'm talking about the career diplomats . . . who all too often may not be making decisions or giving advice to the administration that's in this country's best interest."

Those words, uttered nearly a year after the WikiLeaks release, resonate for a segment of the population whose distrust for the State Department and diplomacy is deep-rooted and ongoing.

NO BIG DEAL

Signs of the disconnect between Washington and its diplomats emerged the same day as the WikiLeaks release. The Obama administration was quick to distance itself from WikiLeaks, from the content of the leaked cables, and occasionally, even from those who wrote them. The lines became so blurred that it was hard to tell if the real problem was WikiLeaks or the cable writers. At worst, diplomats overseas were either disenfranchised from the foreign policy establishment or made invisible. The tone around Washington was dismissive.

"I want to make clear that our official foreign policy is not set through these messages, but here in Washington," Secretary of State Clinton said at a November 29 press conference, leaving the role of U.S. diplomats in foreign policy an open question.

White House spokesperson Robert Gibbs joined the effort to downgrade the cables, saying, "By its very nature, field reporting to Washington is candid and often incomplete information. It is not an expression of policy, nor does it always shape final policy decisions." Listeners were left to wonder what was the point of having diplomats, if all they offer is incomplete information and they don't shape policy decisions.

Defense Secretary Robert Gates also dismissed the idea of any real damage. "I've heard the impact of these releases on our foreign policy described as a meltdown, as a game changer, and so on. I think those descriptions are fairly significantly overwrought. The fact is, governments deal with the United States because it's in their interest, not because they like us, not because they trust us, and not because they believe we can keep secrets." Gates insisted information sharing would continue. "Is this embarrassing? Yes. Is it awkward? Yes. Consequences for U.S. foreign policy? I think fairly modest."[20]

Gates offered a historical perspective, quoting John Adams,

to illustrate that WikiLeaks was nothing new. "How can a government go on, publishing all of their negotiations with foreign
nations, I know not. To me, this appears as dangerous and perni-
cious as it is novel." To Gates's way of thinking, WikiLeaks was a
more modern version of the back rooms in telegraph offices where
diplomatic dispatches were routinely decoded before being sent
onward.

In an understandable rush to minimize the crisis, the cable writers
were minimized too. Washington's dismissive tone often focused on
the relative weight and importance of the cables, rather than the leak
itself. That had the unfortunate ancillary effect of associating the diplomats with the embarrassment. Absent from the State Department,
White House, and Defense Department response was any mention
that diplomats are members of the U.S. foreign policy community
who contribute to informed internal debate, enhanced by the fact
that they live, work, and often speak the language in some of the
world's most remote and complex countries.

Instead, Washington spokespeople were quick with indignation
over WikiLeaks' putting sources at risk, a fact they mentioned often.
What they always failed to mention was that one of the most damaging cables, instructing diplomats to collect cell phone and credit card
information on foreign diplomats working at the United Nations,
actually came from Foggy Bottom.

The Washington line was a success, of sorts. A few commentators
furthered the misalignment between the field and Washington by
opining that the diplomatic reporting was not much more than a
collection of gossipy cables, such as one citing Muammar Gaddafi's
relations with his voluptuous Ukrainian nurse, and was of negligible
impact on foreign policy.

But there was a downside to the minimization. Frederick Hitz,
senior fellow at the University of Virginia's Center for National Security Law and former CIA inspector general, said the attempt to minimize had gone so far that the government had substantially weakened

its own case against Assange. "American officials are working over-time to downplay the seriousness of the leaks. And as embarrassing as they are, that's not the standard of prosecution."[21]

Asked if it wasn't ironic, inconsistent, or even hypocritical that Secretary of State Clinton's much-publicized Internet Freedom Initiative, articulated in a Newseum speech in January 2010, was in conflict with those like Assange who were pushing the boundaries of that freedom, Hitz agreed. "They are walking a tightrope, to be sure. In one sense transparency is good, in another seeing your own diplomatic cables displayed on pages of the *New York Times* is disquieting."[22]

Clinton's remarks to the State Department traveling press on January 9, 2011, seemed to bear out his observation. "I think I will be answering concerns about WikiLeaks for the rest of my life, not just the rest of my tenure as secretary of state. I've told my team that I want to get one of those really sharp-looking jackets that rock-and-roll groups have on tours. And I could have a big picture of the world, and it could say 'The Apology Tour.'"

Clinton's public remarks furthered the idea that it was an etiquette flap rather than a security breach, repairable with exhausting rounds of polite visits and reassuring phone calls. Despite a humorous delivery, her message suggested that only thanks to endless work had the matter begun to fade.

"I have been very, very much involved in reaching out to leaders and others who have concerns about either the general message of our confidential communications being exposed in this way or specific questions about their country or themselves," she said. "That aspect has receded a lot. I've done an enormous amount of work, as have other members of our government, but it still is in the atmosphere."

Hitz's warning would prove prescient. By 2013 it was clear that the Department of Justice was unlikely to mount a case against Assange, with most legal experts agreeing that his role as recipient of leaked material was different from that of Private Manning's.

What no one knew on that Monday morning in November 2010 was that WikiLeaks was only the first of many incidents in which government secrets, large and small, would be revealed. Edward Snowden was waiting in the wings. The Russians would tweet an eavesdropped conversation in which the State Department's assistant secretary for European affairs and the U.S. ambassador to Ukraine would scheme over who should and should not be in a future Ukranian government. Revelations that America was not alone in spying would come to the fore.

But the most important disconnect was far more subtle. From one topic to another, the cables reveal a rift between diplomats' pragmatic and realistic view of what was possible in the world of 2006 to 2010 and Washington policymakers' far more ideological and ambitious agenda.

Chapter 2

- - - - - - - - - - - - - -

ANTI-AMERICANISM:
Let's Burn the Flag!

- - - - - - - - - - - - - -

Trying to get foreigners to like us is the default endeavor of the State Department's public affairs office, and in my view, it's largely a waste of time.

—*James Glassman,*
former Under Secretary
for Public Diplomacy and Public Affairs April 16, 2014

- - - - - - - - - - - - - -

ON A FRIGID WEEK IN EARLY JANUARY 2008, NEWLY elected Representative Keith Ellison (D-MN) stood at the U.S. ambassador's residence in Oslo, chatting with a group of Norwegian immigrants from Africa, Asia, and the Arab world. Ellison represents one of the most traditionally Norwegian-American constituencies in the United States, but what made his visit noteworthy was that he was the first Muslim elected to Congress (and also the first African-American elected to the House of Representatives from Minnesota). His swearing-in ceremony with a Qur'an once owned by Thomas Jefferson had made headlines.

The Oslo event ran overtime as Ellison fielded questions about how he could represent a country "at war with Islam"; what he thought about reparations for slavery; and whether he was able to speak freely in the United States as someone who criticized Bush administration policies. The embassy, highly pleased, reported that Ellison "helped counter simplistic and irrational anti-Americanism."[1]

This is Norway, a friendly ally. Like many Western European countries, it has welcomed Muslim immigrants who have integrated with varying degrees of success. Events across Europe since WikiLeaks suggest meetings with immigrant communities ought to be an important part of American diplomacy. But American officials don't always do this effectively.

Cases in point were the misadventures of Karen Hughes, under secretary for Public Diplomacy and Public Affairs, who embarked on a widely publicized "listening tour," in 2005 in which she sought out encounters with Saudi, Indonesian, Turkish, and Egyptian audiences. In contrast to the triumphal reports from Oslo, the embassies that arranged Hughes's visit were mostly silent. They left it to the *New York Times* and *Washington Post* reporters who traveled with Hughes to describe the tenor of her meetings. Elite Saudi women disputed Hughes's notion that their lives needed improving, saying, "Well, we're all pretty happy."[2] Turkish women confronted her with heated complaints about the Iraq war, "turning a session designed to highlight the empowering of women into a raw display of anger at U.S. policies in the region."[3] American reporters lampooned Hughes for tirelessly introducing herself as a "mom" and for "her tin-eared assurances that President Bush is a man of God."[4]

There are no leaked cables touching on these gaffes and awkward moments. High-level official visits like Hughes's require reports from embassies—but custom dictates that the visitor clears the cable, making it nearly impossible to offer an unbiased account. Embassy Cairo skirted the issue and reported only on Hughes's meeting with Prime Minister Ahmed Nazif.[5] Embassy Riyadh dodged the issue by noting Hughes had brought books for a library and requested more of the same.[6] Embassy Ankara solved the problem by reporting on Turkish media coverage of Hughes's visit, which it characterized as fair and factual. The diplomats left it to *Hurriyet*, Turkey's influential daily, to describe the scene. "She had some difficult moments when many of the women criticized U.S. policy in Iraq. A KA-DER member . . . called on the United States to end wars that lead to poverty. Hughes responded that as a mother, she also did not like war, but added that sometimes war is necessary to protect the peace."[7]

Embassy reports on the visits by Ellison and Hughes illustrate a long-standing reliance on public diplomacy as a corrective to polish the rough edges of U.S. foreign policy. While all nations understand the need for public relations, Americans may be unique in their persistence in reaching beyond governments to engage directly with the people. Speeches make careful distinction between foreign leaders, who may be out of favor, and foreign people, who never are. Even in countries in which participatory democracy is a pipe dream, American diplomats routinely meet with people far from power, operating on the theory that even if their vote doesn't count, their opinion might. They reach out to subgroups such as immigrants in Norway, women in Saudi Arabia, and dissidents in Russia. Doing this effectively takes skill and insight. While delivering a message to the foreign ministry, a mainstay of traditional diplomacy, is easy, winning friends for America is harder.

Public diplomacy cannot be a cure-all for unpopular policies. But the habit of forging policy in Washington and tasking diplomats with implementing it sets up a disconnect. Confronted with images of angry foreign crowds burning the flag, policymakers wonder why diplomats don't do a better job; diplomats wonder why policymakers are surprised by protests and why they aren't more interested in their knowledge of the local scene.

Diplomats who specialize in public diplomacy have at their disposal a toolkit that offers traditional soft power—academic exchanges such as the Fulbright program and cultural offerings such as jazz ambassadors—and hard power programs, such as international broadcasting in local languages and engagement with media. Visits from prominent U.S. experts from the worlds of sports, entertainment, academia, or politics are essential components of that toolkit, all of which is aimed at increasing understanding and enthusiasm for America.

Public diplomacy falls in and out of favor with policymakers. At the end of the Cold War, Congress saw little need to fund it. Having won the ideological war against communism, it seemed clear that the world was rapidly embracing democracy and free market models. Practitioners argued in vain that public diplomacy is a long-term investment. It is also costly and maddeningly difficult to show results. Cultural programs have been particularly vulnerable to skeptics who are unpersuaded the world needs another American quilt exhibit, another Fulbright grant, or another jazz concert. These critics demand proof that such programs make a difference in global public opinion. They seek to tie public diplomacy programs to one essential question: What can we do about the way the world views the United States?

After 9/11 Washington became obsessed with anti-Americanism. Successive polls taken by the Pew Research Center Global Attitudes Project showed astounding drops in support even from staunch allies, with some approval ratings in the teens or single digits.[8] Polls by Gallup and Zogby, which covers the Middle East, produced similar results.

How bad was it? One Pew report showed America's approval rating in Germany had plummeted from 78 percent in 2000 to 30 percent by 2007. Some shakier allies were even more dubious about the United States. In Turkey, approval ratings were at a dismal 9 percent; and in Greece, another NATO ally, only 34 percent held favorable views of the United States. That drop in Greece was further documented by a February 2010 U.S. Embassy Athens cable reporting that an astounding 73 percent of Greek military officers believed Greece would be better off in a military alliance with Russia.[9]

The Pew Research Center's Global Attitudes Project in 2008 noted that "in Muslim nations, the wars in Afghanistan and particularly Iraq have driven negative ratings nearly off the charts . . . In the view of much of the world, the United States has played the role of bully in the school yard, throwing its weight around with little regard for others' interests."[10]

The Pew surveys reported that public opinion in countries less closely linked to the United States was even worse. In Argentina, only 16 percent of the public had a favorable view of the United States in 2007; in Pakistan the total was 15 percent; Egypt was at 21 percent.[11] While public opinion polls can be a blunt instrument for measuring fickle and nuanced attitudes, they also can be an important bellwether of dramatic shifts.

Pew surveys revealed complaints that America acts unilaterally; doesn't take into account the interests of other nations in formulating policy; relies too much on military force; does too little to address the world's problems, many of which it causes; and has widened the gulf between rich and poor. "On matters ranging from promotion of democracy to globalization to international security, the rest of the world became openly skeptical of America's word and intentions over most of this decade."[12]

Pew's late president, Andrew Kohut, told a congressional committee that anti-Americanism is an intensively held opinion, which makes it difficult to change, and that "it is no longer just the U.S. as a country that is perceived negatively, but increasingly the American people as well, a sign that anti-American opinions are deepening and becoming more entrenched."[13] Embassy reporting cables substantiate the data and provide context for the low percentages.

The polls, along with growing numbers of anti-American incidents, led panicky policymakers to set up countless panels, commissions, and studies, all charged with fixing America's public image problem. Almost invariably, Washington insiders convened these efforts without soliciting insights from the diplomats who had witnessed firsthand this global no-confidence vote. The commissions and their conclusions, when contrasted with the reporting cables, expose borderline disarray between Washington and the field.

THE MANY WAYS TO HATE US:
TALES FROM ABROAD

After 9/11, Washington may have been seized with the need for outreach to Muslims, but embassies all around the globe were reporting
to Washington about the depth and extent of anti-American sentiment that went well beyond the Muslim world. There seemed to
be no overarching theme but rather a fury based on each country's
circumstances. Angry mobs torched the U.S. embassy in Belgrade
on February 21, 2008, because the United States recognized Kosovo.
Populist Venezuelan dictator Hugo Chávez made outrageous statements that fomented a new wave of anti-Americanism across Latin
America. Protestors in Zimbabwe didn't like U.S. sanctions; Canadian television shows featured plots that emphasized U.S. lawlessness.

Embassy officers were close enough to smell the tear gas and
smoke from burning effigies, and some cable writers were enthusiastic in describing the more outlandish lengths to which countries,
governments, politicians, and local media would go to tweak the
eagle's beak.

The U.S. consulate in Jeddah reported that a North African astrologer, locally renowned for his accurate forecasts, predicted that President Bush would be assassinated sometime in 2007. The claim was
quickly posted to the Islamic extremist Al Sahat website. Internet
visitors left prayers, known as *doa'a*, for the assassination to occur,
giving a grim new meaning to the idea of praying for leaders. Within
days, the site had recorded more than 24,000 hits.[14]

In the Gulf region, Embassy Manama reported the good news that
commemorations for the Shia holiday of Ashura were less offensive
in 2007. "The U.S. and Israeli flags nailed into the street for people
to walk on were not present this year."[15]

In Islamic countries, Friday sermons are a good way to gauge
anti-Americanism, and on a March day in Khobar at the Imam

Ahmad bin Hanbal mosque, Sheikh al-Qahtani did not disappoint. A consular official sat through his sweeping views of American misdeeds throughout history, starting with the colonists' slaughter of Native Americans, running right up to the fluctuations in the stock market. He admonished his congregation "never to believe America's failed propaganda war deceiving Arabs and Muslims alike"; derided what he called failed American efforts to improve its public image in Arab and Muslim countries; and ominously warned that "things may even get worse as long as Guantanamo, Abu Ghraib, Afghanistan, and Palestine remain fresh in people's minds."[16]

In Saharan African, U.S. Embassy Nouakchott described a rash of groundless, paranoid press reports of alleged U.S. spying. One news story noted the chargé was seen in the company of a uniformed U.S. military man (a bodyguard), and several papers alleged that the Marine House (a dormitory for off-duty marines attached to the embassy) was a secret CIA prison. Peace Corps volunteers were also accused of spying, and one paper offered proof through photos of the U.S. embassy cafeteria and the chargé at a ceremony for U.N. Human Rights Day. The cause of all this hullabaloo? The chargé had called a recent coup a coup, rather than using the preferred politically correct term, "event."[17]

Strained U.S.–Zimbabwean relations are nothing new, so a cable from the embassy in Harare shrugged off a protest of a thousand chanting youths bused in from rural areas, wearing matching t-shirts emblazoned SANCTIONS ARE CRIMINAL and carrying professional-looking placards, referring to U.S. sanctions against the government of longtime strongman Robert Mugabe. They booed, pumped fists, sang political songs, and called for war with America. After a strong finish that included taunting the local guard force, the crowd moved discreetly down the street to receive payment.[18]

Sometimes, embassies struggled to know where to begin to counter outright lies and disinformation. In one of the more bizarre examples, Tajikistan's Ministry of Internal Affairs published a pamphlet saying

that Afghan farmers began producing opium poppy at the behest
of the U.S. government; that Americans profited from this business; and that the United States wished to destroy Persian, Islamic,
and former Soviet societies through drug addiction. Embassy Drug
Enforcement Administration officers met with the commander of
the ministry's narcotics unit, where they were treated to "an angry
tirade from the unit chief, who defended the allegations, claimed
they were true because they could be found on the Internet, said the
U.S. government had in fact done much worse than the allegations
in question, and insulted the embassy officers and the ambassador."
The DEA officers walked out of the meeting.

Not willing to give up so easily, the ambassador went to the commander's boss, the interior minister, who disavowed the pamphlet,
said he had not authorized it, and had not yet had time to examine
it. The embassy offered an understated comment: "Old Soviet and
more recent Russian propaganda against the United States influences
individual officials in Tajikistan. This incident highlights the public
diplomacy challenge we face in defending U.S. interests here."[19]

Latin America offers an abundance of equally bizarre rhetoric. It's
hard to see why the United States would bother dignifying Hugo
Chávez's utterances with a response. He once compared George
W. Bush to Hitler and warned that exporting Halloween to Latin
America was tantamount to terrorism; he also told the U.N. General
Assembly that Bush was "the devil himself" and had left a smell of
sulphur in the Assembly chamber.[20]

But Chávez had lots of company in the region. Piling on from
anti-U.S. stalwarts such as Cuba, Nicaragua, and Ecuador might well
be expected, but even Brazil exhibited entrenched, generations-long
anti-Americanism. In an analysis of foreign ministry leadership,
the embassy noted that one of the three senior-most diplomats was
"virulently anti-American, and anti–first world in general. He has
advocated extreme positions . . . that Brazil must develop nuclear
weapons—and as the senior official in charge of personnel matters,

issued a required reading list of anti-American books that has only recently been toned down."[21]

American popular culture—music, films, and television shows—and its commercial orientation rarely represents the best of U.S. culture. American diplomats worried about conclusions Egyptians and Saudis would draw from watching *The Simpsons, Desperate Housewives,* and *Friends.*[22] And yet, one Saudi television executive told the embassy that American television is "winning over ordinary Saudis in a way that Alhurra (a U.S.-funded Arab-language satellite television network) and other U.S. propaganda never could." In the ultimate irony, the executive said the programming had been so effective that it was widely assumed the U.S. government must be behind it.[23]

Far from the Muslim world, Embassy Ottawa gave a run-down of anti-Americanism Canadian-style on several TV shows. In a humorless analysis, the writer alleged "the level of anti-American melodrama has been given a huge boost . . . as a number of programs offer Canadian viewers their fill of nefarious American officials carrying out equally nefarious deeds in Canada while Canadian officials either oppose them or fail trying." The writer described episodes and plots featuring CIA rendition flights, schemes to steal Canada's water, and F-16s flying in for bombing runs in Quebec to eliminate escaped terrorists. The writer, who seemed to have momentarily forgotten that this was merely entertainment, warned that "twisting current events to feed long-standing negative images of the U.S.—and the extent to which the Canadian public seems willing to indulge in the feast—is noteworthy as an indication of the kind of insidious negative popular stereotyping we are increasingly up against in Canada."[24] The author somehow missed an earlier and much-beloved Canadian show, *This Hour Has 22 Minutes,* with Rick Mercer's weekly feature, "Talking to Americans," in which he enticed prominent American politicians (including governors and presidential candidates) to comment on ridiculous statements designed to show how little Americans know about Canada.

Spy-versus-spy antics in Nouakchott and the latest rants from Chávez in Caracas are amusing and mostly harmless, but it's quite another thing to read thoughtful reporting from intelligent observers in key countries like Russia, Turkey, or France. Embassy officers described their conversations with sophisticated opinion leaders who showed the depth and complexity of anti-Americanism.

Istanbul media representatives offered a thoughtful analysis of what they described as a deep and potent anger and mistrust of the United States. One editor explained that the views of Turkish youths toward the United States were not fundamentally anti-American but a reaction to Bush administration policies toward the Middle East, Iraq, Iran, and the PKK (the Kurdistan Workers' Party). Another editor criticized Bush's use of the word *crusade* in describing the fight against terrorism, which the public perceived as anti-Islam.[25]

In 2007, Russian analysts linked anti-Americanism to unpopular U.S. policies, including missile defense. Both pro-Kremlin and liberal analysts told U.S. diplomats that anti-Americanism was popular across all major political parties and helped forge a political consensus in favor of a resurgent Russia playing a more assertive role internationally. They said some Russians see the United States as playing the role of puppeteer, encouraging misbehavior by Poland and the Baltics and trying to set the "new" Europe against Russia's "old" partners.[26] This distinction between new and old Europe surfaced frequently following the collapse of communism and was often shorthand for a view of a still-divided continent.

Despite the well-publicized U.S. "reset" on Russian relations, prominent Russian analysts told assistant secretary for European Affairs Philip Gordon that U.S.–Russian relations had continued their slide. One asserted that anti-Americanism "was a pillar of Russian foreign policy," citing Russian public opinion polling that showed the percentage of Russians who believed the United States presented the greatest terrorist threat had grown from 8 percent in 2007 to 26 percent in 2009. Turning to the July 2009 meeting between President Barack Obama and then–prime minister Vladimir Putin, analysts said that while there was a temporary uptick in U.S.–Russian relations, "darker forces" were consolidating. While anti-American sentiment had been muzzled immediately after the meeting, it persisted. The United States was an easy target and kept the Russian people mobilized. The analysts noted that Obama's speech at the New Economic School in Moscow was seen by only 1 percent of the public, and Russian television only gave "half a sentence" to the civil society forum, another U.S.-run feature of his visit. They concluded gloomily that "Russian leadership had no interest in showing Obama's visit in a positive light."[27]

In a separate conversation, the political director of the French Ministry of Foreign Affairs, Gérard Araud, offered the U.S. ambassador a French interpretation of Russia's negative fixation with America. Araud, who had returned from Moscow the day before, described a meeting in which he and his boss, Foreign Minister Philippe Douste-Blazy, had barely sat down when Putin launched into "a half-hour anti-U.S. harangue bringing together a catalog of complaints and charges about U.S. behavior." Araud said "Putin offered up a 'rambling' indictment of the U.S., 'linking all the dots'—U.S. unilateralism, its denial of the reality of multipolarity, the anti-Russian nature of NATO enlargement, the U.S. in Central Asia—as he described a 'U.S. plot against the world.' Araud said he could only interpret Putin's tirade as an expression of pent-up resentment and frustration stemming from 'hundreds of years of Russian history' and in particular the humiliation of the immediate post–Cold War years."[28]

Turning to the complexities within the French-American relationship, Araud, who met in 2007 with a congressional delegation led by Representative John Tanner (D-TN), offered a "historical disquisition on the differences between France's and Britain's post-war relationship with the United States. He said Britain tries to "ride the tiger," influencing U.S. policy behind the scenes. "This is what they have tried to do on Iraq: With what success, we might ask?" France, he explained, tries to defend its interests as an independent player. "We're trying to exist and to exercise our right to have our own opinion, including on how to address international crises. That means that we may agree in some cases—as on Iran where we work extremely closely, coordinating daily. In others, as in Iraq, we disagreed, and still do. This is not anti-Americanism, it is France developing its own analyses and exercising its own policy."[29]

While anti-Americanism was a "pillar" of Russian foreign policy, differing with the U.S. was explained as a "defining element" of being Canadian. In an extraordinary conversation with Canadian Liberal Party leader Michael Ignatieff's chief of staff Peter Donolo, Consulate Toronto's consul general reported on Donolo's exposition on the importance of differing with the United States.

> Donolo went on at length about how important it is to Canadians to be seen as different from Americans. He said this difference "defines us" . . . and noted PM [Brian] Mulroney had been a U.S. "lap dog" in a way even [Prime Minister Stephen] Harper was wary of. He recalled once calling White House Press Secretary Michael McCurry after President Clinton had been "over the top" in praising Prime Minister Jean Chrétien, asking that the president be "less generous lest he hurt the PM politically." McCurry laughingly said it was the first time a foreign leader had ever asked for less love from the president rather than more. "Things are easier with a Democrat in the White House," he added, "but we should always remember this need for difference." He speculated that Canada staying out of the Iraq war might have saved free trade by convincing Canadians that they need not fear political integration with the U.S., so economic integration was less threatening.[30]

Such subtleties are important in understanding how to think about anti-Americanism and the ways it plays out in different countries and on different foreign policy themes. This kind of information might have been helpful in the many Washington-based discussions on the phenomenon. On any given day, U.S. diplomats will have to deal with the sophistication of a Donolo or an Araud, but also with the crazy accusations of the Tajik narcotics commander. With points of objection this disparate, a local focus, rather than a Washington-directed one, is a better approach.

As a postscript to the examples above, the United States was not the only country occasionally caught off guard by bizarre local reactions to routine diplomacy. When the Swiss embassy in Bishkek decided to celebrate fifteen years of Swiss-Kyrgyz cooperation on development assistance programs with billboards superimposing a small and understated Swiss flag, which contains a cross, over the Kyrgyz flag, which features a stylized interpretation of a yurt, all hell broke loose. A member of parliament angrily asked the prime minister why the Swiss had been allowed to "deface" the national flag. The Kyrgyz government quickly ripped down all advertising; the keynote speaker canceled his participation at the anniversary event; and the Swiss chargé received a summons to the Kyrgyz version of the attorney general's office. In a meeting with the U.S. ambassador afterward, the baffled chargé insisted the logo had been preapproved by the Kyrgyz National Commission on the State Language. Nonetheless, the angry Kyrgyz parliamentarian had the last word: "If this had been Turkey, there probably would have been a war."[31]

PUBLIC DIPLOMACY: THE WASHINGTON PERSPECTIVE

Countering anti-American sentiment is a fundamental part of public diplomacy, which until 1999 had been the mission of the U.S. Information Agency (USIA). With its slogan "Telling America's Story to the World," its work ranged from awarding Fulbright scholarships to broadcasting news through an extensive international network that included Voice of America along with other regional outfits.

Although some would consider this propaganda, the United States has always been ambivalent about that term. Congress passed the Smith-Mundt Act of 1948 to forbid the use of U.S. government propaganda within America's borders, lest the government propagandize its own citizens. The word carries a freighted history, given its association with the Nazi Germany war machine, yet there was consensus in the early 1950s that America needed to be aggressive about countering Cold War–era distortions and disinformation, especially from the Communist world.

By the 1990s, disinformation was also coming from the developing world. One of the most malicious and persistent rumors was the baby parts scandal, in which foreign media accused Americans of stealing babies in order to harvest their organs for ailing U.S. children. The repulsive story cast a pall on legitimate adoptions and became remarkably difficult to refute. The story was fueled by reports that technology was making organ transplants a more common medical procedure, along with the advent of organ transplant tourism (the phenomenon of adult citizens in poor countries willing to sell their organs to wealthy recipients). The idea of stealing babies for their organs became more plausible.

If asked, embassy public diplomacy officers would have denied they trafficked in propaganda, arguing that countering run-of-the-mill disinformation kept them far too busy to engage in darker operations. They would have added that their days were filled with programming, organizing both academic and professional exchanges, cultural representations, and press events for their ambassadors and Washington visitors, along with battling back endless and groundless rumors and misinformation.

Despite the broad range of activities, the end of the Cold War signaled to Congress that there was no longer a need for the agency, and the late senator Jesse Helms led an effort to abolish the USIA, which closed in late 1999. Most of the agency's 6,400 employees—of whom about a thousand were foreign service officers—were absorbed into the State Department. The broadcasting arm of USIA—with its

Voice of America radio in forty-five languages, Radio Free Europe/ Radio Liberty in twenty-eight languages, and Radio Free Asia, Radio Martí, and TV Martí—was spun off into a newly created federal agency called the Broadcasting Board of Governors.

The rough road of consolidation is relevant to the leaked cables and anti-Americanism. The cables reveal a State Department struggling to understand public diplomacy and how best to deploy assets of personnel, budgets, and the programs it had unexpectedly acquired.

The State Department was not alone in its quandary. Following fast on the heels of the demise of the USIA, 9/11 made the scrutiny of the nation's public diplomacy platforms all the more intense. It would be hard to count the number of blue ribbon panels, special commissions, congressional hearings, op-eds, and scholarly reports that focused on what to do not only about public diplomacy in general but anti-Americanism specifically. (Practitioner-scholar Richard T. Arndt counted more than thirty by 2006.)[32] In time, anti-Americanism became so exclusively linked to violent extremism from the Muslim world that the concepts became inseparable. To see anti-Americanism through such a narrow lens, and to link it almost solely to a religion not well understood in Washington, set the stage for a powerful misconception. It also meant that public diplomacy risked being judged by an impatient Congress and others solely on its ability to move the needle in public opinion polls.

Both the Bush and Obama administrations tended to view anti-Americanism as the single most alarming feature of the Muslim world, especially in countries such as Pakistan, Egypt, and Iraq. As policymakers focused more on Islam, they became trapped in a cycle in which public diplomacy was linked to anti-Americanism, which was in turn linked to Islam.

Public diplomacy practitioners were quick to point out that post-9/11 studies on public diplomacy were "overwhelmingly interested in what could be done in Washington; very few addressed what happens overseas. The views of the people responsible for implementing public diplomacy overseas were largely absent."[33] Former ambassador William Rugh wrote that most commission members "had not been career officers with field experience; instead they have been Washington-based policymakers or short-term political appointees."[34]

The many commissions seemed to skate over empirical data from public opinion research, echoed by a few experienced voices that put forward a similar message: the problem lay in U.S. policies, not the messaging programs. Rugh, a public diplomacy officer who served most of his career in the Arab world, wrote that "despite 60 years of U.S. public diplomacy programs trying to reach Arab public opinion, Arab criticism of the United States reached unprecedented levels largely because of disagreement with U.S. policies themselves."[35]

The Government Accountability Office (GAO) took a pragmatic approach, looking into staffing since the 2002 implementation of the Diplomatic Readiness Initiative (DRI), which was meant to remedy years of budget cuts that had left the State Department without the personnel to fill overseas positions. The study found that the DRI, which enabled the State Department to hire one thousand additional employees, had been consumed by the insatiable need for staffing in Iraq and Afghanistan. Public diplomacy positions suffered some of the most severe staffing gaps.[36] Several embassy cables support this analysis. Even Embassy Riyadh, surely a crucial post-9/11 operation, wrote, "Our greatest need in Saudi Arabia is for qualified officers and staff to carry out this PD strategy. For most of the past two difficult but critically important years, we have been operating at half strength in terms of American officers, yet we have seen more than one promised public diplomacy hand diverted to other posts. We need to assign language-qualified, at-grade, PD-cone officers to the existing public diplomacy positions at Embassy Riyadh and the two Consulates General in Dhahran and Jeddah. In addition, in order to implement this strategy successfully, we need four new public diplomacy officer positions."[37]

The GAO also focused on the foreign language deficit. Two of its studies from 2006 and 2009 concluded that more officers need to speak more languages—and at higher levels of proficiency.[38] In 2003, former ambassador Edward Djerejian had said that within the entire foreign service, only five officers spoke Arabic well enough to discuss and debate issues on Al Jazeera television.[39] His observation quickly became the new benchmark for language proficiency. GAO studies bought into the idea of increased language competence, along with more officers and more programs. But the focus on language leaves unanswered the question of why so many Spanish-speaking countries in Latin America, including Argentina, Bolivia, and Venezuela, also have abysmal anti-American numbers, despite the fact that many foreign service officers speak fluent Spanish.

The Office of Management and Budget was even more harsh, rating public diplomacy field operations as "not performing—results not demonstrated." Its study claimed overseas programs had difficulty measuring impact; that few public diplomacy programs linked budgets to performance; and that there was not a broad overarching U.S. public diplomacy strategy."[40]

This deficiency in assessment is striking. While the many commissions in Washington agonized about public diplomacy, few grappled with what metrics might offer an impartial way to judge success. Despite their convenience, public opinion polls cannot be a reliable standard for gauging the effectiveness of public diplomacy actions. Too many variables influence public attitudes, and an isolated incident in one place may pull down numbers everywhere. Nonetheless, it is clear that between 2006 and 2010 the public diplomacy community had not been able to offer its own standards for effectiveness, and in the words of practitioner Joe Johnson, "If you cannot define success, you'll never succeed."[41]

THE IMPACT OF CONGRESSIONALLY MANDATED REPORTING

The many panels neglected to examine one important trend: the impact of congressionally mandated reports. By their nature a scorecard-type evaluative report, they unmistakably sound like judgments on the policies, culture, and cooperation of other countries. This reporting work, which draws heavily on embassy staff time, helps fuel anti-American resentment. Even the friendliest nations bristle at the presumptiveness of the United States passing judgment on how they handle sensitive areas such as human rights, religious freedom, and counternarcotics.

One safely retired practitioner wrote, "It strikes many of us as ludicrous, for example, that our small embassy staff in Reykjavik has to devote many hours to preparing an annual human rights report. Instead of repeating, year after year, that the government of Iceland respects in every important particular the liberties of its citizens, they could be out talking to Icelanders about America."[42] Such brave sentiment emerges from those currently serving who make a similar point by chronicling foreign governments' outrage.

Embassy Moscow wrote about the blistering reaction to the International Religious Freedom Report, saying that the Ministry of Foreign Affairs (MFA) sneered: "It seems that the authors decided not to bother themselves with releasing updated information" and called the IRF report "a politically biased document distorting the facts, which deliberately misrepresents the Government of Russia's stellar record of protecting religious freedom."[43] The report attacked an increasingly authoritarian Russian government for its treatment of minority Russian religions as well as its judicial restrictions against Jehovah's Witnesses and the Church of Scientology. The cable writer could not resist a sneer right back, acidly noting, "Since other countries may not be familiar with Russia's long tradition of inter-faith harmony, the MFA kindly offered to 'try to help them understand.'"

The French MFA offered a more sophisticated response to the International Religious Freedom Report for France, having within its bureaucracy a bureau focused on religious affairs. The embassy reported that a follow-up meeting to the report focused on methodology, and the French may have won a point, noting that the State Department quoted results of a poll from Catholic newspaper *La Croix,* which did not use scientific methods. The French also insisted the burqa debate (the outlawing of women wearing burqas in public places) should be left as a judicial matter.

Embassy reporting reveals that the State Department struggled mightily to gain traction on its annual Human Rights Report. The document ended up prolonging discussion of abuses at Abu Ghraib prison, which while uncovered in 2003 lingered long after as a convenient example of U.S. hypocrisy.

China bristled at the criticism in its Human Rights Report, which focused on tight government control of dissent, and the detention, harassment, and house arrest of human rights and democracy activists. "We urge the U.S. to examine its own human rights problems and not use human rights as an excuse or publish human rights reports in order to interfere with others' affairs," the government stated. "The U.S. practice of throwing stones while living in a glass house is a testimony to the double standard and hypocrisy of the U.S."[44]

The Czech Republic's prime minister Mirek Topolánek was irate to read that the State Department did not think the Czechs had a stellar record respecting the rights of the Roma (itinerant people of northern Indian origin who face prejudice and difficulty integrating into European mainstream life). "To the report from the U.S. State Department I can only say that a country that allows torturing of prisoners can hardly teach me about how human rights have been violated here."[45]

The U.S. embassy in Buenos Aires noted that the Argentine government's extreme sensitivity to any public criticism whatsoever posed a problem for all the annual congressionally mandated reports, even fairly innocuous ones. "The April 1 release of our perennial Investment Climate Statement, which covers the foreign investment climate here, for example, generated concern within the GOA [Government of Argentina] despite its extremely understated tone. We are working to assuage their unease through private conversations and publicly putting the report in its proper context."[46]

The congressionally mandated reports offer one of the clearest glimpses of the disconnect on anti-Americanism. While idealists may still see the country as the last great hope of the downtrodden, defenseless, and victimized people of the world, its shift in recent years as the world's foremost military power burdens it with unwelcome publicity about rendition flights, torture at Abu Ghraib, and civilians killed in drone strikes (a report and film of which preceded the WikiLeaks diplomatic release). Not only do the many reports underscore the U.S. loss of credibility, but in countries with single-digit approval ratings, the text of these reports is simply another irritant.

The International Religious Freedom Report, which provides an assessment on the status of religious freedom in every country in the world, presents particular challenges because it illustrates cultural differences. It is a blunt tool with a rigid format that does not allow for context. It leaves Germans feeling that their treatment of Scientologists and the French that their ban on burqas are seen in the United States as equivalent to how the Taliban treats women. A section titled "Improvements in Respect for Religious Freedom" speaks approvingly of some German states' willingness to allow Islamic religious instruction in public school classrooms—something that would be constitutionally challenged in the United States.

American-style religion, with its televangelist millionaires, West-borough Baptist protests at funerals, anti-Islamic rants by pastors, and eternal court fights over prayer in schools and crèches in town halls, may be something of an acquired taste. Embassies run into trouble translating the U.S. constitutional requirement of separation of church and state in countries that see no need for such separation. Other countries are skeptical the separation exists at all, citing U.S. support for Israel, statements from elected officials that the United States is a Christian nation, and President George W. Bush's previously mentioned remark of a U.S. crusade against terrorism.

Yet another congressionally mandated report, the International Narcotics Control Strategy Report, exposes the U.S. to gibes that the report comes from a country that fuels demand for drugs and has among the highest number of drug users. Worse still, according to critics, the report is issued by a country where certain states have legalized the use of some drugs, a strategy long advocated by many Latin American countries. Countries wonder why they should continue to work with a partner with such blatant double standards. The reporting template assesses a growing list of countries touched by global narcotics trafficking according to a number of criteria: institutional development, supply reduction, drug abuse awareness, treatment, corruption, national goals, and bilateral cooperation. Some of the countries on the list, such as Afghanistan, undoubtedly pose a threat. Others, such as the UK, Canada, and Germany presumably have adequate laws in place to combat narcotics without scrutiny from the U.S. Congress.

Of course, advocates argue that the virtues of the congressionally mandated reports outweigh imperfections; that the good should not be the enemy of the best. The reports on trafficking and human rights give victims and those who cannot speak for themselves a measure of hope. NGOs also write reports, but none have the universal resources or reach of the U.S. government, which still counts for a great deal. The annual Trafficking in Persons reports seem to come under less attack and have revealed a once invisible group of victims held captive in gruesome circumstances.

Perhaps future rounds of commissions and panels focused on public diplomacy could incorporate more voices from the field and the front lines. They might also explore whether human rights, human trafficking, counternarcotics cooperation, and religious freedom might be assessed in less dogmatic ways that would allow policymakers to preach less and learn more—one of the ostensible rationales for all the reports. But until that happens, it is important for those exploring the roots of anti-Americanism to understand that whatever good the reports might bring must be balanced against the clear opportunity for America-bashing they provide.

THE LEADERSHIP PROBLEM

America's efforts at public diplomacy are riven with disconnects between Washington and the field that start at the top. Public diplomacy has suffered mightily from poor direction. Three administrations struggled to find and retain adequate leadership, largely because they were unclear about the skill set needed; because finding qualified leaders proved difficult; and in a few cases, because Senate approval was lengthy or uncertain. Underlying all of this was policymakers' dual uncertainty about the nature of anti-Americanism and the nature of public diplomacy, the tool with which policymakers expected to counter it.

The State Department's under secretary for Public Diplomacy and Public Affairs, sometimes dubbed America's top PR agent, oversees three bureaus: Educational and Cultural Affairs, Public Affairs, and International Information Programs. These three bureaus spearhead the nation's effort to engage foreign audiences. The Bureau of Educational and Cultural Affairs (ECA) handles all manner of youth, academic, and professional exchanges as well as cultural programming. The Bureau of Public Affairs (PA) responds to domestic and international media on U.S. foreign policy topics. It houses the spokesperson's office and runs the daily noon press briefing, crafts answers to media inquiries, and arranges interviews with State's top policymakers. The Bureau of International Information Programs (IIP) creates multimedia and digital communications products to promote people-to-people conversations about U.S. foreign policy priorities.

Since 1999 there have been nine under secretaries, interspersed with vacancies of up to fifteen months at a stretch. A report from the Advisory Commission on Public Diplomacy noted the position has gone unfilled 30 percent of the time.[47] Just as concerning as those long vacancies, the tenure of incumbents has been short, ranging from barely six months (Margaret Tutwiler) through two years, three months (Karen Hughes). There was one under secretary in the waning days of the Clinton administration; four in the Bush administration, and at this writing four in the Obama administration.

Three of the nine had very close connections to the president: Evelyn Lieberman was deputy press secretary and then deputy chief of staff in the Clinton White House; Karen Hughes was a trusted Bush confidante and White House counselor; and Margaret Tutwiler had served as State Department spokesperson and ambassador to Morocco. Three came from industry: Charlotte Beers had been chairman of both Ogilvy & Mather and J. Walter Thompson; James Glassman had been executive editor and/or publisher for magazines such as the *New Republic,* the *Atlantic,* and *U.S. News and World Report,* among others; and Judith McHale was president and CEO of Discovery Communications and creator of the Discovery Channel. Obama appointee Tara Sonenshine had an eclectic career that included ABC's *Nightline,* stints at NGOs such as the International Crisis Group and the International Women's Media Foundation, as well as time spent as executive vice president of the federally funded U.S. Institute of Peace. Kathleen Stephens was a career foreign service officer designated as a placeholder while awaiting Sonenshine's confirmation (her tenure lasted only two months), and current incumbent Richard Stengel is a journalist with sixteen years of experience

as managing editor at *Time* magazine who also collaborated with
Nelson Mandela on his autobiography.

These are all smart people. Every one of these appointees brought
impressive accomplishments from lengthy careers—in other fields.
Their eclectic professions touched on at least some aspects of public
diplomacy—communications, television, advertising, journalism,
and publishing. Nonetheless, none had truly successful tenures as
under secretary; each struggled to help public diplomacy find a foothold in the State Department; and all failed to make meaningful
inroads in combating anti-Americanism.

The State Department publishes an organizational chart on its
website, a challenge even for experts in complex structures to compre-
hend. Critics claim the department has become more unwieldy as it
has acquired other agencies such as the Arms Control and Disarmament Agency in 1997 and the U.S. Information Agency in 1999, and
taken on additional foreign assistance responsibilities from the U.S.
Agency for International Development. The secretary of state heads
the department, and near the top of the chart are slots for six under
secretaries covering political affairs; economic growth, energy, and
environment; arms control and international security affairs; public diplomacy and public affairs; management; and civilian security,
democracy, and human rights.

It is telling that many of the State Department's under secretaries for the other five divisions have been career officers, not political
appointees. The nine above-mentioned incumbents' experience pales
against distinguished career officers such as Patrick Kennedy, under
secretary for Management, or Thomas Pickering, Marc Grossman,
Nicholas Burns, and William Burns, all former under secretaries for
Political Affairs. These career officers have all been ambassadors. They
brought decades of experience at embassies and consulates as well as
intensive experience inside the State Department and an in-depth
understanding of other key agencies. They knew how to work with
the National Security Council and other interagency players such as

the Departments of Defense, Commerce, Agriculture, and Energy. They had connections on the Hill, testified before Congress, tackled the toughest policy issues, and met dozens of times with foreign heads of state.

The resistance by all administrations to entrust this key job to a career officer has not gone unnoticed. In frustration at the long-unfilled gaps, a group of thirty-seven former ambassadors and other retired high-level diplomats sent an open letter to Secretary of State Kerry in May 2013 calling for the position to be filled by "a career foreign affairs professional with years of overseas and Washington experience."[48] To no avail.

The under secretary of Public Diplomacy and Public Affairs job may well be harder than its counterpart position in Political Affairs. The latter has boundaries largely defined by tradition and is replicated in most of the world's foreign ministries. There is a tidiness about the many geographic offices, with desk officers reporting to their office directors and up through deputy assistant and assistant secretaries. This structure is more or less symmetrical with foreign ministries around the world, making the routine communication of day-to-day diplomacy relatively easy.

Public diplomacy, by contrast, is a uniquely American job that usually has no foreign counterpart, because the American approach pulls everything under one roof, from hard-hitting policy speeches to long-term academic exchanges like Fulbright scholarships.

While discontinuity and long gaps have made it difficult to lead the Public Diplomacy and Public Affairs division convincingly, the records of the under secretaries have been checkered by their actions as well as their absences. In a few cases, they have been excoriated by both domestic and overseas media. Communications expert Karen Hughes personified the Bush administration's conviction that public diplomacy meant opening a dialogue with the Arab world. As mentioned earlier, Hughes gamely traveled to the trouble spots— Turkey, Saudi Arabia, Egypt, and Indonesia. She brought along a young American Muslim student and tried to connect with female audiences, but critics were quick to pounce on what they saw as the cluelessness of her mission.

Philip Giraldi, a former CIA counterterrorism expert, wrote that Hughes blamed the glitches in her listening tour on U.S. embassies and ordered her senior assistants to shake up embassy staffs and demand a more aggressive delivery of the administration's message. She set up an infamous "echo chamber," designed to keep everyone on message.[49] In a sure sign of discontent, her message to the field, "Karen's Rules," was leaked and published in the *Washington Post,* the *Nation,* and elsewhere. The memo was given to the *Post* by a recipient who noted that "if all were well, nobody would have leaked it."[50]

The rules reinforced an image of micromanagement—for example, Rule #2: "You are always on sure ground if you use what the President, Secretary Rice, Sean McCormack or Senior USG [U.S. government] spokesmen have already said on a particular subject." And Rule #5: "Don't Make Policy. This is a sensitive area about which you need to be careful. Do not get out in front of USG policymakers on an issue, even if you are speaking to local press."

Even an assessment in the usually pro–State Department *Foreign Service Journal* was fairly damning. Shawn Zeller, senior staff writer for *Congressional Quarterly* and frequent contributor to the *Journal,* wrote that Hughes was seen as too controlling. "Many in the field say that Hughes's public relations–style approach to public diplomacy reflects the kind of top-down thinking that works better in politics than foreign affairs. Many of Hughes' initiatives, in other words, started with a dictate from Washington that the field must then follow, with little receptivity to ideas coming from the other direction, they say."[51]

Charlotte Beers was criticized for an attempt to "brand" America the same way she had earned fame branding Uncle Ben's rice. And when Margaret Tutwiler suddenly announced her switch from government public relations to the executive suites of the New York Stock Exchange, the timing of her move, which occurred during the week that the first brutal images of abused Iraqi prisoners at Abu Ghraib were released worldwide, raised eyebrows.[52] James Glassman, who lasted only seven months, seemed not to believe in the job. He wrote, "Trying to get foreigners to like us is the default endeavor of the State Department's public affairs office, and in my view, it's largely a waste of time."[53]

When Judith McHale was rumored to be next in line, the Washington Post's Al Kamen noted that the job "has been especially difficult given Washington's reputation abroad." He shrugged off her lack of diplomatic experience, noting, "We're reminded that this is a job that involves selling a message."[54]

Others were not so sanguine. George Washington University professor Marc Lynch protested that McHale would be "a terrible, terrible selection. The position . . . should go to someone with experience in and a vision for public diplomacy, and who will be in a position to effectively integrate public diplomacy concerns into the policy-making process."[55]

Chaos at the top had consequences below. Weak and absent leaders failed to incorporate the newly consolidated division into the State Department's bureaucracy. The former USIA's largely civil service component ran academic and cultural exchanges with a firewalled budget and worked for years out of the same building at L'Enfant Plaza, six Metro stops and a considerable walk away from the State Department's Foggy Bottom. The sense of remaining separate from the State Department was stronger than the sense of working together. ECA program officers and branch chiefs routinely spoke of the State Department as a separate entity. Both civil and foreign service officers were demoralized, having seen their former agency undervalued and dismantled by Congress, only to find themselves white elephants in a State Department that was mystified and bemused by its newfound assets.

A gap in the middle, among public diplomacy implementers, compounded the leadership gap at the top. Like all FSOs, those assigned to hardship and dangerous posts in Iraq, Afghanistan, and Pakistan serve for only a year. Many were simply not present, since, as the GAO study noted, numerous overseas assignments were going unfilled. A host of other, greater hardship countries are two-year assignments, and the maximum an officer may stay in any country is three years. Given the need to interact with local opinion leaders, nearly all public diplomacy overseas assignments are language-designated, but shortfalls in language skills and the long lead time needed to teach difficult languages compounds the problem. Combined, these conditions created a shortage of experienced public diplomacy officers with language skills and in-depth knowledge of the countries in which their expertise was needed. And the Wikileaks cables illustrate the consequences of that gap.

PROGRAMS IN THE FIELD: FROM MEALS TO IDEALS

For the most part, American diplomats work out of embassies—the lead diplomatic facility that is always located in the capital city. In larger countries, the State Department also staffs consulates, secondary facilities that extend diplomatic reach, headed by a consul general who reports to the ambassador. In some countries, such as Canada, the United States supports not only an embassy in Ottawa but multiple consulates in Vancouver, Calgary, Toronto, Montreal, Quebec City, and Halifax. There is also an American Presence Post (APP) in Winnipeg. APPs are usually single-officer posts with very limited services; they do not issue visas. The State Department also staffs diplomatic missions to international organizations, starting with the United States Mission to the United Nations. Other examples include the International Civil Aviation Organization (ICAO), the Organization for Security and Co-operation in Europe, (OSCE), and the UN's Educational, Scientific and Cultural Organization (UNE-SCO). It is possible to have more than one ambassador in a city. Brussels hosts three—one at the U.S. embassy, one at the U.S. Mission to NATO, and one at the U.S. Mission to the European Union.

The State Department expects all officers, including the ambassador, to engage in public diplomacy, and nearly all embassies and many consulates include a public diplomacy section, headed by a Public Affairs Officer (PAO) whose job is to think strategically about assets to be used in public outreach and to plan programming. These officers perform the obvious tasks—running exchange programs, monitoring the media, and writing speeches for the ambassador. The WikiLeaks cables show there is also room for considerable creativity, and those diplomats proposed and organized an ambitious range of events.

Officers at the U.S. embassy in Paraguay attempted to reach a new audience—people interested in environmental issues—by hosting a bird-watching tour on embassy grounds. They pulled out all the stops, inviting bleary-eyed government officials, NGO leaders, and journalists to a 6:30 a.m. pre-breakfast tour led by bird-watching experts. They published a foldout guide, "Birds of the U.S. Embassy Gardens," that helped visitors identify more than sixty species of birds inhabiting the ten-acre compound. They also assisted with the publication of the companion guide, "Birds of Asunción," which they distributed to guests. The embassy figured there was just something irresistible about bird-watching.[56]

A continent away, the three U.S. diplomatic installations in Italy—Embassy Rome, Embassy Vatican City, and the U.S. Mission to UN Agencies—joined forces to spotlight the United States as a leader in the fight against hunger through a "hunger banquet" at the ambassador's residence. The missions reported that the event divided attendees according to access-to-food proportions found in the world. At the special Thanksgiving reception, 60 percent of the guests were served rice under a tent outdoors; 25 percent ate rice and beans in the residence foyer; and a handful were served a posh meal with wine. The ambassadors wrote that a "hunger banquet might also help soften the USG image in light of the rise in anti-Americanism worldwide . . . and presents an opportunity to discuss humanitarian assistance with embassy contacts not aware of the role the U.S. plays."[57]

In Cuba, where the United States had an Interests Section in lieu of an embassy, the staff tried to turn down the temperature on politics with a baseball-themed Fourth of July reception. Guests dined on hot dogs and popcorn while being entertained with baseball-themed music, videos, and a reenactment of Abbott and Costello's "Who's on First?" Cubans loved the party favors, which included baseballs, baseball cards, and material donated by Major League Baseball.[58]

In the early 2000s, every embassy worthy of the name began hosting iftar dinners, traditionally celebrated to break the fast during Ramadan. In Muslim-dominant countries, these made good sense and had been going on long before 9/11. In countries such as Germany and the United Kingdom, with significant Muslim minority populations, they also worked well. But in countries with few Muslim residents, the dinners smacked of pandering or a desire to check the box on Muslim outreach to satisfy anxious Washington policymakers. They were attended only by Muslim members of the diplomatic corps and interfaith leaders.

Over time, embassies began to look beyond the now-obligatory meal. Embassy Athens and the consulate in Thessaloniki hosted iftar dinners but emphasized to Washington that they were only one element in a sophisticated outreach program to a complex and divided community. While one Muslim community in Thrace dated back to Ottoman times and comprised ethnic Turks, Pomaks, and Roma, it contrasted with a very distinct urban community of recent Muslim immigrants from Albania, the Middle East, South Asia, and Africa. The mission strategy for the Thracian Muslim community focused on exchanges and partnerships with civil society organizations, support for minority rights, and cultural programming, while outreach to the recent immigrant community focused on partnerships with Muslim organizations, religious freedom and refugee issues, and fostering Muslim–host country dialogue.[59] This kind of analysis and targeted programming goes well beyond the somewhat superficial thinking on iftar dinners. Embassy London created a counter-radicalization multi-agency working group to improve its understanding of a very complex UK Muslim community. It made the point that one-size-fits-all programming doesn't work in a single country, or even in a single city. "Programs are shaped to fit particular neighborhood needs and dynamics, recognizing that the diversity of Muslim communities precludes a monolithic set of responses."[60]

U.S. Consulate Jeddah wrote that even a short-term event can require exhaustive and elaborate planning. It created an American Culture and Commerce festival from scratch in the Saudi city of Abha. The post hoped the event would engage broader, younger, and harder-to-reach audiences outside major cities and educate Saudis about U.S. culture, education, and commercial partnerships. The four-day event featured a gala VIP opening, English teacher training workshops, presentations on study in the United States and visas, panel discussions, presentations to local businesses, and much more. The post proudly reported that some eight thousand people attended, many of them students. And yet, scant funding from Washington sent the consulate scurrying to find sponsors and partners. Why Washington stinted on an event that seemed to hit all the bells on Muslim outreach is mystifying.[61]

Embassy Benin coupled iftar and Ramadan with the idea of service and organized the first-ever community blood drive at the Cadjehoun Mosque in Cotonou in response to President Obama's call for an interfaith day of volunteer service.[62] Mauritania brought an American Muslim couple to interact with locals, a foreshadowing of a frequent and popular programming effort to bring American Muslims to audiences overseas.[63] But even innocuous events such as iftar dinners can be controversial. Embassy Asmara, operating under some of the most hostile host country conditions anywhere on the globe, reported that the government of Eritrea shut down its iftar dinner, sending a diplomatic *note verbale* (an unsigned diplomatic note written in the third person) expressly forbidding the planned meal. This came after the embassy's official protest of Eritrean security forces roughing up a U.S. public diplomacy officer and many of his guests as he hosted a public event at a rented auditorium.[64]

Embassies far from the Muslim world also tried new forms of outreach. In Buenos Aires, the embassy wrote in November 2008 about its efforts to combat the highest level of anti-Americanism in the Western Hemisphere, a status that had persisted for six years. A cable reviewing attempts to reverse the trend found a formula for success in relentless media outreach (several times a day), focused attention on youth, and augmented involvement with NGOs and community activities. That said, the embassy had a lot of help. Writer Tom Wolfe came for the International Book Fair; figure skater Michelle Kwan met with youth leaders; violinist Joshua Bell performed, as did headliners such as Ozomatli, Toto, Béla Fleck and the Flecktones, the Black Eyed Peas, and reggaeton stars Wisin and Yandel. The State Department chose an Argentine to receive the Secretary of State's International Women of Courage Award and funded exchange projects for the country's high school students and English teachers. Yet measuring the results of all this activity remained difficult. The post noted, "We are beginning to see our [public opinion] numbers head north again," falling prey to the use of public opinion polls as a measure of success.[65]

As Buenos Aires's efforts indicate, public diplomacy costs money, and the cables show embassies thinking beyond the next meal, pitching Washington with programming ideas and funding requests they linked to wider strategic plans to advance U.S. interests. Larger posts, such as Buenos Aires and Riyadh, sent multipage requests for elaborate and multifaceted programming. Smaller posts, such as Paramaribo, looked for amounts as small as $13,350.[66]

Any thoughtful reading of the cables leads to the conclusion that designing public diplomacy is a task for those on the ground, not those in Washington. No Washington panel could anticipate the subtle differences of the Thracian Muslims. A hunger banquet would never work in countries where hosts deem it a point of honor to offer guests their very best—a cold bowl of rice would be an unpardonable insult. It worked in Rome because diplomatic receptions are plentiful and food is never in short supply.

Although anti-Americanism had infinite variations, too much of the public diplomacy toolkit from Washington continued to be standard issue: exchanges, cultural programming, and American speakers. And plenty of embassy proponents of activist programming argued that conquering public opinion was only a matter of adequate resources skillfully used. In a frenzy, posts mounted program after program while Washington continued to pursue a foreign policy that was certain to alienate.

TO KNOW US MIGHT NOT BE TO LOVE US

Given the implacable and pervasive nature of anti-Americanism, it is time to consider the assertion propounded by former Under Secretary James Glassman at the outset of this chapter. Is trying to get foreigners to like us a waste of time?

Perhaps Glassman failed to acknowledge the strength of the American desire to be liked. Obama took up the fight at a town hall meeting in Strasbourg in April 2009. Acknowledging that "there have been times when America has shown arrogance and been dismissive, even derisive," he also chided a uniquely European style of anti-Americanism that clearly annoyed him. "In Europe there is an anti-Americanism that is at once casual, but can be insidious . . . these attitudes have become all too common. They are not wise. They do not represent the truth. They … fail to acknowledge the fundamental truth that America cannot confront the challenges of this century alone, but that Europe cannot confront them without America."[67]

Obama's words were politely received in Strasbourg, but they did not spark discussions back home about whether work to combat anti-Americanism is worth pursuing. Obama spoke for the optimists who believe that anti-Americanism can be conquered. No one is asking (or at least not very loudly) whether the United States should accept that anti-Americanism is the price paid for pursuing unpopular policies. And no one has yet proven that fear of losing the world's good opinion has ever constrained the United States from taking action. The idea that world public opinion should be part of any policy decision-making process was famously articulated by the USIA's director, Edward R. Murrow, who said, after dealing with the results of the 1961 Bay of Pigs invasion, "Dammit, if they want me in on the crash landings, I'd better damned well be in on the take-offs!"[68] Murrow was arguing that it is unreasonable to turn to public diplomacy practitioners only when it's too late. They deserve a seat with policymakers at the takeoffs, too. It's still a valid request today and still ignored.

From Argentina to Zimbabwe, the leaked cables show embassies operating according to a predictable pattern. Posts attempt to gauge the depth and virulence of anti-Americanism, hold earnest discussions with opinion leaders, and then plan programs aimed at moving the needle of public opinion. The underlying assumption is that if diplomats could only perform enough outreach, sit down with enough people, and engage in enough useful dialogue, they could solve the problem. Rather than sound out the depths of the harm caused by disasters such as Abu Ghraib, Guantanamo, and drone strikes, diplomats appear to have become uncritical believers in the power of their own programs. Happy talk and can-do cables full of public diplomacy triumphs seem aimed to please policymakers rather than educate them on what might be wrong. When in doubt, the common solution is to plead for resources to do even more programming. Too many cables cater to Washington's insatiable demand for success stories, when a more courageous stance might have been to write about failure and to insist that some of Washington's policies were so unpopular, no amount of clever programming would turn the tide.

While embassy reporting was energetic—and frequently colorful—in describing anti-Americanism, it was less than candid in pushing back on the policies that caused it or insisting on a seat at the policy table. Yet experienced diplomats such as Richard Arndt insist that "policy is not just *a* factor, it is the *only* factor." If getting people to like us were easy, it would have been done long ago. The fact that it is so hard suggests two alternatives: either work in new ways to achieve it or agree with Glassman that it is a waste of time.

Of course the WikiLeaks operation was itself an example of anti-Americanism. Assange, speaking of his motivations, told the *New York Times* that the United States had become "the greatest threat to democracy," with a government and society dominated by the military, its people cowed into conformity by what he called "the security state." His anti-American views were a magnet for supporters and volunteers drawn from all over Europe who made common cause with him, and U.S. government pressure only galvanized them.

America ought to welcome a discussion that includes outlier and iconoclastic ideas like Glassman's and others'. Asking uncomfortable questions is the foundation of a thoughtful approach. The dozens of commissions on public diplomacy spurred no revolution in thinking because the usual suspects in Washington cannot or will not think differently. Until someone convenes a panel with diplomats fresh from the field, the sounds of protests still ringing in their ears and the tear gas still smarting in their eyes, we won't have the dialogue we need to move public diplomacy in new directions.

Such a panel might start with this observation from Anthony Quainton, former director general of the foreign service and former ambassador to Peru, Nicaragua, Kuwait, and the Central African Republic. "We've made the assumption for five years now that everyone wants Western-style democracy and capitalism. Well, the reality is that that assumption may be wrong, and then you are really swimming upstream."[69]

Chapter 3

CRISES:
"Post Will Continue
to Monitor the Situation"

- - - - - - - - - - - - - - -

The night is filled with a constant cacophony of sounds: mostly chanting and the singing of hymns, but interspersed with screams of grief, prayers shouted from loudspeakers and barking dogs.

—*U.S. Embassy, Port-au-Prince*
January 16, 2010

- - - - - - - - - - - - - - -

SOMETHING IS WRONG. IN SECONDS A CHARMING foreign boulevard goes from postcard perfect to a war scene. A peaceful protest turns ugly. Strikers block major roads and the smell of burning tires fills the air. The usual urban sound track judders to a halt amid gunshots, running footsteps, and the clang of hastily cranked shop shutters. The leaked cables from 2006 to 2010 included reporting on political crises including the assassination of Benazir Bhutto in Pakistan; coups in Thailand, Guinea, and Honduras; the Israel-Hezbollah-Lebanon war; and the Russia-Georgia war.

Sometimes Mother Nature delivers the disaster. The power fails

and cell phones start dying. The hotel air conditioning stops working; so do the toilets. Water is no longer safe to drink. Rumors are
everywhere, but facts are scarce. The years 2006–2010 saw major
earthquakes in China, Italy, Chile, and Haiti; massive bushfires in
Australia; floods in Jeddah; and a deadly cyclone in Burma. These
equal opportunity calamities struck rich and poor countries alike,
although poverty affected recovery rates.

More subtle but just as devastating are economic crises. In 2008 an
unprecedented economic disaster unfolded on a global scale; millions
of people lost their jobs, homes, pensions, or life savings. The reactions
of their governments varied as they dealt with underlying structural
weaknesses in their economies. In Europe, it brought about the near
withdrawal of Greece from the eurozone—and the near joining of
Iceland. Jobless rates in southern European countries approached 25
percent, and the debt-to-GDP ratio in Greece neared 150 percent.
Debate over where to lay blame prompted nasty exchanges. While
leaders fulminated, austerity measures led to widespread riots, strikes,
and the fall of one government after another. Welcome to chaos, the
frequent offspring of crises.

American diplomats have a responsibility to protect American
citizens in a world full of unsafe places. Of course, the easiest way to
protect them is to convince them to stay home. The State Department
issues stern travel warnings for specific countries, instructing Americans to "reconsider their travel plans in light of current political tensions and the possibility of violence." The U.S. government would like
Americans to stay away from—at this writing—some thirty-seven
countries. Some brook no argument: North Korea, Iran, and Syria.
But other countries slapped with travel warnings have historical and
complex American connections, such as Mexico, Israel, Colombia,
El Salvador, and the Philippines. Americans live and work in these
countries; many more have deep family ties to them. While the State
Department hopes Americans will stay away, embassies deal with the
inevitability that Americans will be there, all the same.

Americans are globe hoppers. They work in NGOs, church groups, charitable organizations, civil society, and for media outlets reporting on all of the above. They run everything from health clinics to banks to educational exchanges for students, professors, and entire universities. They are contractors and advisors, people with sought-after skills who are admired—and hired. American consular officers help their fellow citizens overseas in dozens of ways. They issue passports to newborns and help eighteen-year-olds register to vote. They handle the minor crisis of a backpacker who lost his passport in a local bar, but they also deal with citizens who are ill, injured, or dead. For the American community abroad, the embassy is a first responder.

American embassies are in a unique position to chronicle and analyze these crises, and sometimes to predict them. In a natural disaster such as the 2010 Haiti earthquake, cables read like chapters in a gripping narrative. Long after television reporters had left the scene, embassy officers chronicled the painstaking efforts to put Haiti back on its feet. The cables depict an embassy improvising through broken lines of communication and infrastructure, coordinating assistance and response, and displaying the professionalism of an experienced consular corps working flat out.

In many such situations it is Washington that has the global view—embassies might not be able to see beyond the haze of tear gas, smoke, or wreckage. In the global economic crisis, for instance, embassy roles were bound to be limited. Most focused on the value they could add by describing how events played out in their host country, knowing that their observations were only a small part of a complex picture. On the other hand, during more traditional crises, embassies knew they had the full attention of Washington—but for only a limited time. The Haiti earthquake was neither the first nor the last. It was preceded by quakes in Sichuan, China, and L'Aquila, Italy. It was followed a month later by a Chilean earthquake of an even greater magnitude, which in turn was followed, about a year later, by a massive earthquake and tsunami in Japan.

In the WikiLeaks cables, diplomats provide details that take readers beyond the headlines. They describe how Iceland's economic pain came from the disarray of its officials, who seemed unable to summon the will to phone Washington. They illustrate how the unfathomable response of the military junta in Burma to Cyclone Nargis arose from a tradition in which omens matter, soothsayers are routinely consulted, and numerology governs decisions. Cables on Honduras describe a deeply polarized country's efforts to address a coup that seemed to have an equally polarizing effect in Washington.

EMBASSY AT THE EPICENTER: THE HAITI EARTHQUAKE

The magnitude 7.0 earthquake struck at 4:43 p.m. on Tuesday, January 12, 2010, when the roads were busy, children had been dismissed from school, and shops were full of customers. Security camera footage of panicked guards in the National Palace gives some idea of the terror, while aftermath photos of dust rising from the gigantic white edifice, with its three domes either collapsed or at jarring angles, give an idea of its power. None of the fourteen government ministry buildings in Port-au-Prince was left intact.

Deputy Regional Security Officer Peter Kolshorn recounted in DipNote, the State Department's official blog, how he raced to rescue embassy staff.

> All I could see was dust and gasoline flowing down the road. The severity of the situation hit me when I walked down the street to an embassy housing complex and saw a car in the driveway … but no house. I looked over the edge of the ridge and saw the

crumbled remains of the house and people buried in rubble. An embassy officer was buried up to her waist, face covered with dirt and blood and calling for help. To the left, a man tried to free himself from the rubble. Further to the left, an arm protruded from the wreckage. My head was spinning as I contemplated how to get them out.

Kolshorn described the indescribable:

I was nauseated from the gasoline fumes all over the street. The walking wounded appeared like shadows out of the dust. I made radio contact with my boss and asked for a vehicle to transport the injured . . . Information began to flow in, both from the embassy radio and people on the street: the National Palace, Hotel Montana, and the Caribbean Market had all collapsed; roads were impassable; and embassy employees were unaccounted for. It was a nightmare.

With no vehicle, Kolshorn improvised stretchers from ladders and metal gates.

The trek down the hill seemed to take forever, as we moved slowly to avoid the injured and dead who covered the road. Sounds of praying and screams of loss and pain filled the air. It was horrific. We heard the cries of children beneath the rubble; we stopped and with other survivors we managed to free one.

All told, it took Kolshorn seven hours to get to the road and reach transport, "a moment of elation in the nightmare . . . Then, the chaos really began back at the embassy."[1]

The embassy unleashed a tour de force of reporting, sending 162 cables, the first one transmitted seventy-two hours after the earthquake and running until February 28 (the final day of the tranche of leaked cables). Still to come, months later, were a cholera outbreak and disputed presidential elections.

Many of the cables were situation reports, or sitrep cables, painstakingly detailing each damaged aspect of Haitian society: transport, including ports, airports, and roads; infrastructure, such as electricity and water; hospitals and clinics caring for the injured; and conversations with both Haitians and the international community on how to set up one of the most comprehensive recovery efforts ever attempted.

By any standard, Haiti is a special case. It usually ranks at the bottom of any development list in the Western Hemisphere, and the UN Development Programme (UNDP) ranks it at 166 out of the 187 countries it measures.[2] It is often buffeted by natural disasters; it suffered four hurricanes in 2008. Even without disasters, nearly a fifth of its ten million people are considered "food insecure."[3] Although it lies just seven hundred miles from the United States, the tragedy of its endemic poverty, corruption, and dysfunctional governments make it feel like another world. Haiti's people have lived through decades of military interventions, dictatorships, and seemingly entrenched political instability. For years the United Nations has been in-country, helping to quell political violence and ensure stability. At the time of the earthquake, the UN Stabilization Mission in Haiti, known as MINUSTAH, was the most recent incarnation of the organization's presence.

Sadly, MINUSTAH lost 101 people, including the secretary general's special representative, his principal deputy, and scores of senior staff, when their headquarters at the Hotel Christophe crumbled. Tragedy touched the U.S. embassy as well. Cultural Affairs Officer Victoria DeLong was killed when her home collapsed. A total of 11 U.S. government workers, ranging from embassy local staff to Centers for Disease Control workers, died. In all, 104 Americans were killed out of a population of some 45,000 American citizens living and working in the country, some of whom carried both U.S. and Haitian nationality.

The first sitrep from the embassy was grim.

We continue to experience severe aftershocks. It is estimated that half the embassy residences are structurally unsound and uninhabitable ... Post continues attempting to contact the Government of Haiti Ministers, several of whom are reported injured by the Haitian press. The Ambassador has been unable to reach any GOH officials by phone ... MINUSTAH's response has admittedly been hampered by the fact that of the estimated 400 UN staff in the Hotel Christophe, approximately only 50 made it out.[4]

The embassy was quickly concerned about the absence of any police presence, particularly worrisome because as jails collapsed, almost all the prisoners escaped. Many police were killed, others were seeing to the needs of their families, still others had no means to get to work. Some worked in civilian clothes, their uniforms left in their destroyed homes. Police vehicles were useless without fuel. Communication was cut off because police stations had no electricity and could not keep phones or radios charged. Roving gangs looted with impunity and large numbers of people wandered the streets.

"Looters dragged a USAID contractor from his vehicle at gunpoint on January 13 as he was leaving the parliament, after spending hours digging out bodies, including two dead Senators, Michele Louis and Jacque Wilbert. Thieves shot his vehicle and pulled him out; he gave them his cash, then got back into his car and left the scene."[5] Adding to the grimness, "the Petionville police station is also plagued by citizens who are depositing the corpses of victims on the property."[6]

Getting help into Haiti was a logistical hell. Flights could not land at the damaged airport for the first two days and were diverted to the Dominican Republic, Haiti's neighbor on the shared island of Hispaniola, notwithstanding the fact that the only highway connecting the countries was too damaged for vehicles. Ships bringing in cargo could find no viable berths—many jetties lay underwater. There was no gas for vehicles, no service for cell phones, no electricity for lights, and people were increasingly desperate for food and water. Massive amounts of rubble and unburied cadavers hampered recovery efforts. A reporting officer described the street scene: "Damaged vehicles remain abandoned in the middle of the road, some with drivers and passengers still inside. An increasing number of bodies, many uncovered, line the streets and are beginning to decay."[7]

And a few hours later:

> After nightfall, living in Port-au-Prince is an eerie and surreal experience. The city is mostly dark, with very few vehicles on the streets. The odor of decaying corpses is beginning to permeate the air. The night is filled with a constant cacophony of sounds: mostly chanting and the singing of hymns, but interspersed with screams of grief, prayers shouted from loudspeakers and barking dogs. After an aftershock occurs, the background noise increases in a wave of screams rising from the city.[8]

Secretary of State Clinton flew to Haiti at the request of President René Préval, arriving four days after the quake in a Coast Guard cargo plane; however, even she was not immune to the airport congestion. The embassy reported, "Préval cited the fact that the Secretary's plane had to circle the airport and delay landing due to air traffic as an example of the lack of (aid) coordination." Préval told Clinton that his only means of communicating with the prime minister and cabinet members was "by having them arrive at his residence by motorcycle."[9]

The secretary and her team set in motion the assistance and coordination that was to follow for months. While in agreement over most issues, Clinton noted that Préval and Prime Minister Jean-Max Bellerive were resistant to the idea of refugee camps to house the 1.5 million homeless, an idea for which there was no good alternative.

She effectively made the decision for them. "We need to work to sell them on the idea," the secretary told the embassy. "Haiti is still in shock, but now they can see and hear the response."[10]

By the end of the first week, signs of improvement began to emerge. U.S. government agencies are nothing if not specialized, and soon embassy sitreps evolved into detailed damage assessments of each sector of Haitian society, with a can-do strategy about how to get things up and running. The embassy's Narcotics Affairs Section took on the police stations and prisons; U.S. Navy engineers focused on the ports; USAID's Food for Peace, partnering with the UN's World Food Programme (WFP), took on the task of delivering food to two million people. To illustrate the challenge, the embassy reported, "Due to inaccurate information, WFP transported commodities for 5,000 people, but 20,000 people arrived to collect food rations. To resolve the situation, WFP reduced the supply per person from 5 to 3 days."[11]

The embassy officers seemed eager to report glimpses of recovery; gradually the tenor of their reporting changed from horror to cautious optimism. Their cables tell Haiti's story from many angles: from the shock of destruction to efforts to get organized to signs of new life and hope. For example, the roads got slightly better. A trip from the Dominican Republic, normally about an hour, had taken five hours post-earthquake, but was soon down to three. By day twelve the embassy reported fuel deliveries had restarted, bringing the mixed blessing of more vehicles on damaged and rubble-strewn roads with massive traffic jams and long delays. Banks and wire transfer companies began to disburse funds, and fruit and vegetable street vendors slowly returned.

Organizing health care for a vulnerable population was another huge undertaking. The USS *Carl Vinson* and the USNS *Comfort* arrived to offer 1,000 hospital beds, with 10 operating rooms, 24 surgeons, and 130 nursing staff on board. The ships were attached to a huge effort on land to assess local hospitals and clinics and supplement medical assistance, primary care, and disease prevention.

At its peak there were 67 international search-and-rescue teams, comprising 1,918 staff and 160 dogs. "Recent search and rescue operations in Haiti are unprecedented, resulting in the largest number of known rescues in an international response. To the surprise of many, live rescues were still conducted 11 days after the earthquake, far surpassing the expected 72-hour window of survival."[12]

Soon cables began focusing on a private sector eager to get back to work, especially the garment industry. Owners met to coordinate efforts to get factories up and running—their employment and foreign earnings were seen as a key aspect of recovery. About 30 to 40 percent of the country's production capacity had been damaged.[13]

All too soon, on February 28, the WikiLeaks cables stop, long before Haiti had completed its path to recovery. Nonetheless, the intensity of embassy coverage offers a case study in the early stages of disaster recovery and a chance to deconstruct, step by step, the architecture of one of the most massive and complex recovery operations ever mounted. Readers see firsthand how embassies cope, improvise, and organize. The embassy reporters had the advantage of knowing the terrain, with many officers having worked other crises elsewhere. They reported on crucial but less newsworthy items, personalized the accounts, and guided the initial planning and relief efforts. The embassy was widely praised for the professionalism of its actions, but its reporting was also a tour de force.

In an interesting footnote, the death toll of the quake remains hotly disputed. The U.S. government and independent aid workers place the toll at anywhere from a low of 46,000 to 160,000. The Haitian government is accused of deliberately inflating the numbers from its initial count of 230,000 (widely seen as inflated and unsubstantiated) to 316,000 on the first anniversary of the quake as a means of getting more assistance.[14] In contrast, the military government in Burma did exactly the opposite in the aftermath of Cyclone Nargis, essentially stopping the count at 138,000, for fear that acknowledging a higher number would lead to political instability.

In fact, they were right.

CYCLONE NARGIS AND THE WINDS OF CHANGE

Half a globe away from Haiti lies Burma, with a population of nearly fifty-four million, making it almost as populous as Italy, with a geographic size larger than France.[15] Located on the Bay of Bengal, its neighbors include Bangladesh, India, China, Laos, and Thailand. Like Haiti, it also ranks low on the UN Development Programme's scale, coming in at 148 out of 187. But in Burma's case, the lack of development can be traced to the military junta that ran the country from 1962 to 2011, following a socialist one-party model with occasional periods of martial law to suppress protest and reform movements. Its most famous pro-democracy dissident, Aung San Suu Kyi, endured years of house arrest and harassment before her party, the National League for Democracy, won by-elections in 2012, which led to her gaining a seat in parliament. By late 2015, her party had won a majority of seats in parliament.

The United States imposed severe economic and investment sanctions on Burma in 1997 through the Office of Foreign Assets Control. Subsequent reviews reinforced and expanded prohibitions on importation of products of Burmese origin or on any sort of U.S. investment in Burma. Other countries and organizations, including the European Union (EU), imposed similar sanctions. Burma ended decades of isolation with a visit from Secretary of State Clinton in December 2011, which in turn led to the gradual lifting of some sanctions and additional meetings between Burmese president Thein Sein and President Obama in 2012 and 2013.

The country's size and geopolitical significance give added meaning to the story of Burma's cyclone—a remarkable tale of destruction and transformation. The cyclone also offers proof that military juntas can be undone by their own bad habits—crony capitalism, corruption, and the isolation that comes from not being answerable to an electorate. Cyclone Nargis killed tens of thousands of people, but it was the disarray it wrought among the ruling generals, exposed as uncaring, incompetent, and paranoid, that helped to spell the regime's end.

The cyclone, a rare low-altitude storm with 120-mph winds, was the worst natural disaster in Burma's history. It made landfall overnight on May 2–3, 2008, and sent a storm surge up the densely populated Irrawaddy River Delta. Nargis arrived a week before a previously scheduled national referendum on a new constitution, to which pro-democracy activists were urging a "no" vote.

The embassy reporting was prescient. Days before the cyclone touched land, U.S. diplomats had warned, "The GOB [government of Burma] has traditionally turned down international assistance, as it did after the 2004 tsunami . . . the regime may be especially averse to assistance at what they consider a politically sensitive time."[16] And in its first report following the disaster, on May 5, the embassy again emphasized that the scale of U.S. assistance would depend on the willingness of Burmese government authorities to accept it.[17] Later that day, the embassy's chief of mission exercised disaster assistance authority, declaring that "the disaster is beyond the capability of the host government to respond, and is of sufficient magnitude to warrant U.S. government assistance, and that it is in the best interest of the U.S. government to respond."[18] Those criteria are required under U.S. law to set up a formal disaster relief operation.

Subsequent cables depict an exasperating fight with the government. The junta leaders, perhaps revealing their naiveté about the strategic and technical elements of a massive assistance operation, were reluctant to allow commodities, aid workers, and aid assessors to enter the country. Burmese recalcitrance frustrated the efforts of the entire international community. The generals, hunkered down in their newly built capital of Nay Pyi Taw, two hundred miles north of the hard-hit Delta region, seemed unaware of the scale of the disaster. According to the embassy, this was because no mid-level underlings had the courage to inform them. Old and out of touch, the generals believed humanitarian assistance could be confined to deliveries of bottled water at the airport; they had no idea of the sophistication and coordination a modern humanitarian aid operation requires. The generals resisted any notion of the need for aid workers on the ground, confident they could handle the complexities of distribution. When they could not, they gave their people a new reason to wish for their removal. With each passing day, lives were needlessly lost. The discovery that those who ruled were incapable of caring for their people opened new avenues for pro-democracy activists.

A few days following the cyclone, the embassy warned that although Burma had requested international assistance, it was not yet ready to permit entry of either UN or U.S. government assessment teams, "so they should not make any travel plans."[19] This soon became a refrain, as the embassy described the extensive damage and the many signs that Burma's leaders were in denial. Despite the destruction of the Irrawaddy Delta, including the collapse of 95 percent of the buildings, "the Minister of Social Welfare asserted Rangoon [also known as Yangon, the former capital, and still the country's commercial center and most populous city] was 'not severely hurt; not very big damage.'"[20]

The embassy immediately saw the political implications of the cyclone, noting that the regime was determined to continue with the constitutional referendum on May 10, a week after the cyclone hit, albeit with at least a third of Burma's population unable to vote. "This unprecedented humanitarian disaster has knocked both the regime and the pro-democracy opposition off their game. Both are grappling to respond. While the regime continues to make claims of recovery that people know are untrue, and to dismiss the need for international expertise to provide humanitarian relief, the generals may have to reverse course in order to assure their own survival."[21]

The embassy, still located in Rangoon, offered details of the immediate challenge of a massive cleanup. The government relied on army personnel but left them woefully ill equipped. "They can be seen around town trying to dismantle fallen trees with little more than knives and brooms."[22] The embassy was also affected, reporting rather quaintly, "We received one chainsaw from Bangkok today and we will receive 4 more chainsaws within one or two days. Post has requested 2000 MREs [meals ready to eat], and Embassy Bangkok will send us batteries."[23]

The storm's destruction had huge economic implications for the Delta region, Burma's outlet for export earnings. It sank eighty registered ships in the Rangoon River, cutting off access to the port and oil refinery. A refinery business source told the embassy that the government's practice was to clear sunken ships with divers who "use saws and machetes to cut the ships into pieces. This can take up to six months for one ship."[24]

But the humanitarian catastrophe was of primary concern. "UN local staff in Labutta reported a make-shift camp of 100,000 people has been set up with nothing to eat or drink. Corpses are floating everywhere, contaminating local waterways that people use for drinking water because they have nothing else."[25] Two weeks later, the embassy's concern mounted. "The GOB has yet to come to terms with the fact that it does not have the capacity to respond to this disaster ... Relief supplies to date have not reached most of the victims in the region two weeks after Cyclone Nargis slammed into the Delta."[26]

Soon the focus shifted to the prolonged delays in issuing visas for international relief workers. The embassy quoted sources saying that no high-level government officials dared to describe the full scope of the disaster to the seventy-five-year-old senior general, Than Shwe.

Unpleasant pictures in the media reportedly make the Senior General retreat even further into isolation. According to our contacts, Than Shwe is above all concerned with saving face and holding onto power.

. . . Meanwhile PM Thein Sein and the eight ministers on the national rescue committee reportedly have become more desperate. Sources told us Thein Sein expressed fear to [the third-ranking general] that 60,000 had lost their lives already and up to 300,000 could, if water, food and medicine were not delivered quickly.

. . . Than Shwe's isolation and paranoia know no bounds. All fingers point to him as the obstacle to delivering the humanitarian assistance the Burmese so desperately need, just like he is the obstacle to an inclusive political dialogue. Our many contacts are visibly distraught as they watch Burma's humanitarian catastrophe worsen by the day because of the intransigence of Than Shwe. The question is who is brave enough to shunt Than Shwe aside? Most Burmese tell us no one. Other senior officials may passively sit while thousands needlessly die rather than challenge Than Shwe.[27]

The international relief community was equally exasperated. Assistance teams languished without visas for weeks, and the Burmese government actually turned away sixty-two medics who arrived on a chartered relief flight from Bangladesh. The UN's World Food Programme suspended relief shipments to Burma after the regime refused to release supplies from one of its flights.[28]

Then, suddenly, the picture changed. A U.S. C-130 relief flight, accompanied by Pacific Command's Admiral Timothy Keating, USAID administrator Henrietta Fore, and other American officials, was allowed to land on May 13. It was quickly followed by two more flights the following day and five the day after. In an understated description of behind-the-scenes diplomacy, the embassy wrote, "On May 11, the Chargé met with the Chinese Ambassador to discuss the possibility that Burmese authorities may object to Admiral Keating's presence on the C-130. After further discussion, the Burmese authorities agreed not to object to the admiral's visit."[29]

The rarity of the chargé's meeting suggests the extent of Chinese alarm over Burma's resistance to aid—and the fact that many of China's investment projects may have been suffering. "The opaque nature of China's economic involvement in Burma is compounded by the reclusive nature of the PRC diplomatic presence here. The Chinese embassy regularly rebuffs requests for meetings and information from the Rangoon-based diplomatic community."[30] The embassy was keenly aware of Chinese economic influence in Burma. An economic cable noted that Chinese investment had increased dramatically over the past decade, visible in hydropower, oil, gas, mining, and construction projects. Officially, China was Burma's third-largest trading partner, after Thailand and Singapore, but embassy sources speculated that unofficial trade might be ten to twenty times the official trade value.

Once on the ground, the delicate conversations between the U.S. delegation and the Burmese went nowhere. "The meeting went as we expected. The Burmese delegation, which did not include anyone with decision-making authority, was pleasant and cordial, but made no firm commitment to accept U.S. assistance beyond relief supplies flown into Rangoon.... If it was not clear before, it is now: the Burmese Government, at this time, welcomes the donation of commodities to assist with cyclone relief and only that."[31]

On the other hand, the visit received an unprecedented amount of government-controlled news coverage, including nearly seven minutes on national television and pages of newspaper photos. "To most ordinary Burmese, the positive coverage of the deliveries of U.S. humanitarian aid was extraordinary... a real breakthrough. Today in Burma, where we have been unable to place even the most innocuous press release ... we are enjoying the most positive attention we have ever received."[32]

In later analytical reporting, the embassy revealed that the senior generals believed the United States was about to launch an invasion. It was inconceivable to them that a U.S. naval carrier could sail near Burmese territorial waters with no motive other than logistical support for humanitarian efforts. The chargé wrote, "While it would also be nice to think that our Nargis assistance had positively changed minds, it appears more likely that fear of a U.S. invasion prompted the opening... The fear of invasion was real, according to a variety of our contacts in the regime."[33] Pro-democracy activists agreed, telling embassy officials later that the regime understood military might, "and only the presence of U.S. military ships had forced the generals to allow relief workers access to the post-Nargis Delta."[34]

Willingness to accept aid did not last long. Despite a call from UN Secretary-General Ban Ki-moon urging immediate issuance of visas to UN aid workers, Than Shwe was unresponsive. The embassy noted that the UN humanitarian assistance coordinator was not allowed to enter the country until May 18 and made no progress in obtaining permission for his international staff to visit the field. Other reputable international bodies, such as the Emergency Rapid Assessment Team of the Association of Southeast Asian Nations (ASEAN), of which Burma is a member, were also denied permission to visit the field, as was the European Union's commissioner for development and humanitarian aid.

Indeed, the Burmese regime continued to ignore reality. Subsequent cables document how the on-again, off-again approach to visas became a pattern, with international aid workers almost as desperate to get in as the people they hoped to reach. "As we have seen too often, the GOB will make a concession and then start backtracking... The senior generals cannot resist micromanaging everything."[35]

The consequences came home to roost at an international donor conference staged three weeks after the cyclone hit. "The regime's hope for a cash-rich pledging conference fell flat as donors held on to their checkbooks... GOB hoped the conference would net billions of dollars to rebuild the ravaged delta. Donors instead chose to remind the generals that there is no free lunch."[36] Despite the regime's disappointment, the embassy doubted that the donors' scolding would change the regime's behavior.

To understand the intellectual distance Burma's leaders had to travel, a cable discussing prospects for the International Committee of the Red Cross to work in Burma noted that it took nine months for Burmese officials to hold a substantive discussion with the organization, which they viewed as "toxic."[37] Burmese journalists were jailed for reporting on Nargis victims who dared to complain about the regime's slow response.[38] The regime continued to toy with aid workers' visas, delaying renewal for the directors of CARE, Pact, and Save the Children, while denying renewal for two senior UN officials, a WHO epidemiologist and the UNDP country representative.[39] Driving home the point, the embassy wrote that, as further proof of the regime's paranoia, "the Orwellian-sounding Cartoon Exhibition Supervisory Committee" had pulled four cartoons from an exhibition to raise funds for cyclone victims.[40]

Yet the embassy reporting offers evidence that the cyclone led, at least indirectly, to profound changes. Diplomatic colleagues suggested that the continuing international humanitarian presence had opened a small political space in the country as local NGOs got involved in the distribution of humanitarian aid.[41] The embassy agreed, reporting, "Relationships between villagers and local authorities are changing and villagers are taking actions to ensure the aid is distributed transparently and evenly." The continuing international relief effort "has the potential to move Burma towards democratic change by instilling participatory decision making and notions of accountability at a grass-roots level. The regime has opened opportunities to work with Burmese civil society to an unprecedented degree." A World Bank expert in social impact analysis noted people were beginning to hold their leaders accountable. Civil society was starting to expand.[42]

The cyclone brought changes in Washington, too. Embassy reporting and increased international attention on Burma raised awareness of a long-stagnant diplomatic relationship, possibly creating room for new thinking. Half a year after the cyclone, Secretary of State Clinton ordered a policy review. By August, Senator Jim Webb (D-VA) made the first congressional visit to Burma since Senator John Kerry had visited in 1999. The following month, Clinton announced changes in the United States' Burma policy at the UN, saying that "engagement versus sanctions is a false choice." She was the first secretary of state to visit Burma in more than fifty years. She wrote enthusiastically about her growing relationship with pro-democracy activist and Nobel laureate Aung San Suu Kyi and her frustration over the country's hesitant progress toward democracy, noting, "It is sometimes hard to resist getting breathless about Burma."[43]

LET'S CALL IT A COUP:
THE CASE OF HONDURAS

Latin America has such a sorry legacy of overthrown governments that one assumes every embassy must have an *In Case of a Coup* hand-book. There are certain depressingly familiar triggers. Presidents chafe at term limits or refuse to accept election results; constitutions are capriciously changed; and the roles of the executive, legislative, and judicial bodies and, above all, the military become jumbled. Neigh-boring countries have the bad habit of harboring fugitive leaders who never seem to face justice. Those same neighbors nonetheless vote to expel the offending country from regional organizations and self-righteously recall their ambassadors.

The Honduran coup of June 28, 2009, was a six-month diplomatic odyssey, with elements of both drama and farce: a president whisked out of the country in the dead of night in his pajamas, a forged letter of resignation, and plenty of double-talk—not all of it from Honduras—about how the coup had actually preserved democracy. Unlike natural disasters, in which the U.S. goal is to minimize death and suffering in a country and help it rebuild, political crises require a broader range of solutions. Frequently the U.S. has its own favored outcome, a factor that had huge implications in Honduras.

The immediate events of the day in question are the only uncontested aspect. At 2:30 a.m. on Sunday, June 28, 2009, Honduran president Manuel Zelaya, in office since January 2006, was hustled out of bed by the military and forcibly flown to Costa Rica. The pajama detail became such a consistent part of the narrative that when Zelaya later met Secretary of State Clinton, he joked that as a result of the Honduran coup all Latin American presidents had learned to sleep with their clothes on and their bags packed.[44]

Zelaya was replaced by Roberto Micheletti, the president of the Honduran National Congress and next in the line of succession. Micheletti, who served from June 28, 2009, through January 27, 2010, was cold-shouldered by the United States and most other nations and international organizations as a de facto president who had deposed a democratically elected one. However, the back story and cast of characters are important. The left-wing Zelaya had outraged Honduran conservatives by forging alliances with Raúl Castro of Cuba, Hugo Chávez of Venezuela, and Daniel Ortega of Nicaragua. He raised suspicions when he called for a poll to gauge public interest in his plan to change the constitution, a change that would allow presidents to serve two terms. Critics saw this as a means of unlawfully remaining in power. The Supreme Court upheld a lower court ruling blocking the referendum, and the Honduran Congress, attorney general, and human rights ombudsman all agreed that Zelaya had violated the law. Nonetheless, Zelaya pushed on with his plan for a June 28 poll that would in turn authorize a full referendum and requested that the military prepare ballot boxes. The ranking general refused and Zelaya fired him, which led to the resignations of the defense minister and several other officials. Both the high court and the Congress ruled that the firing was unlawful, triggering the crisis that led to the coup.

The trail of U.S. embassy cables reveals a remarkable behind-the-scenes effort to get Zelaya reinstated, an effort that cost the United States some diplomatic capital along with the ire of conservatives back home, who argued that the coup came in the nick of time to rescue Honduras from Venezuela's path. The cables also reveal the limits of even the most intense U.S. pressure, as one initiative after another failed to accomplish the Obama administration's stated goal of returning Zelaya to office.

The deposed president embarked on peregrinations worthy of a deposed monarch, hobnobbing with anyone who would give him a platform from which to rally supporters. Zelaya gained more prominence as a deposed president than he had ever achieved while in office. Consider this portion of his exhausting itinerary: After being summarily deposed on June 28, he landed in Costa Rica but moved on to Nicaragua a few hours later to represent Honduras at a regional meeting; he then flew to New York to make a speech before the UN on June 30. On July 5, he tried to land in Honduras aboard a Venezuelan aircraft while twelve thousand supporters swamped the airport. His plane circled, but the sight of military vehicles on the tarmac dissuaded him from landing.[45] He ended up back in Nicaragua and later El Salvador, where he was joined in a press conference by the secretary general of the Organization of American States (OAS) and the presidents of El Salvador, Argentina, Ecuador, and Paraguay.[46] He met Secretary of State Clinton in Washington on July 7, who persuaded him to work with the mediation of Óscar Arias Sánchez, the Costa Rican president and recipient of the Nobel Peace Prize in 1987.[47]

Zelaya stayed for a time in Managua and then staked out a spot on the Nicaraguan side of a border town. He finally snuck back into his own country on September 20 and holed up in the Brazilian embassy, where his entourage created chaos for his hosts. In the aftermath of U.S.-brokered elections, which he advised his followers to boycott, Zelaya made an unsuccessful attempt to flee to Mexico on December 9 and was finally granted safe passage to the Dominican Republic on January 27, the day of the inauguration of the next Honduran president, conservative Porfirio Lobo Sosa. Throughout this period, his supporters protested at rallies that sometimes turned violent, leading to injuries and some deaths, and sparking fears of descent into civil war.

Zelaya was a controversial figure from the outset of his presidency, clashing with Honduran conservatives and media over his populist policies, even before he launched his plan for a constituent assembly to draft a new constitution. Clinton described him as "a throwback to the caricature of a Central American strongman, with his white cowboy hat, dark black mustache, and fondness for Hugo Chávez and Fidel Castro."[48] Many American conservatives applauded the coup. They saw Zelaya as the most recent in a disturbing trend of left-wing Latin American leaders: Lula da Silva in Brazil, Daniel Ortega in Nicaragua, Rafael Correa in Ecuador, Evo Morales in Bolivia, and of course Hugo Chávez in Venezuela. They also saw Chávez's hands (and money, and mischief) all over Zelaya. Venezuela had reportedly printed the ballots that would have been used for the referendum. The embassy reported that Chávez was so eager to see Zelaya restored to office that he arranged for food, weapons, and supplies to be brought into Honduras from Nicaragua for the use of Zelaya's supporters, leading many Hondurans to believe that "Zelaya is planning to return to retake the presidency violently, and with Venezuelan support."[49]

The embassy reported that the coup divided the Honduran public almost evenly. The opposition insisted the action was in defense of democracy against a would-be dictator. The Supreme Court president and the human rights commissioner both spoke in favor of the coup, as did members of Congress from the opposition and Zelaya's own party. The Roman Catholic archbishop of Honduras, Cardinal Oscar Andrew Rodriguez, endorsed the coup on live television and implored Zelaya not to return for the good of the country.[50]

The coup also divided opinion outside Honduras. The majority of the international community was unswayed by pro-coup arguments. The UN called for Zelaya's immediate and unconditional restoration. Faced with an ultimatum from the OAS to restore Zelaya, de facto President Micheletti withdrew from the group (a move of dubious legality) on July 2. The European Union recalled its ambassadors, and both the Inter-American Development Bank and the World Bank "paused" their loans to the country. The embassy reported that virtually all Honduran political and personal contacts "displayed a high degree of naiveté over how the coup would be perceived by the international community."[51]

Nowhere did the quarrel play out more erratically than in the United States, where gyrating opinions on the coup illustrated the disparate perceptions among Washington, the embassy, and the American body politic. Conservatives charged that the State Department mishandled it from the start; liberals said that Clinton's efforts to restore constitutional order, many of which are documented in the WikiLeaks cables, resulted in a tainted new government, a horrific upswing in human rights violence, and deeper poverty for an already impoverished nation. Honduran coup supporters were heartened by comments from prominent U.S. Republicans and the editorial pages of the *Wall Street Journal*, which declared the coup "strangely, well, democratic," giving Hondurans hope that the U.S. government might interpret the crisis as something more benign than a true coup.[52] Their hopes were short-lived.

Was it a coup? President Obama was pretty clear, saying on June 29 that "the coup was not legal" and could "set a terrible precedent." Clinton was more nuanced, saying the situation "had evolved into a coup," but that the United States was "withholding any formal legal determination." Clearly playing for time, she added, "We're assessing what the final outcome of these actions will be. Much of our assistance is conditioned on the integrity of the democratic system. But if we are able to get to a status quo that returned to the rule of law and constitutional order within a relatively short period of time, I think that would be a good outcome."[53]

American political commentators seized on Honduras as the first real test for Obama and Clinton's foreign policy. The theme of the Obama administration siding with Latin American leftists like Zelaya was picked up by the right. Commentator Mary Anastasia O'Grady wrote that Hondurans were being "pressured to restore the authoritarian Mr. Zelaya by the likes of Fidel Castro, Daniel Ortega,

[and] Hillary Clinton."[54] The *New Republic* said Clinton's Honduras policy was "a mistake in search of a rationale."[55]

Writers on the left were not much kinder. Mark Weisbrot of the Center for Economic and Policy Research railed against what he saw as conflicting statements from the White House and the State Department and assailed the department's neutrality in its reply to a query from Senator Richard Lugar, which he said appeared to blame Zelaya for the coup.[56] Reuters wrote that the Honduran crisis had divided Washington. "Earlier this month, 16 Democratic Congressmen wrote to Obama urging him to freeze the assets of coup leaders. But a group of Republican senators has sought to hold up confirmation of State Department appointments due to the administration's support for Zelaya, an ally of Venezuela's leftist president Hugo Chávez."[57] Despite the Republican encouragement, Hondurans were caught off guard by the mixed reaction in the United States, and the embassy reported, "They have expressed surprise and dismay at the USG response, stating that they feel abandoned by the USG."[58]

The leaked cables reveal that the embassy played an enormous role throughout the crisis, maintaining a frenetic rate of activity as it dealt with realities on the ground as well as in Washington. The embassy was deluged with so many congressional visits in the six months between the coup and the inauguration of Lobo that the *New York Times* noted, "The situation wasn't helped by Republican members of the United States Congress who traveled earlier to Tegucigalpa to cheer on the coup makers (they appear far more concerned about Mr. Zelaya's cozy relations with Venezuela's Hugo Chávez than democracy)."[59] Embassy cables reveal that the ambassador complained to Óscar Arias about how a congressional delegation led by Connie Mack (R-FL) had attended a high-profile meeting with de facto President Micheletti, which "had not been helpful to our efforts to find a democratic and constitutional solution to the crisis, since it gave Micheletti the hope to hang tough and not negotiate on the issue of the quick return of President Zelaya."[60]

A key actor in the crisis was Ambassador Hugo Llorens, an experienced career foreign service officer in charge of an embassy of 450 staff from fourteen U.S. government agencies, 180 Peace Corps volunteers, and at least indirectly responsible for 500 U.S. military personnel at Soto Cano Air Base. (Its presence made it unlikely from the start that the United States would ever completely abandon Honduras.) His embassy's prolific coverage of the coup and documentation of efforts to restore democracy offers a day-by-day (and sometimes hour-by-hour) description of U.S. diplomacy. His embassy wrote seventy sitreps and many additional cables providing context on human rights, media, political personalities, and ongoing negotiations, totaling more than eight hundred cables in the five months between the June 28 coup and the election on November 29 of a new president.

Llorens's involvement raises questions as to whether the United States crossed the line from helpful neighbor to agenda-laden interloper. Was the considerable coercion the United States exercised justified? Was the stated U.S. aim of restoring Zelaya to office ever feasible or worthwhile?

The embassy played hardball from the start. At a press conference outside the embassy on the day of the coup, the ambassador condemned it. The first embassy report described the mood in grim terms. Broadcast news was abruptly cut off the air; Internet and landlines were down; there were curfews, arrests, and tear gas. "Black smoke was seen rising from the area around the presidential palace around 8:30, apparently from burning tires. One source at a nearby hotel reported seeing a car burning. A military helicopter has been circling low around the area."[61]

The following day, the embassy reported it was maintaining a no-contact policy with Micheletti and his de facto regime, noting that since the U.S. government did not recognize the regime, the embassy would not send diplomatic notes until further notice.[62] By July 8, the embassy announced that a substantial amount of U.S. foreign assistance to Honduras had been suspended, and that much more was under review."[63]

One of the only ambassadors left in the country, Llorens would later call the experience one of the most challenging he had ever faced. The United States could have recalled him, leaving the running of the embassy to a chargé, but would have lost the opportunity to work through the crisis alongside the Hondurans and influence the outcome. The leaked cables suggest that having an ambassador present was an advantage. The intensity of his engagement was remarkable.

The ambassador reported that he spoke with Zelaya "on a daily basis to counter the influence of these radical elements and balance the President's [Zelaya's] perspective."[64] The cables showed he was speaking with Costa Rican mediator Arias almost as frequently, and with members of the entire Honduran political spectrum. He took plenty of criticism for his role. Senator Jim DeMint (R-SC) said he was "the only one in Honduras who thinks there was a coup."[65] Juan Carlos Hidalgo of the Cato Institute called him a "proconsul."

Latin American coups have a way of becoming personal. Llorens housed one of Zelaya's adult children and his family and repeatedly offered safe harbor to Zelaya's wife. On July 1 he sent the defense attaché with three vehicles to her country home to bring her and eight family members to the capital. They spent a night at the ambassador's residence, then moved on to a family home. Weeks later he invited them all to dinner.[66] Sadly, none of this solicitude would prevent Zelaya from turning on him months later.

In addition to near-daily sitreps, embassy officers frequently returned to the theme of the illegality of the coup, concluding in one cable, "We believe the military and the Congress conspired in the coup . . . the actions taken to remove the president were patently illegal."[67] Another cable offered a Who's Who of the Honduran coup, profiling the key actors. The pivotal cable, "Open and Shut: The Case of the Honduran Coup," considered every legal argument and concluded that it was indeed a coup.[68]

The embassy and the State Department had a vested interest in proving that a coup had occurred. This allowed them to impose a range of sanctions and exert leverage against Honduras, ranging from cutting off significant aid to canceling military exercises and revoking visas of de facto regime members. The heft of U.S. involvement in Honduras gave it far more leverage than more symbolic cut-offs by the EU and other nations. Had the Obama administration determined there was no coup, none of these actions would have been available. They also chose the mediator. No one doubts Arias's stature, but the initiative to ask him to mediate was Clinton's.

The cables take for granted that Honduras's political environment was worse off for having undergone a coup. The fact that some polls indicated a majority of Hondurans supported the coup was distressing to the embassy, which insisted nonetheless that the coup was a setback to Honduran democracy.

Talks under Arias began in Costa Rica on July 9, and the embassy shifted gears from worrying about the legality of the coup to expressing frustration over intransigence from Micheletti and his team. The cables make clear that Arias saw the ambassador as a key partner. For example, he called Llorens on July 13 to see if Llorens had been able to "soften the position of the de facto regime."[69] In response, the embassy launched what it called "a full court press to get Micheletti to reinstate Zelaya."[70] In fact, a key part of what became known as the San Jose Accords was Zelaya's reinstatement—something which never happened. Arias and the ambassador spoke six more times before the end of July. Despite a phone call from Secretary of State Clinton, Micheletti balked at signing any accord, and by late July Zelaya told the ambassador the Arias talks were a failure.

What to do? The ambassador and Arias conferred, and Llorens noted that the United States continued to "pause" economic assistance and had completely suspended military aid. The next step was to pressure regime officials by withdrawing their diplomatic visas, a step urged by both Arias and Zelaya. In fact, visa revocations had begun on July 28 with the top four Micheletti officials. Another round of revocations targeting more Micheletti associates came on September 10; they continued throughout the fall and into the new year.

The embassy also put pressure on Zelaya. The ambassador described to Arias a meeting he had with Zelaya in Managua in which he urged him "to put on his presidential suit," take the diplomatic offensive, and work for a diplomatic solution on the basis of the Arias plan. He told Zelaya that his activities on the Nicaraguan-Honduran border had earned him bad press coverage. His opponents had labeled him a radical and reinforced the perception of his close ties to Venezuelan president Hugo Chávez.[71] It is unusual for an ambassador to speak this sternly to a head of state, even one who has been deposed.

A few weeks later the ambassador and Arias were again sharing concerns—this time about Micheletti's intransigence. Arias worried that the regime was seeking to stall and delay and did not seem fully committed to reaching a deal. He suggested that the United States needed to increase the pressure on the business community and "consider taking away their visas and possibly freezing their bank accounts."[72]

On August 26, the embassy did something unprecedented. It stopped issuing U.S. travel visas to *everyone* in Honduras, with the exception of those seeking emergency care or permanent immigrants. This action took the conflict—and U.S. pressure for a resolution—to all Hondurans. Grandmothers hoping to attend weddings, students hoping to study at U.S. universities, and families hoping for a trip to Disney World were now out of luck.

Even that drastic step produced few concrete results. Zelaya roiled the country anew with his return to Honduras on September 20. When he took sanctuary at the Brazilian embassy, Micheletti's team beefed up security, worried that Zelaya's supporters would reinstate him by force. Ignoring international law governing the sanctity of embassies, the de facto regime turned off the Brazilian embassy's water and electricity and surrounded the compound with security forces who assaulted people. The U.S. embassy had to step in and convince the regime to restore services and stand down. The Brazilian chargé described in graphic terms to his American colleagues what it's like when a political refugee shows up at your embassy. He described the situation inside as tense, with Zelaya and one hundred and fifty supporters occupying most of the compound and running a well-organized political operation despite outside efforts to jam communications, and despite appeals from the Brazilian foreign minister to Zelaya to maintain a low profile.[73]

After a month of this, Washington dispatched the heavyweight team of Assistant Secretary of State for Western Hemisphere Affairs Thomas Shannon, Principal Deputy Assistant Secretary of State Craig Kelly, and National Security Council Senior Director for Western Hemisphere Affairs Daniel Restrepo. After exhaustive talks, the delegation obtained agreement from Zelaya and Micheletti to resume stalled negotiations, which culminated in the signing on October 29 of the Tegucigalpa/San Jose Agreement, which would have restored Zelaya and allowed him to finish out his term.[74] The cable triumphantly describes it as "an historical reversal of a Latin American coup through peaceful negotiation. Work remains to implement the accord, but we believe the political will exists to do so." This assessment turned out to be wildly optimistic. The embassy also announced that in a gesture of support for the agreement, it would reopen its nonimmigrant visa section.

Less than two weeks later, Craig Kelly was back in town, trying to put implementation back on track.[75] It was clear that Micheletti was simply playing out the clock until the election. Kelly met with Zelaya (but according to the reporting cable not with Micheletti), and Zelaya maintained the upcoming election would not be valid without his reinstatement and declared he would call for a boycott. Kelly was back in town a third time a week later, and a more realistic Zelaya admitted there was no chance for his reinstatement before the elections. Kelly also met with business leaders close to Micheletti and urged them to pass on the message that he should step down. In this at least, the United States was compelling, and Micheletti agreed to take a "leave of absence" on the eve of the elections.

The prolonged and unresolved governance situation made for an uneasy election. Turnout was disputed, but it was probably between

45 and 50 percent. The embassy reported that "November 29 was a great day for Honduran democracy and the Honduran people displayed great civic commitment in expressing their will in the ballot box."[76] In fact, few international observers saw this as a full return to democracy, largely because nothing about the coup had been resolved, rendering elections somewhat meaningless. The conservative candidate won, 56 to 36 percent. Even here, the country felt the weight of the embassy when the Supreme Electoral Tribunal (STE) results were delayed by the losing party, which had expressed concern that the preliminary results were not tallied correctly. "The Ambassador spoke to STE President and told him that in the interest of the country and of transparency to issue the results. He then called the losing candidate and urged him to drop his objection given the wide margin of his loss."[77]

This micromanagement of the election process suggests intervention can become a habit, and that by election day, the previous months of intense focus had so fixated the embassy on removing Micheletti that it was inconceivable to leave it to the Hondurans to muddle along on their own, or to accept anything less than a clear-cut outcome. Despite the celebratory tone of the cables, the United States won nothing. Zelaya was never restored to the presidency. Defiant to the end, Micheletti did not actually leave office until January 21, when he declared another leave of absence, this time for good.

The crisis ended with a whimper. Former president Zelaya flew off to the Dominican Republic the same day President Porfirio Lobo was inaugurated. Very few foreign presidents showed up for his inauguration. Even stalwart Arias demurred; he was disappointed that Lobo had not done more to get Micheletti to step down sooner. The rest of the world looked with suspicion on the election process; the U.S. view of it as relatively free and fair was not widely shared. Lobo inherited a country distracted by a climate of lawlessness that gave it the highest murder rate in the world. Human rights had grievously deteriorated. Honduras faced a long, slow path emerging from international isolation, and the country has yet to emerge from political polarization. The question remains whether the embassy's energetic involvement in the coup aftermath ultimately served Honduran interests.

ICELAND'S OLD TESTAMENT ECONOMICS

To paraphrase Tolstoy, all prosperous countries are alike. But in the global financial crisis of 2008, each country pursued its own unhappy route to bankruptcy. The crisis affected so many individuals, industries, and countries that were it not for the fact that it was bloodless, it would easily dwarf all the political and natural disasters of this era combined. Ordinary people lost their jobs, their homes, and their pensions. Decades-old financial institutions evaporated overnight. Countries didn't know what to do.

"Global" was an appropriate modifier for the crisis. One of the players needing rescue was Citigroup—an institution with more than 300,000 employees in more than 100 countries that handled $2 trillion of the world's payments every day. Another, AIG, had 74 million policyholders in 130 countries.[78] Suddenly these behemoths and many others, such as Bank of America, Chase, Merrill Lynch, Morgan Stanley, Bear Stearns, and Lehman Brothers, were being called financial death stars. Former Treasury secretary Timothy Geithner described what happened succinctly: "Borrowers took too many risks, creditors and investors were way too willing to finance those risks, the government failed to rein in those risks, and then was unable to act quickly or forcefully enough when panic hit."[79]

In the week of October 6, 2008, a distracted Washington watched the stock market tank in its worst week since 1933. The market dropped 50 percent from its 2007 peak. Deciding who to blame was a question for politicians rather than economists. Geithner used the phrase "Old Testament justice" to describe a strong public sentiment that the bankers who drove the system into the ground should be punished, not bailed out. Geithner, on the contrary, believed in government intervention. He argued that all financial crises are essentially about confidence, and while restoring confidence might have little to do with justice, the approach leaves everyone better off.

The crisis also wreaked havoc in Europe, where economies both in and outside the European Union are tightly linked. Europeans are in the habit of talking to one another, and there are plenty of mechanisms for high-level meetings and coordination. But what about the periphery—countries that are not members of the G-20 or the EU but were reeling from financial disaster all the same? These smaller ponds, in which U.S. embassies were major players, offered economic officers extraordinary access to finance ministers and other fiscal policymakers. Embassy economics officers have a wide range of contacts, since they handle not only routine economic policy issues but also scientific issues such as energy, global warming, climate change, and environmental sustainability.

For an economics officer in 2008, almost no place in Europe was smaller or more interesting than Iceland. Its version of the global financial crisis was a strange mixture of incompetence, comeuppance, naiveté, and defiance, with a good measure of Cold War politics thrown in. Geithner's Old Testament justice had a different meaning in a country that managed to be furious at Russia, Britain, and America all at once.

Iceland Gets "the Middle Finger"

The most oft-repeated slogan of this period, "too big to fail," certainly didn't apply to Iceland. With a population of 320,000, Iceland is barely large enough to be a city, let alone a country. Its GDP of $13.6 billion puts it on a par with retailers like Best Buy. It only became an independent country in 1944, and it's often said that everyone knows everyone. In 2007 Iceland topped the UN charts as the best country to live in in the world—a status that vanished in the space of a week.

Embassies reflect the scale of the countries in which they work, and one remarkable aspect of the reporting from the small staff at Embassy Reykjavik is its thoroughness. In the run-up to the financial crisis, the embassy had been preoccupied with local reaction to a U.S. decision to close Naval Air Station Keflavik in 2006. Iceland, which has no military forces, was a charter member of NATO, largely because its location provided an excellent refueling point for bombers. This made it a pressure point in the Cold War, and the Soviet Union built a massive embassy in Reykjavik, widely assumed to be a listening post. The embassy description of the espionage atmosphere reads like a version of *Spy vs. Spy*. "It is believed that the Chinese are continuing to utilize their technical and humint [human intelligence] capabilities to conduct industrial espionage. It is also believed that the Russians are monitoring the Chinese actions. The current Russian DCM [deputy chief of mission] in Iceland is considered to be a China expert. The current Chinese ambassador to Iceland is a known U.S. expert. It is unknown if there is any targeting of the mission or any of its employees by the Russians or Chinese."[80]

Despite persistent Russian overtures, Iceland firmly planted itself in the West, but with some significant boundaries. Like Norway, Iceland resisted joining the European Union (although it is a member of the European Economic Area and the European Free Trade Association) largely because it wanted an unfettered hand running its fisheries industry. Icelandic ambivalence about EU membership continued through its financial crisis, when it began the formal entry process at its height, only to draw back in late 2013.

As is often the case, heady days preceded the economic fall. Egalitarian Iceland found itself transformed by a new class of billionaires and the attendant trappings: fancy cars, parties, yachts, and posh apartments in London and Manhattan. Iceland's high interest rates attracted "hot" money from everywhere, bloating its banking sector to unsustainable levels. Ordinary Icelanders found they could get cheap loans in other currencies, allowing them to finance homes, cars, and vacations in yen, dollars, or pounds. Big-thinking entrepreneurs borrowed foreign currency to buy European boutiques, Eastern European telecommunication companies, a Danish airline, and—for more than $100 million—the West Ham United soccer team. "For the first time, one could have a career in Iceland as a bodyguard."[81]

As early as April 2006, the embassy reported that credit rating agencies and international financial firms had released "a torrent of reports raising questions about the state of the Icelandic economy and stability of Iceland's major banks. This public doubt about solvency caused a marked drop in the value of the Icelandic krona and of shares on the Icelandic stock exchange." The embassy warned that rating agency Fitch had raised concerns in February, followed by Moody's and Standard & Poor's. "The various reports run the gamut from concluding that the Icelandic financial sky is falling to the view that despite a few economic indicators being out of balance, the Icelandic economy is sound and the negative prognostications wildly exaggerated."[82]

The cable laid out the facts: Iceland carried a large current account deficit, high inflation, high personal indebtedness, and high levels of short-term foreign debt carried by Iceland's three major banks. But the embassy wasn't certain any of these risky practices were fatal. It argued that much of the debt was caused by three huge capital investments—two aluminum smelter projects and a massive hydroelectric power plant, developments that would on the whole be good for Iceland.

Fourteen months later, in a June 2007 scene setter for visiting Under Secretary Nicholas Burns, the embassy swung into cheerleading mode. "You'll see ample evidence of a continuing economic boom in Reykjavik, thanks to utilization of fish and energy resources and leveraging of assets to invest abroad. The Viking spirit of risk taking, acquisition, and swift decisiveness have all helped multiply Icelandic holdings in Europe."[83] This tendency to equate national character with economic success and failure would appear again in embassy financial reporting from Greece, Spain, and Italy, when Germans, among others, blamed the economic collapse on their colleagues' character traits.

Icelanders themselves were happy to capitalize on their Viking reputation when it suited their narrative. The country's president described Iceland's new generation of investors as "having qualities we have inherited from our ancestors," and said that "those who venture out into unknown territory deserve our honor."[84] Prime Minister Sigmundur Davíð Gunnlaugsson, whose term followed the worst of the crisis, said, "Icelanders, as descendants of the Vikings, are highly individualistic and have difficulty putting up with authorities, let alone oppression."[85] This streak of independence (some might say stubbornness) made it difficult for Icelanders to deal effectively with the international financial community, as the embassy noted.

Six months before the crisis broke, the embassy warned Washington that Iceland's economy had "gone wobbly," with currency depreciating to near record lows and price hikes of 10 percent in a country in which most consumer goods are imported. The central bank's prime interest rate rose to 15 percent. The prime minister unhelpfully blamed foreign investors and said Iceland would consider "setting a bear trap" to punish them.[86] The casting about for a scapegoat would become a constant theme as the crisis worsened week by week.

By the end of September 2008, the post reported that the Icelandic krona's value had fallen almost 50 percent since the start of the year; inflation had reached 14.5 percent, and Icelanders were clamoring to adopt the euro. The government, seemingly for lack of any better ideas, bought 75 percent of the shares of Iceland's third-largest bank. "This is the first significant government intervention for the Icelandic economy during the recent crisis and comes after a week of harsh criticism for perceived inaction—in particular, for not managing to include Iceland in the 24 September exchange agreement between the U.S. Federal Reserve and the central banks of other Nordic countries."[87]

The Fed had made $30 billion available to Denmark, Sweden, Norway, and Australia to ease money markets and improve global liquidity.

By October 7, it was clear that the government intervention was too little too late. A team from the International Monetary Fund (IMF) arrived at the invitation of the prime minister, who somberly addressed the nation on television about a series of emergency actions. The embassy duly noted that "he closed his address with 'God Bless Iceland,' a phrase rarely used by politicians here."[88]

At this point Russia injected an interesting East-West gambit into the mix, offering a €4 billion loan. The embassy reported that officials angrily said Iceland had no choice but to turn to Russia. They claimed their "friends" in the West had let the country down. Acting Foreign Minister Össur Skarphédinsson took off the gloves in a morning radio interview. "He said it hurt, and added that after about 50 years of a special relationship with the U.S., the only thing Iceland got now was the middle finger."[89] The chairman of the opposition Progressive party piled on, saying President Bush did not turn out to be a friend when needed, and asked Parliament to send Russian president Putin a thank-you note.

Why did Iceland feel America had let it down? Could it be, the embassy wondered, because they actually had not called Washington? It reported, "Despite public assertions that some of Iceland's friends had failed to provide help, the Embassy does not believe the Icelanders have adequately checked out all possibilities of cooperation with U.S. entities. We urged Iceland representatives to reach out to U.S. authorities immediately so that 'our friends said no' means they really asked the right questions."[90]

The embassy, clearly irked by the "middle finger" quote, worked overtime to resolve the question of why Iceland felt abandoned. In a separate cable the same day, the embassy reported that it was trying to determine "with whom the Icelanders spoke in the U.S. and supposedly approached for help in their ongoing financial crisis." It turned out that, apart from earlier talks with the New York Fed, no one in Iceland's government had spoken to any U.S. official for more than a week! Worse still, the embassy's source, a senior Central Bank official, said that the Central Bank had not spoken with anyone at the U.S. Treasury Department other than the Iceland desk officer.[91]

The embassy went to work. Here was a country in over its head, which did not have the right phone numbers and had not sorted out how to work through a global financial crisis with U.S. financial institutions. The next day the embassy reported it had brokered a deal with the minister of finance, who was on a plane to Washington. "Post persuaded the Minister to agree to meet with senior Treasury officials while in the U.S. . . . We would hope this meeting will help Icelanders think through the present crisis and move from a stopgap reactive approach . . . It should also make clear to them how the U.S. can and cannot be of assistance and point them in the direction of other options."[92]

The United States was not the only country dealing with Icelandic ire. The embassy reported that Icelandic officials were "infuriated" with Britain after a nasty spat over the fate of unsecured deposits in Ice-Save accounts. These high-interest savings accounts had attracted large numbers of depositors from the UK and the Netherlands, but Iceland was no longer able to guarantee the deposits. "The British apparently invoked anti-terrorism laws created in the aftermath of 9/11 to freeze Icelandic assets in the U.K. Relations are under strain following U.K. Chancellor Darling's announcement that he seized the U.K. assets of Icelandic banks, and the media reported that the PM Brown wants to sue the Icelandic government to refund British depositors."[93]

It would be hard to overstate Iceland's wrath. The Ministry of Foreign Affairs external trade director told the embassy that if Britain had pulled a stunt like this with France, "a war would have broken out by now." The Iceland media created an online petition, "Icelanders are not Terrorists," which collected more than eighty thousand photos and signatures—about 25 percent of the population—to send to British Prime Minister Gordon Brown.[94] Things got even nastier a week

later when Iceland Central Bank governor Davíð Oddsson opened his
meeting with U.S. Treasury officials by comparing Gordon Brown's
actions to Mussolini's.[95] Graffiti around Reykjavik depicted Brown
with a Hitler mustache.

The embassy busily laid conduits for more communication. By
October 20, it reported that the Iceland foreign minister would be
calling Secretary of State Clinton to ask for a U.S. contribution of $10
billion as part of the foreign loans needed to get through the crisis.
On October 24, the embassy reported that the Icelandic Central
Bank had gone to the New York Fed asking for a $1 billion loan or
a currency swap.

Icelanders themselves were not always on the same page. Oddsson,
a Thatcherite free marketeer who privatized many of Iceland's state-
run industries during his earlier stint as prime minister, was rumored
to be behind the Russian loan. He fought hard against an IMF deal
(and stubbornly defended the krona and resisted EU membership),
but the embassy reported that bankers and private sector businesspeople were imploring their embassy contacts to convince the Icelandic government to take the IMF loan. (In fact, an agreement was
reached on October 27.) The embassy commented, "The Government
of Iceland is obviously struggling with problems of coordination and
turf in dealing with the financial crisis. Away for the first couple of
weeks of the turmoil (due to brain surgery) the Foreign Minister is
attempting to reassert her normal role in foreign affairs. The Central
Bank, however, is guarding its perceived prerogatives closely—and,
judging from the events of the last few weeks, unwisely.[96]

Iceland's strategic location may have been its strongest card. The
idea of a Russian loan got the attention of the international community, with reporters asking uncomfortable questions about what Iceland had offered in exchange—landing or refueling rights at Keflavik,
or special exploration rights to gas and petroleum fields? The embassy
became suspicious after things went quiet and wondered if the Russian loan offer had ever existed. Officers asked around, noting that the

Ministry of Foreign Affairs and other official sources had no knowledge of any loan discussions with Russia. One senior MFA source blamed the whole business on "Central Bank shenanigans," saying not even the prime minister had known about any loan discussions at first. Officers hypothesized that Iceland was less interesting to Russia after it failed in its bid to gain a nonpermanent UN Security Council seat in October 2008 or that Russia's own financial difficulties had become a factor. Or that perhaps

> Moscow was never serious about the loan and offered it only as a public relations stunt to boost Russia's image and discomfit the West. (If so, this tactic has not worked all that well: Icelandic polls taken in October 2006 and October 2008 show the same 39 percent of the population favorably disposed towards Russia, though the negatives in 2008 are slightly higher.) . . . In public officials insist the deal is still on the table, in private sources tell us the deal is on the back burner and they want it to stay there . . . [Icelanders] don't like the Russian presence in the North Atlantic and don't want to encourage it.[97]

The embassy also lobbied on Iceland's behalf, making the case that the United States should lend $1 billion of $4 billion required to conclude the proposed IMF loan. The embassy played the Russian card, arguing that Iceland was important to U.S. security; that it was well positioned in the High North, where melting Arctic ice meant increased competition for gas, petroleum, and trade routes; and above all, that it was a friend of the United States. This cable in particular showed that it was impossible to live and work alongside Icelanders and remain unaffected by their plight. The embassy made an unusually emotional appeal.

> Iceland is reaching out with increasing desperation to any available source of help as it confronts one of the most trying crises in

its history. Assistance from the U.S. at this crucial time would be
a prudent investment in our own national security and economic
well-being. The Icelanders take fierce pride in their flawless history of paying back their debts. Whatever the financial turmoil
and uncertainty of the moment, it's a good bet that this economy
of highly-educated, imaginative, and sophisticated people will
take off again. And when it does, and when the competition in
the High North really gets underway, it may be more important
than we can yet suppose to have the Icelanders remember us as the
kind of friend who stands by in fair weather and foul.[98]

Iceland did take off again. The country repaid the IMF loan early,
became a talked-about success story, and by 2014 even climbed back
up on the UNDP index to fourteenth place (but not to its prior
rank in 2007 of first place). Unemployment eased to 3.5 percent and
growth reached nearly 3 percent. Nonetheless, repeated attempts to
get an IceSave bill to refund overseas depositors through Parliament
or public referenda provoked virulent public resistance, ultimately
leading to the prime minister's populist remarks mentioned above.

One of the stranger aspects of the Icelandic crisis was the role of
serious illness. As the embassy reported, in October 2008 Foreign
Minister Ingibjörg Gísladóttir was away in New York, being treated
for a brain tumor. In addition, her deputy, Gretar Mar Sigurdsson,
was suffering from colon cancer. And Prime Minister Geir Haarde
told the nation on January 23, 2009, that he would resign for treatment for esophageal cancer. That's a lot of leadership distracted by
life-threatening illnesses.

Icelanders who felt spurned by foreigners might have been glad
to see nature come unexpectedly to their aid. One of Iceland's many
volcanos, Eyjafjallajökull, began rumbling on March 20. By April
14 it sent up a massive cloud of ash that covered much of northern
Europe and disrupted air traffic for weeks. No doubt many in Iceland
found the symbolism satisfyingly appropriate.

CRISIS DIPLOMACY

Diplomats rarely get the luxury of working to a schedule. The more fragile the country, the more likely long-term work plans will be interrupted by major events. These four crises give an indication of the range of problems the U.S. government and its diplomats confront at any one time. They do not happen sequentially. While the embassy staff in Port-au-Prince was consumed with the earthquake, their colleagues in Washington were providing diplomatic backup but simultaneously dealing with wars in Iraq and Afghanistan, not to mention problems elsewhere.

In Haiti, the reporting characterized the enormity of the challenges and portrayed an embassy at its heroic best, well supported by Washington in the early weeks of what became a prolonged crisis. In Burma, the embassy leveraged chaos from a natural disaster to support a small political opening for the dissident community and became instrumental in urging a new administration in Washington to review its policy toward the country. In Honduras, the embassy saw its role as highly principled, standing firm against a coup no matter the consequences, despite navigating around congressional ideological haymakers with different views. And in Iceland, the embassy's traditional work of connecting foreign government officials with the right people in Washington suddenly became a crucially important effort that helped Iceland find its path toward financial recovery.

Chapter 4

- - - - - - - - - - - - - -

TRAVEL:
To the Ends of
the Earth

- - - - - - - - - - - - - - -

*Several tribes practice Donyi Polo, a religion worshipping
the sun and the moon, whereas others practice animism.
Missionaries have made few inroads here. Polygamy is
permitted and practiced by some tribal elites. Two of the
tribes exist in a master-slave relationship.*

—*U.S. Consulate Calcutta*
January 18, 2005

- - - - - - - - - - - - - -

THE LAGOS OFFICER WAS HAVING A ROUGH TRIP. HE
had set off to assess tourism prospects for seekers of *Picathartes
oreas*, the gray-necked rockfowl that is one of Africa's most prized
birds, in the company of a Discovery Channel producer, the owners
of a birding tour company, a naturalist, and a BBC correspondent
who reported on the group's odyssey through a small corner of
southeastern Nigeria. The officer described a trek over barely pass-
able clay track and rickety bridges with holes so large that the team
had to carefully position wood planks so their vehicles would not

tumble into the streams below. Things got worse when they reached the Okomu National Park access road, which was an obstacle course of disabled vehicles. Even the BBC's 4x4 was stuck for hours.

"The lodge was a shock," the officer wrote. "It looked derelict inside: shabby walls, peeling linoleum, black mold on the doors and ceiling, and furniture likely banned by some international convention. The potentially picturesque thatched hut built as a dining area needed some serious attention and cleaning (termite tubes climbed untended up wood surfaces to the roof)."

The bird-viewing canopy platforms offered great views, but the intrepid diplomat had to climb one hundred and thirty feet up the side of a tree to reach one, a physical feat for which, he wrote tongue in check, the post danger differential rate was inadequate.

Going home was no better. "The Benin/Lagos expressway was a complete showstopper. The divided highway is always a horror show ... The constant problem of shakedowns by police at the country's ubiquitous roadblocks is beyond annoying." When the group finally returned to civilization, they stopped at a casino in Lagos. "We found a dozen waiters asleep on the kitchen floor and the croupiers asleep with their heads on the green baize."[1]

This is why people join the foreign service. They hope for the moment when they can truly feel far from home. Anyone who has ever sat on the Beltway, Interstate 95, or the Ventura Freeway might well fantasize about driving a 4x4 across Africa. The travails only serve to make the eventual arrival more meaningful. The officer who made this trip will dine out on this story for the rest of his life.

One of the least celebrated facts about the WikiLeaks cables are the tales of life beyond the capitals. Foreign service officers can easily fill their days with the routine matters of diplomacy, as witnessed by the reams of dutiful cables on démarches delivered, scene setters for VIP visitors, and congressionally mandated reporting. But for many officers, the same yearnings that led them into the foreign service also tempt them to leave the comforts and confines of the capital. They know that while globalization ensures they'll find the same stores in Gainesville and Guatemala, another world awaits on the back roads.

It would be easy to dismiss the reporting officers as travel writer wannabes, but they bring something different than the Paul Therouxs and Rick Steveses of the world. They were already working in these countries before they set out, and after their trips into the hinterlands they returned to their embassy desks enriched. There was a policy point to these trips, ranging from human rights to religious freedom, refugees and migration, or environmental degradation. They had enviable access, through their government connections, to places that might be restricted or off limits to tourists. They also had access to people who matter—cultural, tribal, and religious leaders from chieftains to the pope.

Diplomats who travel and write home about it unwittingly illustrate one of the great divides between officers serving abroad and their colleagues in Washington. Their cables about rural realities can challenge assumptions about what matters most. Washington's bias as a capital city inclines those working there to seek out interlocutors in power or those who might likely come to power. These are often Western-educated "people like us" who work in ministries, parliaments, universities, or newsrooms that resemble the Washington work environment. It's easy to see them as the logical counterparts to any foreign policy conversation.

But Mao did not find his followers among the Mandarins. Diplomatic encounters with Turkmen truckers, Papuan separatists, and the garage bands of Tehran should widen Washington's worldview. They seemed to have widened the views of the cable authors.

It takes good writing to demonstrate the many ways cultural traditions trump political ideology. It takes insight to explain why tribal clashes should merit the attention of the desk-bound officer in Foggy Bottom. And it takes an imaginative foreign service officer to connect two opposite poles and answer the "so what?" factor. The delightful aspects of the WikiLeaks cables are the descriptive passages written with curiosity, empathy, and wonder. While Washington politicians obsessed over Islam, one officer actually performed the Hajj and wrote movingly about each phase of his pilgrimage. Another explained that in Thailand, Islam's greatest challenge may come not from the West but from the much older influence of traditional seers and mystics. And in Laos, a polite query about religious freedom turned into a rant from the elders on how Christianity had made their young people lose respect for the ancestors.

Those in the field held one unbeatable advantage over Washington—they had the time and the means to seek out remote locales that their colleagues could only read about. Their treks were purposeful and deliberate. Their cables made a contribution to the world's understanding of inaccessible places and the people who live there. The great irony is that while Julian Assange and his team denounced the diplomats for duplicity, these cables attest to a dedicated group of individuals who undertook incredible journeys in search of understanding.

GETTING THERE IS HALF THE FUN

Airplanes cannot land everywhere. Highways become two-lane roads, dwindle to one lane, and then peter out. And where roads are poor, cars are not always the most useful vehicle. The diplomats used every means of transport from dugout canoes to snowmobiles. Occasionally, they walked.

Here's an officer writing about a forgotten corner of southern China: "It is not easy to get to Xilin. The nearest commercial airports, in Nanning and Kunming, are both at least nine hours away by public transport. The nearest train station is still more than a couple of hours away. From there it takes a few more hours to get to Baise."

And here's a description of a January trip through Tajikistan: "The small rehabilitated airport in Garm operates only in summer, while camels are still used for transport in Jirgitol District."

Kathmandu consular officers warned: "Road travel on Nepal's circuitous, narrow highways is treacherous and grueling. Although we never covered more than 200 kilometers on any day, every day's drive involved a minimum of six hours. Along the way, we witnessed the aftermath of 20 major head-on collisions, more often than not between buses and large carriage trucks."

The consul general of Vladivostok wrote: "Krasniy Yar is an eleven hour drive from Vladivostok, the last four hours over a rough snow road (*zimniki*) cut through the woods ... During this visit the temperature was minus 37 Celsius."

And finally, an intrepid trio in Suriname wrote with jaw-dropping nonchalance: "Emboffs [embassy officers] traveled four days by dugout canoe down the Tapanahoni and Marowijne rivers."

There is something to be said for slow travel. The abruptness of an airplane trip ill prepares travelers for the contrasts ahead. Four days by dugout canoe might be extreme, but the officers were probably more acute observers after their senses had a chance to acclimate to a different world.

The above excerpts are but a small sample of travel cables—sagas, really—that dwell at length on distance, time, and rural lives. The officers were perhaps unconsciously demonstrating that the feat of getting there can be an education in and of itself, even before meeting a single person. And then, when they did, the cables got even more interesting.

NOW THAT YOU'RE HERE . . .

Xilin, mentioned above, the westernmost county in the Guangzhou consular district, is a poor and rural part of southern China. Simple banking presented the visiting officers with their first challenge. Although there was one bank, there were no cash machines, and credit cards were not accepted. The officers presented a 50 renminbi note (worth U.S. $6.25 at the time), which was the first one the shop-keeper had ever seen. "In the end, we had no choice but to be short-changed . . . Even the small Mao bills, treated dismissively in China's cities as disease-carrying, wallet-cluttering wastes of ink and paper, are important monetary units in Xilin."

Culturally, the visitors found the place still ran like an old-school Communist stronghold. "The town awakens each day to the strains of the national anthem and other patriotic songs broadcast through loudspeakers."

Sanitary conditions were appalling. "Even the small settlements astride the main, two-lane highway of the county were quite squalid. At one of these settlements, the restroom facilities at the local government center were described by EconPolAsst [economic-political assistant] as the worst he had seen in his life—no small feat for a Guangzhou native."

But the most unsettling custom was revealed when the travelers checked into their hotel. "Prostitution did not seem to be a discreet trade in Xilin. In the first hotel where we stayed, for example, a condom was thoughtfully provided in each hotel room, discreetly stashed in the cylinder of a toilet paper roll, with no mention of extra charges for use."[2]

★   ★   ★   ★

HALF A WORLD AWAY, officers from Embassy Paramaribo spent four days in a dugout canoe, determined to make contact with the Njuka Maroons (descendants of escaped slaves), who had not been visited by any embassy personnel for seven years. In pursuit of their goal, the officers happened upon a burgeoning illegal gold mining industry run by Brazilian and Chinese immigrants who had been exploiting a no-man's-land with no Surinamese law enforcement or government presence.

Their itinerary into the interior reads like a geography quiz: they went to Dritabiki, Manlobi, Stoelmanseiland, and Loka Loka—all

villages along the Tapanahoni and Marowijne rivers. The dugout
canoe was one of many challenges.

> As no suitable housing could be found in Manlobi, the second
> night's destination and a village of about 1,000 individuals along
> the Tapanahoni river, Emboffs spent one night in a gold mining
> camp across the river from the village. The camp consisted of a
> bar, a restaurant, and a store which sold overpriced supplies. Some
> 20 Brazilians, 5-10 of whom likely were commercial sex workers,
> and a few Maroons lived on the site.[3]

The informal gold mining and the environmental degradation
it caused were the major discoveries of their trip. The officers saw
hundreds of tracts of land mined for gold deposits washed down by
rainwater from the slopes above, along with fifteen floating suction
dredges excavating for gold in the riverbeds. The machines were operated twenty-four hours a day by Brazilians who paid royalty fees to
the closest Maroon village. The officers carefully documented the
widespread selling and use of mercury in the mining areas (a dangerous but cheap means of extracting the gold). Their concerns about
mercury damage to drinking water sources made their trip useful for
environmental as well as sociological reasons.

South of Suriname, the Amazon and Andean regions offered
equally enticing frontiers for embassy officers posted to Brazil,
Colombia, Ecuador, Peru, and Bolivia. They evaluated economic
development, prospects for ecotourism, environmental problems,
and the status of indigenous people.

Bolivia is undeniably beautiful, with fossils in Sucre, salt flats in
Potosí, and rain forest in Pando, but government support to develop
tourism in these areas is very limited. "The people in the government now aren't from Pando—they don't know the rain forest and
it's hard to get them to care," lamented one ecotourism expert to
embassy visitors.

Despite the underdevelopment, the region attracts hordes of back-packers, and environmentalists shudder as more so-called eco-lodges spring up. The border town of Guayaramerín hosts a wildlife park that an officer described as "a glorified backyard zoo. Amazon birds, monkeys, capybaras and jaguars huddled in cramped cages while visitors snapped photos. . . . When asked where he obtained the animals, the owner responded, 'you can buy anything in Bolivia if the price is right.'"[4]

In a perverse example of how lack of infrastructure creates a kind of dark tourism, thousands of thrill-seeking mountain bikers flocked to "The Road of Death" to ride down the steep ten-foot-wide unpaved path that offers no guardrail between the biker and the two-thousand-foot drop below. "Not everyone gets the 'I Survived Bolivia's Death Road' t-shirt handed out by tour companies at the end of the trip," the officer wryly noted. "At least 13 bikers have died on the road in the past decade."[5]

Embassy reporters from Bogotá noted that Colombia was also struggling to build viable ecotourism, despite substantial help from a USAID-sponsored initiative, which provided small grants to indigenous communities. A chronicle of an ambassadorial visit to Amacayacu National Park noted that it was home not only to pro-tected flora and fauna but to indigenous communities that lived in the park and helped care for vulnerable species. The cable spelled out the challenge in stark terms: the Amazonas department, one of thirty-two statelike political divisions, is Colombia's largest but has only forty-eight thousand inhabitants, 53 percent of whom lived in a sixteen-kilometer strip along the Amazon. The area was woefully short of infrastructure, with only twenty-five miles of paved roads and few hotel rooms. The economy contributed less than .05 percent to Colombia's GDP, and there was no comprehensive plan to attract high-income "boutique" tourists.[6]

★   ★   ★   ★

A WORLD AWAY FROM the rivers and mountains of South America, but with the same spirit of exploration, embassy officers took to the backwaters of the post-Soviet world—contested villages in Georgia and forgotten rural spots in Central Asia. While Moscow and Saint Petersburg are as cosmopolitan as any part of Western Europe, the remote parts of the former Soviet Union provide landscapes littered with the rusting automotive hulks of Zhigulis, Trabants, and Wartburgs, all of which served as apt metaphors for the hasty abandonment of Soviet-era decay and the isolation of those left behind.

The troubles of ethnic Georgians in the breakaway region of Abkhazia are emblematic of the problems of people whose national identity may not change as fast as their borders. A year after the 2008 Russian invasion of Abkhazia and South Ossetia, embassy officers ventured into Gali, a border town within the UN security zone.

Emboffs observed decrepit housing, execrable roads, collapsing schools, insufficient health care facilities, horse drawn carts and insect-threatened hazelnut trees . . . The nuts are the primary source of income, with profits from the fall harvest needed to last the whole year.

The aspect of life in Gali most immediately and glaringly apparent to a visitor is the appalling state of the roads. The longest stretch the main road extends without massive road damage is perhaps a couple hundred yards . . . The roads in the villages, off the main road to Sukhumi, are even worse, with gaping holes every few yards. Although the UNHCR's [UN High Commissioner for Refugees's] four wheel drive SUV handled the rough spots well enough, the horse drawn carts and old Zhiguli sedans the locals use likely encounter major difficulties.[7]

Ethnic Georgians hinted at shakedowns when they crossed back and forth across the border and described the many ways their language, history, and culture were being erased. The officers described a dying village with depressing prospects, still occupied by Russian troops and Abkhaz forces, and one from which young people flee for better futures elsewhere.[8]

On the other side of the Urals, the Central Asian republics of Tajikistan, Turkmenistan, and Uzbekistan, with their borders like interlocking jigsaw pieces, offer a physical landscape as challenging as the political one. It is easy to understand why embassy officers might want to take to the roads and explore something less contentious than the halls of government.

Tajikistan offered an irresistible temptation to diplomats stuck in Dushanbe one January: a visit to the Rasht Valley to see rural life in winter. The locals begged them to wait until summer, warning of perilous road conditions in the mountains. Undaunted, the officers loaded their vehicle with meals ready-to-eat, sleeping bags, and bottled water, and headed off to Garm, six hours northeast from Dushanbe on the road to Kyrgyzstan.

> EmbOffs enjoyed blazing snow-covered scenery as drivers slowly maneuvered through icy mountain roads at 25–30 kilometers per hour. Occasionally men from villages dressed in furry hats and beards came up to shovel dirt on the mountain paths to provide traction for passers-by. Vehicles small and large maneuvered between rockslides on the icy roads, carrying people and goods, such as new Chinese minivans, into the country.[9]

They also saw firsthand how harsh winters affect daily life. With only two to four hours of electricity a day from mid-October to mid-April, they made a very quick visit to School Number 1, where "shivering pupils bundled in coats dutifully wrote in their notebooks."

Evidently the group survived to make another excursion eight months later—this time covering two thirds the length of the 1,344-kilometer Tajik-Afghan border, where they found more poverty-stricken villages and a rapidly developing western route for Chinese goods.

In the Tajik mountain village of Zing just downstream from the Darvaz border crossing, 165 families survive on remittance income from family members working in Russia, pensions, and family gardens. A shiny mausoleum marks the entrance to the pomegranate and apple tree–lined road. Residents often live over 90 years in this mountain town known for its honey sold in two-liter bottles. Across the river from Zing, Afghans transport goods via donkey along the mountain path to their houses the same shade of brown as the dirt. The Afghan side is within throwing distance of Tajikistan and EmbOffs watched as an agile Afghan boy clambered off the thin mountain path to retrieve sticks for firewood from further down the mountain.[10]

ANTHROPOLOGY 101:
ANCIENT PEOPLES

Embassy officers were clearly fascinated by encounters with indigenous people, most of whom live in some of the globe's remotest corners. Tribal peoples were challenged by creeping modernity, intergenerational divides, and contentious relations with national government officials, who were often of different ethnicities. Officers were alert to human rights abuses and evidence of political and economic marginalization, but their stories suggest a far more complex picture.

Where does India end and China begin? The answer to that riddle encompasses practices dating back to the British Raj: a long-unresolved border war and a fiercely xenophobic collection of tribes for whom modern nation states such as India and China are abstract concepts. A glance at a map of Arunachal Pradesh, India's most isolated and least developed state, shows why the question might be relevant. Bhutan, Nepal, and Bangladesh nearly converge to leave Arunachal Pradesh's connection to the Indian "mainland" hanging by a thread. With one million inhabitants, it is the least populated of all Indian states, home to twenty-six tribal groups, each with its own language and customs, and hundreds of subgroups.

"Arunachal is something of an anthropologist's dream but a political and developmental nightmare," wrote a U.S. consulate officer. Its northern border with China is a dotted line, symbolizing the uncertain feelings of the people (many of whom identify more with China than with India), as well as the cartographers. The border has been in dispute since India's defeat in the 1962 Sino-Indian War. Deemed "sensitive" territory, even Indian citizens need special permission to visit. More than 80 percent of the land is covered in heavy forests, and parts of the state are still largely unexplored. With few highways, helicopters and footpaths are the main ways in and out.

The officer explained that indigenous communities are protected through a system of Inner Line Permits dating back to the days of British rule. No outsider can enter Arunachal Pradesh without an Inner Line or a Protected Area Permit. Neither can they buy land, start a business, or take up employment. Visiting consular staff were prohibited from taking photos with their Inner Line Permit. Yet, the officer noted, the people of Arunachal are unanimous about retaining the permit system. Without it they fear they would lose their lands to people from mainland India.

Villages are administered in consultation with headmen and the elected *panchayat* (local self-government leader). "Several tribes practice Donyi Polo, a religion worshipping the sun and the moon, whereas others practice animism. Missionaries have made few inroads here. Polygamy is permitted and practiced by some tribal elites. Two of the tribes exist in a master-slave relationship."[11]

This is a place few Westerners ever reach.

In a smoky Mishmi longhouse, middle-aged tribal women with enormous plugs in their earlobes stared at the PO [principal officer] as he squatted by the fire and sipped rice beer under racks of charred wild cattle skulls. Asked through an interpreter what they found so interesting, they replied that they had seen "white" people on the cable television in their longhouse but that they had not believed, until just then, that such people existed in real life.[12]

The United States has an interest in the peaceful resolution to the long running Sino-India border dispute, and there may be prospects for U.S. investment in hydropower projects, forest-based industries, or adventure tourism. But with the xenophobic nature of the native Arunachalese and the government of India's reluctance to upgrade infrastructure—especially if some or all of the land will eventually go to China—foreign investment remains a distant hope.

★   ★   ★   ★

SOMETIMES THINGS AREN'T what they seem. In northernmost Thailand's Mae Hong Son province there is a population of stateless people known as Padaung, a subgroup of the Karenni who fled their native lands in Burma in the 1990s; however, they lack refugee status, in part because they live in villages they created instead of official refugee camps. How they came to live in those villages is a story of crass commercial tourism. The Padaung are famous for their "long-necked" women. A custom of placing dozens of brass rings around the neck—which actually force the clavicle bone into a lower position to give the illusion of a longer neck—dates back centuries but had nearly disappeared in modern times.

Ambitious businessmen encouraged the refugee women to revive the tradition, live in Padaung villages, and pose for tourists who were bused in. Hundreds of Padaung saw it as a better alternative than refugee camps. They soon found themselves marketed as a "Thai Hill tribe" and mired in uncertain status. The Thai government refused to classify them as refugees and refused them the right to resettle in third countries, a problem the Chiang Mai consulate said was "endemic for refugees, migrant workers and ethnic minorities near the Thai-Burma border."

The UNHCR representative charged that the women were being kept in a "human zoo," and a human rights group said Thai authorities colluded with Burmese groups to traffic additional long-necked women into these Potemkin-style tourist villages. The Padaung languished in legal limbo, facing the hard choice of either refugee camps or tourist villages without a right to schooling, jobs, or a clear path to legal residency or citizenship.

In a few cases, Padaung women removed their rings as a means of rejecting the exploitation. But the reporting officers inserted a cautionary note, warning that the case of the Padaung is rife with ambiguities. "Despite signs of cultural exploitation, it is not clear what outcome the Padaung themselves want to see. Some have chosen a taste of freedom and economic opportunity in the tourist villages over an uncertain life inside a refugee camp." The consulate report reflected on the frequent hostility between host countries and refugees. Thailand hosts one of the world's largest stateless populations, who must contend with unfriendly and bureaucratic citizenship laws. "This dilemma has left thousands stranded in border camps while many more slip farther into Thailand to work illegally and risk exploitation."[13]

★ ★ ★ ★

IN COUNTRIES WITH which the U.S. has no diplomatic relations, embassies from surrounding countries deploy border area watchers who chat with border crossers hoping to glean insight into a country from afar. Borders drawn on paper maps mean little to rural people for whom seasonal migration is a way of life. Embassy officers in Azerbaijan, a country that sits atop the northern border of Iran, interviewed two ethnic Kashgai people, a semi-nomadic

Turkic minority of about 1.5 million with a history of antigov-
ernment violence. About a third maintain a traditional migratory lifestyle that revolves around sheep and goat herding over a
three-hundred-kilometer stretch of summer and winter grazing
grounds between Isfahan and Shiraz, in central Iran. The seasonal
trek takes three months each way with the help of camels and horses,
although nowadays some herders use trucks to move livestock. The
wool they produce is prized for its high quality and is woven by
the Kashgai into carpets. They have no written language and no
historical national ideology.

One Kashgai interviewee had a PhD in social anthropology; the
other was a Tehran-based Kashgai carpet merchant. Both had been
raised in traditional households, and they offered a fascinating picture
of how a tribal minority is faring in Iran's postrevolutionary era.

Known as the fiercely independent "Lords of the Mountains"
(referring to the Zagros range), the Turkic-speaking Kashgai raided
villages and were regarded with hostility and fear. Once one of the
most violent minority groups in Iran, they engaged in armed resistance against central government efforts to force them into permanent settlements. After the fall of the shah, many returned to their
migratory lifestyle. Although the anti-shah Kashgai leaders were initially embraced by Ayatollah Khomeini, they fell prey to the extremism of the revolution when they rejected Islamic rule and enforced
settlement. As a result, many of their leaders were hanged by the
Revolutionary Guard in 1982.

After the severe repression of the 1980s, Iran's more relaxed policies have encouraged a peaceful political coexistence. Although not
Persian, the Kashgai share the Shia faith—up to a point. The Kashgai
men told officers that the mostly Persian mullahs are tolerated but not
followed. Kashgai women work outside and do not wear the chador
(full covering) except when visiting towns. The PhD left the officers
with an indelible image of how this ancient people are coming to

terms with modernity while, at least for now, maintaining a separate identity. He said that young herders use the Internet and social media, follow the NBA, and listen to rap music. "Economics is achieving what force could not achieve," observed the PhD.[14]

In a media environment in which almost all the news on Iran concerned its nuclear program, this kind of reporting should have been invaluable to Washington. It puts individual faces to the collective label "Iranian," reminds policymakers that Iranian society is diverse, and highlights a domestic narrative that has little to do with Western perceptions.

Turkmenistan abounds with something that would seldom catch a diplomat's attention—truck stops. More than forty thousand Iranian truckers travel to or through Turkmenistan each year, the majority passing through the Farap crossing on the Uzbek border. The embassy officer painted a vivid picture: "As night falls, dozens of drivers congregate at cafes and parking lots, or on the side of the road on either side of the wobbly pontoon that connects the banks of the Amu Darya River and closes to truck traffic at 7 p.m."

American diplomats made a habit of frequenting truck stops to converse with drivers and gauge the political atmosphere inside Iran, a country they cannot visit. The officers wrote about the lively conversations and colorful characters they encountered in the cafes. One rig operator said all his children had emigrated to the United States, Canada, and Europe. "Why does America have a problem with Iran? We're good people—Americans are good people. There are no problems between us."

Ethnic Turkmen were eager to complain about how Iran's Shia majority discriminates against them in a society dominated by ethnic Persians. Turkmen children are forbidden to speak or study their language in school. "Turkmen sometimes marry Persians," one trucker said. "But we never allow them to marry our daughters."

The officers saw the Farap border as an entrée into a sector of Iran's population unseen by policymakers.

None had ever applied for a U.S. visa or had much contact with Americans, although several older members of the group fondly recalled the days when their country was "full of Americans." Everyone we encountered was friendly, hospitable, and appeared comfortable talking openly, in contrast to the truck stop in Berzengi, near Ashgabat, where Turkmen police have a visible presence.[15]

Eight months later, visiting diplomats were stunned to hear how copies of President Obama's Cairo speech had caused a brawl. This much-anticipated speech addressed the Muslim world to generally good reviews. Distributing copies of speeches translated into local languages is a basic part of embassy work. Much of it happens electronically on embassy Web pages, but hard copies are often distributed as well, so American officers had left behind copies of the speech, translated into Farsi, at the truck stop cafe. The friendly proprietor promised to hand them out to anyone interested.

Not long afterward, eight to ten Iranians were eating dinner at the cafe, and she decided to offer them copies of the speech. One driver read the speech and made enthusiastic comments about Obama. A second trucker disagreed, and a heated argument ensued. Several friends joined in on both sides, and before long fists were flying in a full-scale brawl.

The officers noted two divergent views on offer at the truck stop. In general, older drivers were more favorably disposed toward the United States and willing to talk. Younger drivers were more reticent and those who did talk were negative about the United States. The officers apologized to the cafe owner, worried that enlisting her help in sharing the speech had caused trouble. But she seemed to enjoy her role as amateur diplomat, responding happily, "Come back after the 14th, after the President's [Berdimuhamedov's] visit. There will be lots of Iranians here again!"[16]

★ ★ ★ ★

ANOTHER ANCIENT PEOPLE for whom modern states mean little are the tribal people of Papua New Guinea.

Indonesians often say that although Papua is a seven hour flight from Jakarta the province is really 2,000 years away. Papua's several hundred indigenous cultures—each with its own language—are alien and exotic to most Indonesians. Many communities in the Papuan highlands lived with ancient technology until a few decades ago. Long-running tribal wars, usually conducted with spears and arrows, are common in the central highlands. For most Jakarta officials Papua remains mysterious, a dark place filled with tribal conflicts, separatist sympathizers and chronic governance problems.[17]

The separatism is rooted in a sense of inequality. Relations between some 1.5 million indigenous Papuans and migrants from other parts of Indonesia are troubled. The economic disparity between the two groups—migrants are more prosperous—stokes resentment. Papuans lag in health care and education. Malnutrition is common, and malaria and tuberculosis are widespread. The HIV/AIDS infection rate is far above the national average.

But Papua is attractive to international mining companies, some of whom have had a presence for decades. A case in point is Freeport-McMoRan, whose troubles in Papua illustrate how American support for businesses overseas can sometimes trump other foreign policy efforts such as human rights, democracy, and the rule of law.

Freeport-McMoRan has been in Indonesia for forty years, and its copper and gold mining operations there represent 45 percent of the company's income, which also makes it the largest taxpayer in Indonesia. That long history extended through the Suharto era of 1967–1998, when it took political savvy (and payment to local troops for protection) to stay afloat in a country run by one of the most corrupt dictatorships in Asia. To be fair, Freeport also embraced corporate social responsibility—building roads, schools, and hospitals to benefit Indonesians.[18]

But corruption was only one of many problems. The seat of government is in Jakarta, but the gold is in Papua, and, as the embassy explained, Papua can be violent. In addition to separatists, there is an active union movement and determining which groups are behind which actions can be difficult. In 2009 unknown assailants carried out more than a dozen attacks near Freeport-McMoRan's mines, killing several. There have been long-running clashes between Indonesian security firms and Papuan insurgents, and in December 2009, Papuan separatist leader Kelly Kwalik was killed in a shootout. The embassy report stated that he was widely believed to have been involved in a series of shootings targeting Freeport, including an attack that killed two Americans.[19]

This violence was a backdrop to yet another problem—Freeport's need for security. The embassy dutifully chronicled the turbulence,[20] and a *Forbes* magazine article painted it in even starker terms. In addition to using Indonesian troops for protection, Freeport also spent $28 million in 2010 on its own security force. It was sufficiently alarmed to bring in Triple Canopy, a private U.S. security firm staffed by former U.S. Special Forces.[21]

The cables described a disturbing situation in which the Indonesian government used its own troops to protect a foreign mining interest, which in turn supplemented this with its own security forces. Human rights organizations said Indonesian security forces abused Papuans and pilfered the mining operations, some of which were environmentally ruinous. Freeport added to the tension by hiring technicians from outside Papua (who sometimes had better skills), leaving separatists, union activists, and environmentalists frustrated.

The rights of native Papuans gained little traction in this narrative, nor did the separatists who hoped to win back Papua for native Papuans. While any expropriation of Freeport would be a red flag for the U.S. government, many of the union demands seemed modest—a living wage, better working conditions, and more say in the exploitation of Papua's resources.

This is an old, old story that's played out many times elsewhere—Exxon, United Fruit, and W.R. Grace in Latin America, for example. While it is unthinkable that the U.S. government would ever abandon its advocacy of U.S. industries abroad, the embassy cables implicitly pose questions: How many times must we repeat the past? Is there another way to support U.S. businesses while also advancing Indonesian transparency, upholding the rights of indigenous Papuans, and protecting the environment? This remains Indonesia's problem to solve, but when the center of the conflict is a forty-year relationship with a U.S. company that is also its largest taxpayer, there ought to be room for the United States to use its good offices.

ANTHROPOLOGY 201: MODERN PEOPLES

Embassy encounters with people from modern societies whose lives are nonetheless restricted for political, religious, or cultural reasons offer some of the most interesting reading. Social issues in Saudi Arabia and Iran caught the eye of observant officers who strayed from the usual political themes to portray groups ranging from wealthy Hejazis from western Saudi Arabia to Iranian punk rock musicians.

★   ★   ★   ★

TURNING TO SAUDI ARABIA, Americans are often baffled by Saudi tolerance for such a restrictive society. People imagine menacing imams and lurking religious police. Trying to understand why anyone would prefer to live in such a world grips American diplomats, too. The consul general, the lead officer in Jeddah, offered a thoughtful analysis of this question with a stunning opening line:

There is no subject dearer to the hearts of even moderately well-off Hejazis (inhabitants of the Western Province) than leaving Saudi Arabia. The most stilted gathering can be brightened up at once by steering the conversation to a fondly anticipated (or remembered) stint outside the Kingdom.

The writer described social gatherings with people whom she said

bear an interesting secret . . . While outwardly seeming perfectly normal, even a slight acquaintance with them reveals that they are not at all what they seem.

There is a topic absolutely guaranteed to fill the most recalcitrant conversational lull: leaving Saudi Arabia . . . Smiles then light up faces. Voices vibrate more. Even the posture straightens. Men and women begin to talk enthusiastically of the trip they just took, the trip they are looking forward to taking, or their favorite trip of all time about which they are happy to reminisce.

One man (interestingly the majority of these daydreamers are men) mentioned casually that at heart he was a Spaniard "somewhere from Andalucia." Another vouchsafed that Paris was his true home. A third shared that he never felt as well as in England, "Saudi Arabia's historic twin" (a surprise, possibly, to the British).

The officer was amazed at precise details offered regarding airlines, car rental, hotels, and sights, "as if disgorged from a photographic memory. The slightest incident is recalled with pleasure." The downside, inevitably, is a discussion of the return to Saudi Arabia, and the accompanying sadness. "That indeed is the predominant sentiment of the Hejazi returnee: impending doom as individual freedom (what in the West is considered 'normal' life) is to be surrendered to the stifling strictures of Wahhabi Islam . . . No amount of money or status can buy them freedom."

She went on to pose the question—if the Wahhabi lifestyle is so awful, why not change it? The answers were sobering.

This could spell revolution! . . . The overthrow of the monarchy! . . . If there weren't the possibility of escape, maybe we would be forced to do something but since we can periodically leave, we don't have to . . . That's what trips to the West are for.[22]

She concluded with the poignant observation that the greatest frustration among younger Hejazis is never having even been asked what kind of country they want; presumably a less restrictive form of Islamic monarchy.

This cable is dynamite, and it is easy to see why it got the "secret" classification. The diplomat is telling Washington that wealthy, educated, and well-traveled Saudis are essentially disavowing their own society. They find it oppressive, and they have more reason to know than most, since they can compare their country with those they visit.

The officer's frustration with them is equally revealing. Why don't they change their own society? Because they fear the conservatism of the masses and the risk that small modernization gains painstakingly achieved would be lost. The officer was unpersuaded that these elite were in a position to know the views of the masses. Nonetheless, it is clearly easier to dream of one's next sojourn in Paris than to man the barricades in Jeddah.

★ ★ ★ ★

AS A FITTING CODA to these examples of the strange ways in which modern lives and repressive regimes can clash, consider the story of the Iranian garage band Yellow Dogs. In 2009 its members made their way to Istanbul to apply for visas to perform a concert tour in the United States. The consular officers were fascinated by the picture they painted of the underground music scene in Tehran, and their visa interview soon turned into a reporting cable on the lives of Iranian youths. The consulate wrote that the musicians "reinforced the impression that Iranian society spans a far broader and more complex spectrum than many outside observers realize."[23]

The musicians described a scene where "drugs are cheap and easy to find, creative expression is at its most free, and participants are among Iran's most tech-savvy citizens." Some of the group's political predictions did not come to pass, but their images of Iran's youth culture seemed dead on, with their descriptions of hours spent playing video games, watching online TV, and blogging. "They told us with bemusement that they regularly play 'Guitar Hero' online and beat players from the U.S. or Europe. When they tell their online competitors they are from Iran, the other players express shock that Iranians are allowed to use the Internet—and that they are so good at video games."

The Yellow Dogs got their visas and performed on concert tours, were interviewed on CNN and featured in *Rolling Stone*'s Middle Eastern edition, and were highlighted in *No One Knows About Persian Cats*, a film about the Iranian rock music scene. The exposure led to a coveted invitation to play at South by Southwest, and it seemed the group was poised to break out. They never went back to Iran and began a new life in Brooklyn. They applied for and were granted political asylum in the United States.

In one of the cruelest ironies imaginable, two members of the group, along with another Iranian musician, were slain on November 11, 2013, by a fellow Iranian musician who then committed suicide. Articles on the group quoted the embassy cable from WikiLeaks, stressing how the band opened America's eyes to a younger generation of Iranians. "I wish all this attention was just for a new release of an album," said surviving member and lead singer Siavash Karampour. "It took us three bodies to become famous."[24]

THE MANY FACES OF GOD

Embassy reporting about religion suggests that Washington ought to consider the world's faiths more frequently than in the once-a-year International Religious Freedom Report. While politicians talked endlessly about Islamic fundamentalism, officers took a wider view, writing cables describing a variety of belief systems and how they influence local life. Religion and local politics commingle, suggesting that faith and foreign policy are logical, if not always comfortable, bedfellows. They reported on the influence of religions as familiar as Catholicism and as exotic as animism, showing that religion and foreign policy intersect in ways that policymakers might not have contemplated.

Like most other countries, the United States recognizes the Holy See and sends a small contingent of diplomats to its embassy in Vatican City. These officers analyze the enormous reach of Catholicism and its global influence. Some of their cables made the Vatican sound like a hip place, noting Pope Benedict XVI's first foray on YouTube and explaining how the Vatican went green, becoming the first carbon-neutral country in the world.[25] Benedict took an intellectual approach to climate change, linking it to issues from disarmament to the protection of human life to the rights of environmental refugees forced to migrate by the degradation of their natural surroundings.

The cables also described a church that struggled to cope with relentless sex abuse scandals, the first of which broke in the United States in 2002, several years before the issue surfaced in Europe. In Ireland, the abuse revelations of the Ryan Report in May 2009 and the Murphy Report of November 2009 marked an era which officers assessed as one of increasing secularization. "Once ensconced in the Irish Constitution, the Irish Catholic Church reached the height of its prestige and power with the 1979 state visit of Pope John Paul II but it has been falling ever since. At the same time, the Murphy Report reflects Irish shame over the collaboration of Ireland's state bodies, including its schools, courts, and police in the appalling abuses and cover-up that occurred for decades."[26]

U.S. diplomats in the Holy See also wrote about the complexity of managing modern church-state relations. Ecumenism was an important platform for the pope, and the Vatican busied itself mounting interfaith dialogues with Muslims and Jews, among others. The thicket of historical and contemporary complications to this approach were on display in a May 2009 visit to Israel. Pope Benedict XVI spoke at—but not in—the Holocaust Museum Yad Vashem, to avoid seeing an unflattering depiction of Pope Pius XII, who is accused of doing too little to help Jews during the Holocaust. The trip was almost derailed before it got underway, when the pope decided to reinstate a breakaway Catholic group that included Holocaust denier Bishop Richard Williamson. Six months after his Israel visit, Benedict decreed Pius as "venerable" (along with the immensely more popular John Paul II). This act—a first step in a series that lead to elevation to sainthood—reactivated Jewish ire.

Although the pope may be the only religious leader with such a lengthy rule of his own country, the cables also shed light on patriarchs, rabbis, imams, and other religious leaders. Many dealt with the struggles of so-called minority religions, especially native U.S. groups such as Seventh-day Adventists, Scientologists, Jehovah's Witnesses, and Mormons. Explaining the practices of those religions and encouraging other countries to accept their presence was a major challenge for U.S. diplomats.

Germans (among other European nations) have steadfastly refused to grant Scientologists permanent resident visas. Reporting on refusals to two American Scientologists who had hoped to train local church staff, a U.S. officer wrote that the Germans felt the applicants were unable to demonstrate that their cost of living would be met by the Church of Scientology during their one-year stay in Germany and cited the applicants' inability to provide any evidence of health insurance. In other contexts, these objections might have been overcome, but the German official also categorized the Church of Scientology's activities as posing "a threat to Germany's constitutional order" and wondered why the U.S. government was interested in a "residence permit denial case."[27]

In Russia, Mormons, Jehovah's Witnesses, and Evangelical Lutherans struggled to find legal meeting places in a state that excelled at creating a maze of bureaucratic obstacles to worship.[28] Meeting places were also a problem in Shanghai, where the consulate reported that a ruling authorizing expatriate Mormons to meet legally came with strings attached—the rent for the authorized space was one of the highest per head in Asia. In addition, a member of Shanghai's religious affairs board was required to attend and observe services every week—versus once a year under a previous arrangement. And Chinese Mormons could no longer meet in the same location as the expatriate members.[29]

Elsewhere, reporting on religion took on a decidedly non-Western feel. In the Kédougou region of southern Senegal, a political officer visited the Bedik village of Ewol where residents have long resisted both Islam and Christianity in favor of a form of animism. The Bedik escaped from Mali in the twelfth century after the king of Guinea tried to convert them to Islam.

> According to local legend . . . 18 young men were singled out
> to be sacrificed to the traditional spirit they worship. However,
> the devil spirit spared the young men and instead sent a swarm
> of bees which attacked the invading armies, killed the Guinean
> king, and spared them from slavery. In the center of Ewol stands
> a massive baobab tree where the villagers hold their annual sacri-
> fices. The tree is also where, in the past, leading elders were buried
> and where it is believed that their spirits still reside.[30]

Animism also plays a role in Laos, along with ancestor worship, and an embassy officer and a visiting State Department officer found that the farther they traveled from the capital, the further they left the concept of religious freedom behind. In the remote province of Oudomxay, their search for the province's political leaders wound through the multilingual territories of fourteen different ethnic groups. Along the way, they developed an appreciation of the infrastructure and communications challenges the Lao government faces in its northern provinces.

Even in such a faraway region, the officers found evidence that proselytizers had gone before them. They heard villagers complain about tourists distributing Bibles without permission and missionaries coercing ethnic minorities to convert by promising favors. "A con-artist extorted money from poor Buddhists in exchange for promises of salvation after death." They found Seventh-day Adventists and a Calvinist sect forced to conduct religious services in the forest.

In one village, people were eager to gripe about Christianity. "Village elders complained that often cases of conflict arose when families planned important animal sacrifice ceremonies or funerals, and the Christian family members—often younger members—refused to take part. This was an insult to the family and the ancestors."[31]

In neighboring Thailand, astrology, not animism, influences people in high places. The leadership of the Council for National Security visited the famed Chiang Mai astrologer Varin Buaviratlert to protect against ill fortune and pay respect. The officers wrote that "attraction to mediums and mystics cuts across all segments of Thai society, including Muslims." The embassy noted the leaders last visited the astrologer in early November to ward off bad luck that might have stemmed from their September 19, 2006, coup.

Belief in astrology and mysticism is well within the mainstream of Thai culture, which blends astrology and a rich mixture of Buddhism, Hinduism, animism, and elements of the occult into everyday life and decision making. However, the devotion to Varin's wisdom and the cost of flying government leaders up to

Chiang Mai in C-130 military planes has raised eyebrows even among normally superstitious Thais.[32]

In neighboring Burma, the ruling generals favor numerology.

Western rationality is not always apparent in regime decision-making. Than Shwe (a senior general in the junta) reportedly relies on favored soothsayers. We hear one such seer advised moving the capital to the interior because Rangoon would be subject to street disturbances and a horrific storm. Numerology also factors in. Witness the overnight shift to a currency divisible by nines in 1987 and the release of 9,002 prisoners last September, reportedly to ensure an auspicious 2009. Such decision methods may sound strange to us, but they are everyday elements in the lives of many Burmese.[33]

Sometimes the best insights arrive by way of observation. One diplomat went to Mecca to perform the Hajj, an annual pilgrimage that attracts two to three million Muslim worshippers. He wrote that the Saudis' efforts to accommodate the pilgrims, including construction of new bridges and a light rail system, along with the easygoing attitude of crowd controllers and compliant pilgrims, suggested a reflective state of mind punctuated by moments of excitement and joy. The officer-pilgrim described how Saudis dealt with an unusual torrential rainstorm and how public health officials anticipated and dealt with the H1N1 (swine flu) virus.

Part of the religious ritual involves wearing white pilgrimage garments known as ihrams and circling seven times around the Ka'aba, the square granite building at the center of Islam's most sacred mosque, Al-Masjid al-Haram. The officer described the scene:

Pilgrims poured into the mosque at a seemingly endless pace, all jockeying for a position as close to the Ka'aba as physically

possible. Accordingly the ground and lower levels remained jam-
packed both days with many pilgrims on those levels recounting
later that they felt as if the sheer force of the crowd moved them
around the Ka'aba, with their feet hardly touching the ground.
Pilgrims on the two upper floors benefitted from more space and
the picturesque view below of tens of thousands of worshippers
clothed in white moving counterclockwise around the Ka'aba like
a slow-moving hurricane.

The second day of the Hajj, considered the most important, is
known as the day of Arafat, on which pilgrims head towards the
Plain of Arafat, near Mount Arafat where the Prophet Muham-
mad delivered his final sermon. Here worshippers spend the day
in tents praying, reading the Qur'an and reflecting on their lives.
Towards the end of the afternoon most pilgrims exited their tents
and faced in the direction of the Ka'aba to begin offering sup-
plications until sunset. Believing that all prayers on Arafat are
answered, pilgrims pray especially earnestly at this point in the
Hajj, many weeping and shaking with emotion while directing
silent petitions to the Almighty.

The Hajj lasts five days, with most pilgrims spending three of the
nights in the tent city of Mina, which the officer likened to a large
refugee camp, with thousands of tents arranged next to one another.

Camping areas are divided along nationality lines with delegations from each country occupying groups of adjoining tents.
Other tent groupings are reserved for organizations such as the
Organization of the Islamic Conference . . . Most tents are fitted
simply with rugs for sleeping and a small restroom area (toilets and
showers). Higher budget delegations, including royal and ministerial parties, tend to have larger, more luxurious tents equipped
with small beds and upgraded restrooms. Poorer pilgrims sleep
on the streets in any area they can mark out for themselves.

The officer also described the "stoning the devil" ritual, after which pilgrims change out of their ihram and put on regular clothing, which provides the most striking reminder of the international range of the participants. "As pilgrims made their way to stone the devil at Jamarat on subsequent days, many national delegations traveled in large groups, wearing matching garb and carrying their national flags in a spectacle reminiscent of the parade of nations at the opening ceremony of the Olympics."[34]

This compelling description of an event most Americans never witness firsthand is an invaluable effort to bridge a cultural gap, demystify a significant religious act, and provide detail on how the Saudis manage to deal peacefully with enormous international crowds. As part of the voluminous embassy reporting on religion, it offers participatory observation as another means of gathering information and practicing diplomacy.

WHY POWERLESS PEOPLE SHOULD MATTER

The Department of State should not be confused with the National Geographic Society. It is hard to make the case that people living traditional or rural lives are first-line stakeholders in foreign policy. The cables describe a reality in which people far from capital cities are often marginalized, politically and economically. The writing clearly establishes that tribal cultures are stressed by modernization and generational conflict. Indigenous people are on the front lines of globalization's downside—environmental degradation, rampant tourism, and migration, all of which have reached the remotest corners of the planet.

But cables also have to answer the "so what?" question. While earlier generations of American diplomats might not have bothered to venture into the backwaters, today's diplomats do so because they see it as an imperative, and because they see a clear connection between remote people and places and U.S. foreign policy. They have reconsidered who should be on the all-important embassy contact lists. They will always need to meet counterparts at foreign ministries and parliaments, but they are increasingly finding value in meetings with Turkmen truckers, Iranian rock bands, and tribal elders. The back country of Suriname should not have to wait seven years for the next visit.

Culture matters. The officers reporting on their trips and encounters are gently making the case that "people like us" are not the only agents of influence. Seeing the world through the lens of nineteenth-century nation-states is but one vision. Cables from country after country describe people who identify themselves according to their ethnicity, religion, or geography. They will make common cause with like-minded people in ways that sometimes negate the construct of nation-states. On occasion, the view from the village may matter more than the view from the corridors of power. Ignoring that view will leave the United States at risk.

Chapter 5

FRENEMIES:
The Faces Behind Diplomacy

---

*You can either do business with the United States or you can
do business with Frank Zappa.*

—*Secretary of State James Baker*

*Frank Zappa was one of the gods of the Czech underground.
I thought of him as a friend. Whenever I feel like escaping
from the world of the Presidency, I think of him.*

—*Václav Havel, president of the Czech Republic*

Brussels sparkles in the holiday season, with
its Grand Place, the illuminated town hall, and Christmas markets. On December 23, 2009, most people had left their offices for
last-minute shopping, but the U.S. ambassador dropped by the European Union building for the humblest of reasons—to present a con-
gratulatory letter from President Obama to Herman Van Rompuy,
the first president of the European Council.

He was warmly greeted and invited in for coffee with Van Rompuy and his chief of staff, Frans Van Daele, described as Belgium's
"premier diplomat." The ambassador, Howard Gutman, might have

claimed the same title, having charmed everyone to the point that a 2011 profile in Belgian newspaper *Le Soir* lauded him as "someone who could make you love the U.S. again."

The men all knew one another well—Van Rompuy had been Belgium's prime minister before taking up the new EU post, and through frequent interaction, Gutman had come to think of both men as friends. On that relaxed late December day, the EU building was virtually empty. The three chatted amiably, inquired about holiday plans and families, then turned to substantive matters, such as the recently concluded United Nations Climate Change Conference in Copenhagen. Gutman wrote that Van Rumpuy called it "an incredible disaster," and was "as animated and frustrated as I have seen him." He said he had already given up on Mexico City, the venue for the next conference, with Van Daele chiming in colorfully, comparing it to *A Nightmare on Elm Street 2*. "Who wants to see that horror movie again!"[1]

The ambassador wrote apologetically that he merely had meant to deliver the mail, an important clarification in Belgium, where three American ambassadors have to tread carefully to avoid each other's turf. Gutman served as the U.S. ambassador to Belgium, while his colleagues were the U.S. ambassador to NATO, headquartered a short distance from the capital in Mons, and the U.S. ambassador to the European Union, where the liaison function is valuable to both sides, even though the United States is not a member. The new USEU ambassador, William Kennard, had not yet presented his credentials, a necessary bit of protocol allowing the incoming diplomat to introduce himself as the president's official representative in the country. Ambassadors seek to do this as soon as possible upon arrival, but sometimes holidays or schedules intervene. Until this formality takes place, ambassadors cannot engage in official actions, even such mundane affairs as the delivery of a letter from the president. Gutman's instincts to deliver the letter and stay to chat served him well. This is a perfect example of how good contact work in diplomacy gets done.

The importance of carefully building and maintaining relationships is critical to diplomacy. Sometimes it requires nothing more
than the gift of time, and sometimes it leads to real trust and genuine
friendships. The warmth U.S. officials felt for Van Rompuy comes
through in several cables, alongside efforts to explain the importance
of the EU.

At the press conference announcing the appointment of Van Rompuy and EU High Representative Catherine Ashton to their new
posts, the embassy noted that they were asked the so-called Kissinger
question: Which of you will President Obama be calling and which
of you will be calling him? This telling question, "Who do I call if I
want to call Europe?" was meant in Kissinger's time to underscore
the frustration of dealing with a political entity that lacked a foreign ministry yet exercised the chaotic separate foreign policies of its
member states. "Van Rompuy, known for his wit, answered, We are
anxiously awaiting the first phone call!"[2]

Van Rompuy's conservative working style won out over the flash
of his potential opponent, former British prime minister Tony Blair.
The irony of having such a neutral figure at the helm of the unexciting
European Union was not lost on anyone. The U.S. Embassy in Berlin
quoted Germany's *Frankfurter Allgemeine,* which editorialized: "Van
Rompuy is certainly no megastar, who could bring New York City's
traffic to a standstill and let the powerful men in Washington and
Beijing get the jitters. These would have been the qualities of Tony
Blair. However, Van Rompuy does not deserve the insults he had to
hear from an English chuff in the European Parliament. He is doing
a fairly good job in a very calm way . . ."[3]

The insults from the "English chuff" were very publicly delivered
by Nigel Farage, leader of the UK Independence Party, at the European Parliament, a 751-member body of directly elected representatives from a wide spectrum of political parties. "I don't want to be
rude but, really, you have the charisma of a damp rag and the appearance of a low-grade bank clerk and the question I want to ask is: Who

are you? I'd never heard of you. Nobody in Europe has ever heard of you."[4] Farage was subsequently fined, having refused to apologize, and was forced to forfeit $4,000 from his parliamentary salary.

The USEU mission was far kinder, noting that Van Rompuy had once pulled Belgium back from the precipice after a political impasse that threatened to split the nation and praising his skills as a cool-headed negotiator. They portrayed Van Rompuy as a consensus-builder: a quiet man who wrote haiku and used self-deprecating humor to his advantage. When he performed in a comic video, the line that got the most laughs as he tiptoed across the stage imitating a mouse was when Belgian prime minister Guy Verhofstadt said, "Herman is so discreet, so discreet, even when he is there you cannot see him."[5]

The reporting officers' considerable efforts to inject life into this somewhat colorless figure illustrates one of diplomacy's most important tasks—describing key policymakers. Knowing as much as possible about who they are and how they think and predicting their reaction to a wide range of possible initiatives is central to their job. Foreign policy doesn't exist without people, and dealing with people is a crucial part of foreign policy.

Personalities matter. What would a discussion of U.S.–Russian relations be without the image of a scowling Vladimir Putin? And who can think of Italy's Silvio Berlusconi without recalling the 2009 NATO summit when he arrived glued to his mobile phone, until his annoyed host, German chancellor Angela Merkel, finally gave up waiting and ditched him curbside, all of it uploaded for viewing on YouTube?

When the media began sorting through the WikiLeaks cables, reporting on A-list celebrities from the foreign policy world provided an obvious way in. Articles from the *Guardian* and the *New York Times* dealt with world leaders everyone knew—or thought they did. Readers got a look at the "bromance" between Putin and Berlusconi and read how Medvedev played Robin to Putin's Batman. They were titillated by reports that Libyan leader Muammar Gaddafi was never far from his voluptuous Ukrainian nurse and learned that not even eighteen honorary doctorates could suspend the laws of economics for Zimbabwe's Robert Mugabe as he ran his once-prosperous country into ruin.

But the big names were not the only interesting story. The leaked cables offered a wealth of biographic entries on the up-and-comers, the has-beens, the would-bes, the might-be-agains, and others whose positions in their respective countries provided worthwhile insight, perspective, or contradictory views.

Their names would be unrecognizable to most Americans, yet some of these people could become important overnight. Leaders come from the back benches, rural provinces, out-of-power political parties, and occasionally from the ranks of jailed political prisoners, such as the late Nelson Mandela. They get their start as economists, journalists, professors, or pollsters. They work as shadow cabinet ministers before they step into the limelight. The time to find out what makes them tick is before they ascend to the prime minister's office.

The ego that it takes to become a politician often makes for scoundrels; the self-sacrifice it takes to become a human rights activist often makes for saints. There are also the visionaries—voices that stay out of the political lane but whose views become the next big issue. These people might be religious leaders, writers, artists, or filmmakers. To understand a culture is to gain a unique window into a country, so American diplomats visited churches and mosques; attended plays, exhibits, and concerts; watched films and television satires; scanned the newspapers for political cartoons; and were curious about people from all walks of life. Diplomacy has an undeserved reputation for being sedate, decorous, and downright dull. From the embassies' descriptions of their contacts—the people from all walks of life whom they met and conversed with and learned from—it is anything but.

American diplomats needed all their people skills, along with a good sense of humor. Contact work is rarely as civilized as Gutman's holiday coffee klatsch with Van Rompuy. The cables suggest there were plenty of characters who reveled in finding new ways to misbehave, along with people whose stories were genuinely inspirational. Some contacts had power, money, and access. Just as often, they had none.

Contact work encompasses all: the scoundrels and the saints, the artists and the actors, and those who were merely interesting.

MEET THE SCOUNDRELS

It is not a revelation to learn that many national figures are underwhelming, but some fall to such low standards that an undercurrent of revulsion seeps into embassy reporting. One such case involved South African minister of health Manto Tshabalala-Msimang, who made a startling appearance in the headlines of Johannesburg's *Sunday Times*: "Manto: A Drunk and a Thief." A nurse at a hospital in neighboring Botswana accused the minister of stealing a watch from the arm of an anesthetized patient. Tshabalala-Msimang landed in court for stealing hospital supplies and was declared a "prohibited immigrant" and barred from entering Botswana for ten years. A hospital employee quipped, "Everyone here thinks it's hilarious that she is a health minister in South Africa."[6]

She presided at the ministry from 1999 to 2008, during which time HIV/AIDS infected more than four million South Africans, and deaths from the disease doubled. Called "Dr. Beetroot" for her stubborn insistence that a diet of vegetables could cure AIDS, she made headlines when she blocked U.S. funding to assist in the distribution of antiretroviral drugs, effectively sentencing many infected South Africans to death.

Tshabalala-Msimang had personal health problems as well, largely attributed to her alleged alcoholism. She pulled strings to receive a liver transplant that she would not otherwise have qualified for, given her age and condition. Allegedly, she needed the liver because of cirrhosis rather than autoimmune hepatitis, as she claimed. The *Sunday Times* alleged she drank right up to the transplant and continued drinking following the surgery, something the embassy's contacts confirmed.

She came to personify a group of influential Africans known as AIDS deniers, and some critics suggested she be tried for genocide. Others were amazed she outlasted her detractors, but her number one defender was then–South African president Thabo Mbeki, who had spent his early years of political exile in the apartheid era with her, developing a deep bond. She did not leave office until he did. She died of liver failure in December 2009.[7]

Yahya Jammeh, president of The Gambia since 1994 (and evidently for life), also ran head on into Western medicine practices and HIV/AIDS, taking on the mantle of traditional healer. "Claiming healing powers, he paid well-publicized, televised visits to Banjul's principal hospital, visiting patients in their beds, holding the Qur'an over them and rubbing a mysterious elixir over their stomachs. The patients, as shown on the local television news program, invariably responded to Jammeh's treatment by sitting up and saying they immediately felt better."

Embassy officers working in this tiny sliver of a country in West Africa, entirely surrounded by Senegal, grew concerned when Jammeh announced that he would be treating HIV/AIDS and asthma patients on a twice-weekly basis. Claiming to have a cure for HIV/AIDS, "Jammeh gave assurances that patients with the disease would test negative within three days of undergoing his treatment. His patients were to refrain from Western medication while in his care." The post attributed his newfound interest in healing to a "penchant for erratic and sometimes bizarre behavior."[8]

Jammeh also made headlines—far beyond The Gambia—for his foreign policy gambits and homophobic tirades. In a two-hour meeting Jammeh called with the ambassador, he opened by saying, "I want your government to know I am not the monster you think I am." After listening to a lengthy exposition on Gambian foreign policy, the ambassador responded, saying, "perception of [Jammeh] by out-side observers could be attributed in large part to some of his more incendiary comments such as those related to human rights workers and 'cutting off homosexuals' heads.'" [9]

Jammeh responded, "Yes I did make those comments but did I actually cut off anyone's head? Have I ever arrested anyone for being gay? No.... There are gays here in The Gambia, I know that. But they live in secret and that is fine with me, as long as they go about their business in private we don't mind." [10]

Jammeh's views on the subject eventually grew more negative. In a 2013 speech before the UN, he decried "homosexuality in all its forms and manifestations which, though very evil, antihuman, as well as anti-Allah, is being promoted as a human right by some powers." [11]

RUDENESS ON A GLOBAL SCALE

Latvia, a Baltic state admired for its environmentalism, offered an example of one of the most uncouth, obscene, and vulgar politicians ever to hold office. Gundars Berzins, seen by the embassy as the second most influential person in the Latvian People's Party, served as the country's minister of finance from 2000 to 2002, and then as minister of health from 2004 to 2007. The embassy found, to its consternation, that it had become a target for his criticism. He accused the former ambassador of "squeezing Latvians like lemons." With growing dis-may, the embassy watched as a series of interviews he granted to a daily newspaper became sharply anti-American, "full of rude, often obscene statements aimed at various high officials. He accused the Latvian intelligence chief of visiting the embassy two-three times a week and compared him to a kitchen maid for the ambassador."

When the minister of foreign affairs resigned and left Berzins's party, he scoffed, "The little boy should go change his wet pampers, put on the new ones and then come out to the public and reveal his true views on restitution to the Jewish community (adding some anti-Semitism to go with anti-Americanism). . . .

"Berzins did not even spare President Valdis Zatlers, comparing him to a carpet that just lays there which one can urinate or even defecate on. (Comment: The president is reported to have had a colorful reaction in his own right.)" [12]

If there is a common theme among the scoundrels, it is a lack of self-awareness and common sense. A case in point is Kumari Mayawati, an Indian politician who served four terms as chief minister of Uttar Pradesh, India's most populous state. The embassy described a pattern of almost unbelievable abuses of power and vicious reprisals.

One journalist related a story in which a state minister was forced to do sit-ups in front of her as penance for not first asking permission to call on Uttar Pradesh's governor. "When she needed new sandals, her private jet flew empty to Mumbai to retrieve her preferred brand. She employed nine cooks (two as food tasters) and she constructed a private road from her residence to her office to enhance her security." [13]

Things took a more serious turn when Mayawati, long accustomed to throwing birthday parties for herself as a means of acquiring cash gifts, was accused of murdering a district engineer. Mayawati stalwarts visited the hapless engineer and demanded a birthday tribute to the governor. The engineer either refused or did not have the funds. He was tortured and killed in his home. His wife, locked in a bathroom by the assailants, heard her husband's pleas for mercy as he was killed. [14]

Excesses with the trappings of office were a recurring theme in reporting cables. Few Americans will have heard of President Emomali Rahmon of Tajikistan. In office since 1992, Rahmon made a seamless transition from Soviet-era collective farm apparatchik to head of state, and he celebrated his third inauguration with a presidential medallion encrusted with jewels, along with a new Bentley. Tajikistan is one of the poorest of the former Soviet Socialist Republics. It is also one of the most corrupt, ranking near the bottom of Transparency International's Corruption Perceptions Index.

But Tajikistan has geopolitical significance, lying next to Afghanistan. The United States has great interest in security cooperation, and Tajikistan granted unrestricted overflight rights for air transport supply flights into Afghanistan. It also occupies a key node in the Northern Distribution Network ground transit—both of which are essential for supplying U.S. troops in landlocked Afghanistan. This geostrategic importance goes some way toward explaining why U.S. embassy representatives would sit dutifully through Rahmon's lengthy and costly inauguration for a third term that in no way celebrated a democratic transition of power. In fact, they had little choice since inaugurations are routinely a command performance for the diplomatic corps for almost all nations. They did, however, try to give a flavor of the event to Washington readers: "Rahmon's speech emphasized that inauguration day is a holiday for the people of Tajikistan and he invited his guests to 'celebrate like civilized white people' (Comment: no comment). As the party went on, and on, the president took to the stage and began to sing. At this point, the television camera stopped filming."[15]

Racist comments from heads of state are not confined to out-of-the-way countries. Thorbjørn Jagland, a leading Norwegian politician—former president of the parliament, former prime minister, former head of the Norwegian Nobel Committee—also served as foreign minister, where he famously complained on national television about the onerous aspects of his job, "having to go around meeting Bongo from the Congo."[16] That gaff—and a few others—were not enough to block his election in 2009 as secretary general of the Council of Europe, a forty-seven-member body focusing on legal standards, human rights, and rule of law.

Jagland was not alone. In an election campaign speech, North Rhine–Westphalia's minister-president Jürgen Rüttgers said that Romanian workers are not punctual and not able to get the job done as well as German workers. That was bait for Social Democratic Party chancellor candidate Frank-Walter Steinmeier, who said Rüttgers's remark played perfectly into the hands of the "right wing mob."[17]

But transgressions such as these pale against the lengthy rap sheet of Nicaraguan political player Daniel Ortega, whose long-running feud with the United States dates back to 1979. As one of the leaders of the Sandinista revolution and the Sandinista National Liberation Front (FSLN), the political party that overthrew the corrupt Somoza regime, Ortega was infamous during the Reagan years for leading his country toward socialism. Nicaraguan military support for a similarly motivated revolution in El Salvador led the United States to give aid to the Contras rebel groups, probably cementing the foundation for a difficult relationship ever after. Ortega ruled Nicaragua for a generation, from 1979 to 1990. He spent sixteen years out of power and then returned for a second act in 2007—albeit with only 38 percent of the vote—and has been at the helm ever since.

One might think such a long-standing relationship would lead to few surprises. On the contrary, the reporting revealed a U.S. fascination with Ortega, tempered by consternation as the embassy tried to make sense of the motives behind his quixotic actions.

On the foreign policy front, Ortega had an odd penchant for backing losers. His gadfly approach led to a meeting with former Iranian president Mahmoud Ahmadinejad, support for former Libyan leader Muammar Gaddafi, and near-instant recognition of the breakaway states of South Ossetia and Abkhazia in Eurasia. In his own backyard, his tight relationships with Fidel Castro and Hugo Chávez and support for leftist regimes elsewhere in the hemisphere burnished his anti-U.S. credentials.

The embassy cried foul when, in 2009, Ortega used the courts to overturn a constitutional provision that limited him to a single term. The U.S. ambassador's speech at the American Chamber of Commerce denouncing this move spurred an angry mob to attack the embassy, "spray-painting anti-U.S. and pro-Sandinista graffiti on the embassy's security fence, breaking lights and security cameras, defacing consulate signs, and breaking a window... Demonstrators waved FSLN party flags and held signs calling for 'Death to the

Yanquis, Death to Empire' . . . Local police made little effort to control the demonstrations and in some cases facilitated the arrival of protestors."[18] Ortega's move to force constitutional change through the courts worked out well for him. He was reelected in 2011 with 62 percent of the vote and remains in charge at this writing.

Despite tensions in the relationship, the two countries continued to interact. A ceremony marking the thirtieth anniversary of the Nicaraguan army led to an Ortega rant against imperialism and an affront to military protocol.

> In his most belligerent and openly anti-U.S. speech in months, President Daniel Ortega launched into a nearly hour-long tirade on the evils of U.S. imperialism . . . In a direct insult to the Marine Corps Marching Platoon [one of many foreign military units invited to take part in the ceremonies], baking in over 100 degree temperatures throughout the harangue, Ortega pointed to the Marines and said, 'you young soldiers . . . you are not responsible.' . . . He could not resist a final insult—giving only a perfunctory salute to the Marines as they paraded past along with cadets and marching teams from other countries, which got a much longer and more formal salute.[19]

Ortega further exasperated the U.S. by criticizing its assistance to earthquake-stricken Haiti, calling the efforts a military invasion and suggesting they were a subterfuge aimed at installing a military base in the country.[20] When the ambassador protested this mischaracterization, the foreign minister was ready with rhetorical questions. If there was no invasion planned, then why were there so many troops? Why weren't they under the control of the United Nations? The ambassador retorted that Ortega's assertions were absurd and so offensive that Secretary of State Clinton mentioned them at the State Department's annual meeting of Western Hemisphere chiefs of mission.

Just when it seemed impossible for the relationship to decay further, the embassy was caught off guard by Ortega's capacity to mount a charm offensive when it suited his purposes. Small but significant changes in behavior led to a meeting in which "Ortega apologized for the attack on the Embassy, noting that he had personally intervened with the Chief of Police to ensure the Embassy (eventually) had protection from anti-riot units (and for the ambassador himself on the following day). When the ambassador noted concern over the fact that senior FSLN leaders were seen urging on the violent protestors, Ortega somewhat sheepishly acknowledged that at times even he cannot control his own people."

The embassy speculated on a number of motives for Ortega's niceguy act. "In our experience, Ortega's charm offensives are . . . short lived and insincere. Perhaps in the face of his less than successful foreign policy to diversify his donor base . . . he simply seeks reassurance that we plan to stay on here. We will. And hope that this new beginning does not end in disappointment, again."[21]

Despite the love-hate relationship, an American presence was expected at Ortega's inauguration and return to power in January 2007. Embassy Managua described an event that "projected an odd image of disorder, amateurism, and unceremonious conduct, where populism trumped protocol, and security was virtually non-existent." The reporting cable excerpts, describing alternating moments of tedium and hilarity, hint at the risks of keeping VIPs unoccupied for lengthy periods.

The American delegation did not have its meeting with the president-elect until 10 p.m. the evening before the inauguration. The day itself was punctuated with other lengthy delays. The late arrival of President Hugo Chávez of Venezuela left heads of state, royalty, ministers, and other dignitaries waiting nearly two hours in the sun and gave new meaning to the term jockeying for position.

The U.S. delegation was unable to take their seats since the Palestinian delegation was already sitting in them, having been displaced from their own seats by the Central American delegations. By the time Chávez arrived, the seating had turned into a free-for-all, with people taking matters into their own hands, grabbing chairs and moving them at will, blocking aisles and walkways.

As the crowd of the unseated grew, many strained for a glimpse of the (non)proceedings, which acquired the feel of a football rally.

Embassy officers, along with ambassadors and assorted European colleagues who were previously displaced from their seats, stood on the sidelines, alongside a ragtag crowd of Salvadoran guests waving red and black Faribundo Martí National Liberation Front (FMLN) flags and cheering for Ortega. Interspersed among the FMLN and the diplomats were Venezuelans sporting radios and orchestrating the cheering for their leader.

People got testy in the hot sun, and it was duly noted that Crown Prince Felipe of Spain drew noticeably louder applause than Ortega. Many delegation leaders, including Presidents Uribe of Colombia and Calderón of Mexico were noticeably not amused ... The erratic management led several to complain this would be their last inauguration.

When Chávez finally arrived, Ortega further delayed proceedings by ushering the leader around and introducing him to the delegations. Chávez obliged by insulting U.S. delegation head Michael Leavitt, Secretary of Health and Human Services, on the subject of infant mortality.

The long wait was rewarded with a lengthy sermon by Nicaraguan Cardinal Obando y Bravo, "ironically preaching on morality, ethics, and the evils of corruption while convicted embezzler [and former president Arnoldo] Aleman beamed in his seat of honor ... The festivities also featured musical miscues, lapses in formal procedures ... a gun salute that was ill timed and interrupted one of the speakers, followed by the lighting of a larger-than-life neon image of FSLN icon Augusto Sandino." (Aleman's conviction was overturned two years later by the Nicaraguan Supreme Court; all four justices who voted to overturn had ties to Aleman's political party.)

With careful understatement, the embassy noted one of the "more entertaining components" was the commemorative medal ceremony to honor the delegation heads, set to the tune of a classic Nicaraguan folk song.

Although the program announced Comandante Daniel would award the Medal of Latin American Unity Free Nicaragua the task was performed by attractive young women dancers who draped medals over the necks of delegation leaders as part of the choreography. Marking another awkward moment, however, they ran out of medals halfway through, leaving Presidents Calderón and Chávez without their prize. To cover the oversight, the dancers and music continued to play while the first lady improvised.

Instead of giving his formal remarks as programmed, President Ortega closed the proceedings with the departing words, "my people await me," and rushed off to Plaza de la Fe for a rally accompanied by Presidents Chávez and Morales, along with the President of Taiwan (looking as lost as an Eskimo in Africa), who had arrived with several busloads of at least 200 delegates.[22]

WOMEN OF COURAGE

Thankfully, embassies also found plenty of people to admire. The International Women of Courage Award, established in 2007 under then–Secretary of State Condoleezza Rice, gave embassies a platform to extol the bravery and leadership of women who might never attain high office but who had made a dramatic impact nonetheless. "The award honors women around the globe who have exemplified exceptional courage and leadership in advocating for human rights, women's equality, and social progress, often at great personal risk. This is the only State Department award that pays tribute to emerging women leaders worldwide."[23] The honorees come to the United States for the special International Visitor Leadership Program, which provides an opportunity to meet with Americans and make connections that will allow them to continue to empower women in their countries.

The number of honorees ranged from eight to ten in the award's first four years and, perhaps not surprisingly, a number of recipients came from Afghanistan (six) and Iraq (four), both priority countries for U.S. foreign policy. Zimbabwe had two recipients, while others hailed from countries as disparate as Sri Lanka and Argentina.

Embassy Kabul set the stage for readers in a nomination cable describing the indescribable.

> Women in Afghanistan face extraordinary circumstances that frequently prevent them from attending school, working outside the home, or even living free from the fear of becoming the victims of domestic violence. However, the number of courageous Afghan women who fight against pervasive cultural norms to better the lives of all women in their country is outstanding. Despite serious threats to their own safety, sometimes by members of their own families, numerous women in Kabul and the provinces continue their work to advance women's rights in Afghanistan.[24]

One Afghan winner, Mary Akrami, ran two shelters for women escaping domestic violence or forced marriages. "Several women at her shelter have made the bold and virtually unprecedented move of stepping forward and denouncing their abusers publicly and filing court cases against them." A second Afghan winner, Aziza Siddiqui, traveled to remote rural villages to educate women on their rights, organizing meetings in more than fifty villages. Colonel Shafiqa Quraishi, unusual in being a female police colonel who worked for the Ministry of Interior for Gender, Human, and Child Rights, recruited thousands of women to the force and then created unheard-of benefits such as prenatal care and child care. She then managed to get forty-two promotions for women processed in the Afghan National Police—women who had been repeatedly passed over for a decade.

Shokuria Assil, one of only four female members of the Baghlan Provincial Council (roughly the political equivalent of a U.S. state legislature) also championed underdogs. When the Ministry of Education summarily fired three teachers, she challenged the decision and argued that the firings were unjust. She got the women reinstated and eventually convinced a ministry official to apologize publically. This would be impressive in the United States; it was unheard of in Afghanistan. She also advocated for programs for the mentally ill, started a networking group for professional women, and pushed to start a women's driving school.[25]

The winner from Argentina, Susana Trimarco de Veron, is the mother of Marita Veron, kidnapped by a human trafficking ring on April 3, 2002, when she was twenty-three years old. Desperate to find her daughter, Trimarco dedicated herself to exposing the traffickers. Her search through global trafficking networks led to the rescue of ninety-six victims, including seventeen Argentine women who had been forced into prostitution in Spain. The embassy nomination read:

> Trimarco's efforts have led her into dangerous situations, disguised as a prostitute, trolling bars and alleys in search of anyone who might know something about her daughter's whereabouts. She has been threatened, spied upon, and tricked. She has received false leads and death threats, but has not been deterred from her investigations into human trafficking in Argentina. Thanks to her work, the Argentine government is beginning to focus on this crime. 70 cases have been filed in Tucuman province.[26]

The horrible reality is that some of the nominees and award recipients have been physically abused and beaten for their work. Iraqi nominee Najat Shakir Munshid al-Hameedawi was not only a civil society activist, but a district council member and a member of the Baghdad Suburban Services Board. Her duties on the municipal body focused on women's and children's services. At the provincial level, she served as the Istiqlal representative to the Baghdad Suburban Services Board and the chair of the Women and Children's Committee for all of the rural districts of Baghdad. Unfortunately, none of this grassroots work was sufficient to prevent her brutal treatment. The embassy wrote:

> What truly makes Ms. Najat's achievements and tireless efforts amazing is her incredible story of courage. Ms. Najat put her life and that of her family in danger on a daily basis by working for the Government of Iraq and with Coalition forces. She risked her life further by speaking up for her strongly held ideas of democracy and women's rights and against the terrorist groups and sectarian militias who do not want to see a stronger role for women in Iraqi society. The terrorist threat became reality on a Friday in the winter of 2006, when Ms. Najat was violently dragged from her home in front of her family by a gang of Jaysh al-Mahdsi (JAM) Special Groups militia. She was tortured and brought to trial in one of the Sharia courts operated by JAM and sentenced to death. However, on her way to execution, she convinced the executioner that she was innocent and to let her go for the sake of her small children. Her executioner released her with strict instructions to leave Baghdad and Iraq.[27]

Ms. Najat refused to leave and continued her work.

In Zimbabwe, Jestina Mukoko, a former television news broadcaster, turned her skills to the Zimbabwe Peace Project, an NGO made up of four hundred Zimbabweans who monitor human rights, providing the international community with accounts of human rights abuses.

> Her work came to an abrupt halt early one morning, when she was abducted by state security agents, dragged from her home in her nightclothes, and held incommunicado . . . During her abduction, she was tortured by agents who beat her, subjected her to falanga (beating the soles of her feet) and forced her to confess to an alleged plot to mount a terrorist incursion from neighboring Botswana . . . She was repeatedly denied adequate medical care for injuries and medications that went untreated during her detention.[28]

It is reassuring to see a smiling Mukoko in a March 10, 2010, State Department photo standing between Secretary Clinton and First Lady Michele Obama, and it would be logical to assume such high-profile international attention would be enough to ward off further violence. But the Zimbabwean government continued to harass her even after her award, just as she continued, more determined than ever, in her work.[29]

In fact, international visibility can cut the wrong way. One of the 2010 Women of Courage Award winners, Jensila Kubais of Sri Lanka, was so frightened at the prospect of government reprisals that she begged the embassy to revise the citation narrative. "In a meeting with us, Kubais underscored the implications of the wording of the award's citation, noting the importance of avoiding references to her work on 'human rights violations' and focusing instead on her work as a 'minority community leader.'" The embassy noted that Kubais and her group had been threatened by the Criminal Investigation Division of the police and that tagging her as a human rights activist could result in dire consequences. Kubais substantiated this fear by noting that a previous recipient had been vilified in the pro-government press.[30]

Visibility from the award was also a problem for the U.S. embassy in Uzbekistan. The ambassador was summoned to the Ministry of Foreign Affairs, where he was dressed down by an apoplectic foreign minister for the embassy's nomination of 2009 award winner Mutabar Tadjibayeva. The embassy described the "icy tone" of the foreign minister, who concluded the meeting without shaking hands. The embassy was frank about the tradeoffs the award would bring, noting it would likely set back other initiatives, such as Uzbekistan's role in the Afghanistan transit framework, an overland supply route, and the hoped-for return of DEA agents to the U.S. mission. Cooperation had been suspended in 2007, and the embassy frequently raised the possibility of having two openly accredited DEA special agents join the mission—a move that would require Uzbek approval.[31]

The Tadjibayeva case is yet another in which a woman human rights activist was imprisoned for speaking out about government violence against peaceful protestors. "Tadjibayeva suffered horribly in prison, enduring forced psychiatric treatment and long stays in solitary confinement . . . She was placed in an unheated solitary confinement cell in winter for almost 50 days. She developed anemia, low blood pressure, and kidney problems." In truly Orwellian fashion, the prison doctors performed surgery on her but refused to discuss her diagnosis or what the procedure was for. She was released on medical grounds during a June 2008 visit by Assistant Secretary of State for South and Central Asian Affairs Richard Boucher. Both the embassy and the State Department were reticent about whether Boucher had won her release, but both the BBC and the New York Times made the connection. According to the embassy, she continued her human rights advocacy and never shied away from criticizing authorities. She commented to a political officer shortly after her release, "They can break my body but they can never break my spirit."[32]

There is a disconcerting postscript to the Tadjibayeva story. Coming from a part of the world where nothing is ever what it seems, even stories of heroism arrive laden with ambiguity. Tadjibayeva returned her award when she learned that a dissident turned president from neighboring Kyrgyzstan, Roza Otunbayeva, was honored with the same award in 2011. Tadjibayeva said that Otunbayeva, as head of state, bore responsibility for a bloody interethnic conflict in Kyrgyzstan in which four hundred people were killed and thousands injured in fierce clashes between ethnic Kyrgyz and Uzbeks. In a statement she said, "When Mrs. Otunbayeva was a leader of the opposition and was speaking out against injustice, I think then it would have been right to award her. But it is during her presidency that we have seen bloodshed."[33]

The embassy in Kyrgyzstan also had trouble making up its mind about Roza Otunbayeva, leader of the Social Democratic party and former foreign minister. Reporting on a lengthy conversation with her in December 2009 about the ruling Bakiyev family's plans for succession, the embassy was dismissive. "We have little confidence in her information and less in her analysis."[34] Four months later, following widespread rioting that led to the overthrow of President Bakiyev, she was leading the country.

Tadjibayeva was correct; the coup that brought Otunbayeva to power unleashed deadly interethnic violence between Kyrgyz and Uzbeks. But Washington had a different interpretation of her role. The announcement of her award painted Otunbayeva in glowing terms, crediting her as the central figure in ridding her country of authoritarian rule, becoming Central Asia's first female head of state and head of government in a traditional, majority Muslim country, and pulling a divided opposition into a provisional government that kept Kyrgyzstan whole.

Other women of courage nominees stayed away from politics and chose instead to focus on service. North Korean Lee Ae-ran was unable to enroll in university because her family came from a "bad class." Faced with hopelessness, she tried to take her own life by drinking insecticide. U.S. Ambassador Kathleen Stephens picked up the story from there, describing how Dr. Lee Ae-ran finally went to college in 1985, majoring in engineering, when the North Korean authorities opened the doors of science and engineering colleges to those from so-called bad classes.

She left North Korea in 1997 with nine members of her family, and in 2009 she was the first North Korean female defector to receive a PhD. "For many years, Dr. Lee has been helping with the rehabilitation programs for North Korean women who were divorced or have autistic children." She organized Hana Women's Group "to provide leadership training for North Korean female defectors . . . She has been supporting college students of defector families with scholarships. Last year, she created a fund of 30 million won to provide North Korean adolescents with 100,000 won each month for their private tuition fees. She has been stressing to the students 'As long as you hope, you can live.'"[35]

Many of the awardees successfully operated at the margins—filling an obvious need, keeping the government at bay, and connecting with the larger international community. Sister Clauda Isaiah Naddaf (aka Sister Marie-Claude) of Damascus, Syria, was an exemplar of that savviness. The embassy admired—and was intrigued by—the way she had found space to maneuver in the "murky no-man's land" between civil society and the government. Like many recipients, she worked for women who were victims of violence and sexual trafficking. She faced down strict cultural taboos and paved the way for other groups. The embassy was smitten.

A visit with Sister Marie-Claude is never an everyday affair. She sits you down, unveils her vision for assisting women in need, explains the moral framework in which she operates, engages you in a discussion on how we, united, might begin to alleviate suffering, and then you meet the very women and girls to whom she has devoted herself. It is a powerful experience. Her boundless energy, fiery intelligence, and tremendous courage have won the respect of SARG (Syrian Arab Republic Government) officials, diplomats, and NGOs alike. She has stood firm in the face of political indifference and kicked down the doors of cultural constraint to better (and very often save) the lives of women and young girls who have found themselves abandoned, beaten on the street, or slaves to traffickers.[36]

And finally, Hadizatou Mani of Niger tells the story of how, when she was twelve, she was sold into slavery for $500. "I was negotiated over like a goat," she said. Mani was a slave because her mother was a slave, purchased by a man in his sixties who beat her, sent her to work long hours in the field, raped her, and made her bear him three children.

When Niger outlawed slavery in 2003, Mani's master tried to tell the government that she was not a slave but one of his wives. Hadizatou fought for and won a Certificate of Liberation and married a man of her own choosing. Her challenges did not end, however. Her former master sued her for bigamy and she spent six months in jail. According to embassy follow-up reporting, even after her award as an International Woman of Courage, her children still lived with her former master.[37]

The cables offer examples of embassy human rights work that goes well beyond mandated reporting cables. They represent months and years of careful relationship-building and hard-won trust that provided a window into communities fearful of authorities in their own countries. The officers' long-standing relationships with these women personalize the work of human rights and hint at a vast world of impoverished, abused, and unwanted victims.

PEOPLE WHO JUST DON'T LIKE US

The U.S. relationship with Germany is among the most important in the world. Allied since the end of World War II, Germany's industrial strength has been the backbone that rebuilt Europe. The reunification of East and West between 1989 and 1990, with its accompanying risk of a more neutral European position, tested the bonds of that relationship. Since that time, Germany's steady leadership as the single strongest member of the EU has provided further opportunities for collaboration. This is one country whose leaders are household names in the United States. Christian Democrats such as Konrad Adenauer, Helmut Kohl, and Angela Merkel are well-known figures, thanks in part to their long tenures and generally pro-U.S. stances. Social Democrats such as Willy Brandt, Helmut Schmidt, and Gerhard Schröder often pulled at those bonds, causing consternation for U.S. policymakers. In the years since reunification, for the most part, U.S.–German relations rarely make headlines, remaining solid, reliable, and rarely colorful.

No one would ever call the German politician Guido Westerwelle gray. The embassy in Berlin saw him as "a wild card" and warned that his "exuberant personality does not lend itself to taking a back seat to Chancellor Merkel on any issue. If he becomes foreign minister, there is the possibility of higher profile discord between the chancellery and the MFA."[38]

In fact, the prediction was on target in several ways. Westerwelle's Free Democratic Party (FDP) surged to gain 14.6 percent of the votes in the September 2009 elections, making it a junior partner to Angela Merkel's Christian Democratic Union and Christian Social Union coalition. This opened the way for Westerwelle to take on the job of foreign minister, which comes with the title of vice chancellor.

Westerwelle's foray into the realm of foreign policy, with a speech at the German equivalent of the Council on Foreign Relations, came in for scathing reviews. His remarks earned him the nickname of Guido Genscher, linking his ideology to that of his mentor, former FDP foreign minister Hans-Dietrich Genscher. Genscher's penchant for charting a middle course between two superpowers alarmed the United States, which was concerned that his path would lead to German neutrality. The politics of resistance to fully aligning with the United States became known as "Genscherism," a label for Germans

seen as less than fully committed to NATO membership and to a
U.S. presence on the European continent.

The embassy, sketching a biographic profile of Westerwelle in
September 2009 following the FDP's good showing in the election,
found his remarks to be "short on substance, suggesting that Westerwelle's command of complex foreign and security policy issues still
requires deepening if he is to successfully represent German interests
on the world stage."

> He harbors resentment that he has not been taken more seriously
> by the Washington political establishment . . . By his own admis-
> sion, Westerwelle has never seriously harbored a fascination for
> international affairs.
>
> There is a contrast between Westerwelle's increased public sup-
> port and successful leadership of the FDP versus the continued
> skepticism, often bordering on contempt, shown by much of the
> German foreign policy elite toward him.

The embassy continued with a series of damning assessments. "One
foreign policy analyst told poloff [political officer], 'he lacks the gravitas and is seen as too opportunistic to be trusted as foreign minister.' Several Ministry of Foreign Affairs desk officers said they were
not persuaded that Westerwelle 'had the foreign and security policy
expertise necessary.' . . . There was a consensus among desk officers,
driven perhaps by political bias, that Westerwelle was arrogant and
too fixated on maintaining his cult of personality."

The embassy seemed to reach for invidious comparisons. "Like
Dan Quayle in 1992, Westerwelle wants to compare himself to his
mentor, Hans-Dietrich Genscher, but in the eyes of the foreign policy
community, he is no Genscher."

The biggest problem seemed to be his personality—it is clear the
embassy found him hard to like. "Westerwelle found it hard to conceal his resentment toward Washington based on his feeling that nei-

ther its top leadership nor the embassy in Berlin courted him during his time in opposition ... He has little professional experience of the U.S. since he never made extensive efforts to introduce himself to the Washington policy community. Unfortunately our attempts to reach out to Westerwelle were often rebuffed with the excuse that he would only meet with the Ambassador. Only after extensive embassy negotiations with Westerwelle's staff were former CDA [chargé d'affaires] and poloff able to secure a meeting."[39]

Less than a week later, on September 22, 2009, the embassy's postelection analysis insisted that results did not signal change but fretted that Westerwelle's "unpredictability" would require what it euphemistically termed "focused diplomatic engagement."

As it turned out, the embassy had a far more intimate means of understanding the worldview of Westerwelle. It had a source within the FDP, a "young, up-and-coming party loyalist," who offered the embassy documents on many occasions. The source, revealed as Helmut Metzner, "was excited with his role as FDP negotiations notetaker; he seemed happy to share his observations and insights and read directly from his notes and provided copies of documents from his binder." The embassy was extraordinarily lucky to have found Metzner. While cultivating party insiders is the bread and butter of diplomatic work, this level of engagement with a source was unusual, as was Metzner's willingness to serve, for all intents and purposes, as a mole. Unfortunately, for Metzner, it was not destined to last.

Westerwelle struggled to balance his role as foreign minister with his role as party leader. By February 2010, the embassy was reporting Metzner's prediction that Westerwelle would leave diplomacy to the drawing rooms while using straight talk in the world of domestic politics. Straight talk could prove controversial, evinced by Westerwelle's infamous gaffe that "promising people prosperity without work would encourage Germans to indulge in late-Roman decadence" and that working people "are increasingly becoming the idiots of the nation."[40]

Despite the embassy's dubious views, Westerwelle had a long run as foreign minister, from 2009 to 2013. In an interesting footnote, the WikiLeaks cables claimed a political victim: Metzner was dismissed from his job as Westerwelle's chief of staff after admitting he was the source of U.S. insights into confidential negotiations on the formation of the new government.

PLASTIC PEOPLE OF THE UNIVERSE AND OTHER PERNICIOUS ARTISTIC INFLUENCES

Even the most democratic governments have an uneasy relationship with artists and intelligentsia. They go too far, they say too much, they push from the comfortable center of an issue out to the furthest extremes. They make people think—and they also make them nervous. Diplomats seek out writers, playwrights, filmmakers, and musicians and value them for the nuances they can add to an issue. Engaging with artists is one aspect of cultural diplomacy, a catchall term that is often associated with soft power, the idea of espousing foreign policy goals in a less direct and less confrontational way. Cultural programming can be as simple as a traveling exhibit of American quilts, but the savviest diplomats see cultural programming as a two-way street. Local artists serve as a window into the subtleties of the society in which they live and work. Like the figures from other nongovernmental agencies, members of the artistic community provide an alternative view often at odds with conventional wisdom.

Sometimes the controversy they create is as silly as David Cerny's sculpture *Entropa,* which served as the Czech Republic's artistic contribution to its 2009 presidency of the European Union, a rotating honor shared by each member state for six months. The embassy reported that the sculpture, a map of Europe, served as an irritant for its irreverent (either funny or rude, depending on taste) stereotypical

depictions of member states. Some were harmless and predictable—
Denmark was built of Legos, Sweden was an Ikea box; but others,
such as Bulgaria's depiction as a toilet, were insulting. The sculpture
caused the Czech government, already notorious as one of the most
skeptical members of the EU, significant embarrassment and was a
prelude to other disasters in its presidency term.

Sometimes the conflict between intellectuals and the state is
more serious and offers insights into the thinking of the societies
from which they spring. Orhan Pamuk, winner of the Nobel Prize
for Literature in 2006, is probably Turkey's best-known novelist for
works such as *Snow, My Name Is Red, The Museum of Innocence*,
and many others.

In February 2005, in an act that he said was deliberately calculated
to test the limits of free speech in Turkey, he stated, "Thirty thousand
Kurds have been killed here, and a million Armenians. And almost
nobody dares to mention that. So I do." He reinforced these thoughts
in numerous interviews with world media. "What happened to the
Ottoman Armenians in 1915 was a major thing that was hidden from
the Turkish nation; it was a taboo. But we have to be able to talk
about the past."[41]

Pamuk was subsequently charged under Turkey's infamous Article
301, a 2005 law, amended in 2008, which made it a crime to insult
Turkishness or the Turkish nation. The debate Pamuk ignited featured rallies at which his books were burned. He was also the target
of assassination attempts and spent considerable time outside the
country teaching at Columbia University and Bard College.

Pamuk was not the only intellectual to test the waters of free
speech. Turkish-Armenian journalist and human rights activist
Hrant Dink was assassinated in 2007. The seventeen-year-old per-
petrator, once apprehended, openly admitted to the act and expressed
nationalistic pride for it, reportedly saying during his interrogation,
"I don't regret it. I would do it again."[42]

The embassy in Ankara was alarmed by the upsurge in nationalism, writing that it was seeing a lynch-mob atmosphere. "Having gone unchecked, it appears that nationalism is exceeding the bounds of political expediency. In the wake of the Hrant Dink murder, most Turks were stunned by video clips released February 2 that show police proudly taking photos with Dink's murderer before a Turkish flag. The photos fueled rumors of police involvement in the shooting . . ."[43]

Pamuk continued his campaign for free speech, telling Russian magazine *Timeout Moscow* that freedom of expression did not exist in Turkey. He complained that the secular vision of the modern founder of the Turkish state, Mustafa Atatürk, and the politically influential Turkish military's understanding of secularism were completely different.[44]

The Turkish parliament finally amended the infamous Article 301 after an extended debate that highlighted the deputies' divided sentiments. Speaking for many of his parliamentary colleagues, Bekir Bozdag said the law had stained Turkey's image. "Noting the irony of Turkish Nobel laureate author Orhan Pamuk showing the world the beauty of Turkey only to be prosecuted under Article 301, Bozdag said onlookers threw eggs and tomatoes at Pamuk as he entered the courthouse to defend himself against the charge of insulting Turkishness."[45]

The embassy saw Pamuk's case as a bellwether for democracy and came to a pessimistic conclusion. "The fundamental problem lies in the un-reformed mentality of GOT [government of Turkey]) officials, starting with Prime Minister Erdogan, who have yet to fully accept freedom of speech in its broadest form as a core value." Embassy officers said Turkish officials reassured them several times that Pamuk would never be imprisoned, a fact they found more troubling, since it implied officials saw the case as a troublesome one-off, rather than as a test of societal values. They worried that intellectuals without Pamuk's high profile would still be endangered. "A Turkish free speech activist noted numerous speech-related lawsuits Erdo-

gan brought against cartoonists who have lampooned him, as well
as writers and demonstrators whose speech he considered personally
insulting as evidence that the GOT leadership had not embraced the
western concept of free expression."[46]

Turkish discomfort with freedom of expression, as evidenced by
the Pamuk case, was sometimes characterized as the reason Europeans were leery of granting Turkey full membership in the European
Union, but within the EU, countries that were undeniably Western
faced similar problems, personified by writers, filmmakers, and journalists who asked uncomfortable questions that resonated far beyond
their own societies.

The Danish cartoon controversy, which surfaced in September
2005 when a paper published a dozen cartoons caricaturing the
Prophet Mohammed, was one aspect of this problem, and nearby
Netherlands faced several crises as it worked to define the difference
between free speech and hate speech. In November 2004, film-
maker Theo Van Gogh had been murdered by an enraged Muslim
because of his film *Submission*, which dealt with violence against
women in Islamic societies. The Netherlands has one of the highest Muslim populations of any European country—close to one
million, comprising nearly 5 percent of its seventeen million people. Van Gogh's murder led to an explosion of reprisals and fueled
debate that followed on the heels of the earlier 2002 assassination
of Pim Fortuyn, a member of parliament who had run on an anti-
Islam platform.[47]

Geert Wilders, another high-profile anti-Islamic member of the
Dutch parliament, mounted a film attack on the Qur'an called *Fitna*
(an Arabic title meaning disagreement or division among people),
which aired in March 2008. The embassy advised Washington to
view him as more of a hatemonger than a free speech fighter.

Golden-pompadoured, maverick parliamentarian Geert Wilders'
anti-Islam, nationalist Freedom Party remains a thorn in the coa-

lition's side, capitalizing on the social stresses resulting from the failure to fully integrate almost a million Dutch Muslims, mostly of Moroccan or Turkish descent. In existence only since 2006, the Freedom Party, tightly controlled by Wilders, has grown to be the Netherlands second largest, and fastest growing, party . . . Wilders is no friend of the U.S.: he opposes Dutch military involvement in Afghanistan; he believes development assistance is money wasted; he opposes NATO missions outside "allied" territory; he is against most EU initiatives; and, most troubling, he foments fear and hatred of immigrants.[48]

The embassy wrote that release of his film only emboldened him. He campaigned by calling Islam a "fascist religion" and asked voters whether there were "too many Moroccans" in the Netherlands.[49]

On the tenth anniversary of Theo Van Gogh's murder, it seemed his killing was still a third rail for the Dutch. Prominent cultural figures preferred to stay silent, "either because they feared any comments would contribute to further divisions; that comments would be exploited by right wing politicians; or that even the slightest criticism of Van Gogh would be seen as an apology for his killer." Van Gogh's friends claimed "tolerance had become a cover for cowardice,"[50] all of which demonstrate that such a killing harms a whole society, and that the wounds take a long time to heal.

Film has been a powerful way to test political dialogue in countries without Western freedoms. The creative community in autocratic Singapore tested these waters when film censors reversed a ban on *Singapore Rebel*, a film about opposition candidate Chee Soon Juan, but restricted it to adults only. The embassy reported that another film, *Zahari's 17 Years*, about a former political prisoner, remained banned as a "threat to the public interest." The film featured an interview with Said Zahari, a former journalist arrested as a communist conspirator and detained without trial from 1963 to 1979. The censors refused to classify a polemical film entitled *One Nation Under*

Lee (now viewable on YouTube) because it incorporated clips from the banned Zahari film. Yet another film, *Francis Seow: The Interview* (also on YouTube), features footage of the former solicitor-general "who was detained and allegedly subject to harsh interrogation in the late 1980s after he was accused of taking money from the U.S. government to lead political opposition to the People's Action Party. (Singapore also expelled an American diplomat, Hank Hendrickson, in that episode.)"[51] One reason for the easing up may be the authorities' realization that the films are readily available on the Internet.

In some cases, embassy efforts to support artistic works have led to trouble, as was the case with a political film in Nigeria that was at the center of clashes between Muslim traditions and state authorities. The embassy reported that film producer Hamisu Lamido, known as Iyan-Tama, was tried, convicted, and sentenced to fifteen months in prison and a 300,000 naira ($2034) fine for violating censorship laws by releasing the film *Tsintsiya*, a Hausa adaptation of *West Side Story*, without first having it approved by the state censor board. The embassy had a prominent role in the film, ironically having sponsored production of *Tsintsiya* to encourage interfaith dialogue. The case went back and forth through the court system, and Iyan-Tama was granted bail with bond of 500,000 naira ($3390) and released after spending more than sixty days in detention.[52]

Sometimes artists and activists take breathtaking risks. In Azerbaijan, a group of dissidents staged a press conference in which a donkey held forth surrounded by a group of sycophants and furiously writing journalists. As the YouTube video went viral, Azeri president Ilham Aliyev failed to see the humor and threw the offenders—by now known as the donkey bloggers—in jail. Aliyev's country occupies a strategic position, and his NATO overtures, tailored suits, and flawless English make him an attractive political partner. But he also removed presidential term limits, stifled opposition, and wrangled with U.S.-sponsored Radio Liberty when it dared to mock his plan to build the world's tallest flagpole in the Baku port.[53] It took concerted international work, including pressure from President Obama and Secretary of State Clinton, to secure the donkey bloggers' release.

Artistic license is also a challenge in Saudi Arabia. An officer from the U.S. consulate in Jeddah raved about the play *Head Over Heels,* performed before a mixed-gender audience in February 2009. What made it extraordinary, the cable explained, was that it was written— and performed—by a woman and dealt with sensitive themes.

"Maisah Sobaihi's performance included a skit in which a Saudi couple remain married but separate after the husband secretly takes a second wife without wife number one's knowledge or approval. Sobaihi raises the issue of 'misrah' marriages, discreet 'marriages of convenience' in which the man bears no financial obligation to the woman. The fact that a female playwright was able to perform a play with frank dialogue seeking to highlight the challenges and injustices Saudi women face is no mean feat in Saudi Arabia. And perhaps as important, Ms. Sobaihi was able to stage a work in which she freely drops references to sex and women's lingerie before a mixed gender audience."

The diplomat-reviewer had impressive foresight. Sobaihi won a Fulbright scholarship to study at New York University, and in 2013 she was a featured performer at the Edinburgh Fringe Festival. The cable, written four years earlier, is an example of talent spotting from a diplomat who was ever watchful for signs that tolerance for freedom of expression might be growing in one of the world's most challenging environments.[54]

Elsewhere, it was music that provided the inspiration that helped topple hated regimes. At the time of the Czechoslovak Velvet Revolution in 1989, the U.S. embassy had been so lulled into complacency by the seeming eternal presence of communism that few staffers had much contact with dissident Václav Havel. No one was more surprised than former ambassador Shirley Temple Black when Havel, by then propelled to the role of Czech president, said he longed to meet Frank Zappa. Zappa's band, the Mothers of Invention, and their album *Absolutely Free* had been the inspiration for the Czech band Plastic People of the Universe, which had provided the sound track for the Czech dissident community.

Havel, who gained international fame writing absurdist plays that poked fun not only at communism but bureaucracy and pomposity, was a uniquely cultural figure. Forging a close relationship with him and his confidants required a deep appreciation of the influence of the Czech artistic community. Havel set himself the task of making government—symbolized in the enormous Prague Castle—less frightening and more humane. The castle, once the home of the hated Reinhard Heydrich, the Nazi ruler of the Protectorate of Bohemia and Moravia, had been subsequently inhabited by a series of equally frightening communist leaders. Havel set about exorcising the bad karma. He had the castle lit up by set designer Jan Svoboda and then costumed (there is no other word for it) the castle guard using the same artist who worked on Miloš Forman's film *Amadeus* (an Oscar-winning film about Mozart with key scenes filmed in Prague). Havel replaced dusty portraits with modern art and used a scooter to get from one meeting to the next in the building's endless marble corridors. It was perhaps inevitable that the president would invite his musical hero Frank Zappa to Prague and then appoint him an ambassador of trade and culture. Zappa stayed for a time, enjoyed his rock star status, and moved on.

This was too much for exasperated Secretary of State James Baker, who rerouted his plane from Moscow for a stop in Prague, reportedly to rebuke Havel. "You can either do business with the United States or you can do business with Frank Zappa," he warned.[55] Havel must have been dismayed that the American response was as humorless as that of the communists, who never had much use for Zappa either.

Soon enough, Havel's government faced real crises with the break-up of Czechoslovakia into the Czech Republic and Slovakia, and the Merry Prankster days faded of their own accord as the Czech Republic assumed a more traditional role as a state in the heart of Europe, albeit one in which Havel's zany whimsy would linger, along with his wistful motto: "May truth and love triumph over lies and hatred."

AMERICAN VALUES VS. AMERICAN INTERESTS: DO PERSONALITIES TRUMP POLICIES?

This cast of characters offers a small sampling of descriptions from diplomats of the people they encountered across the globe. Were this chapter a full inventory, the scoundrels would far outnumber the saints, and the scoundrels were usually the ones in power. Their poor records on democracy, human rights, and freedom of speech forced American policymakers to choose between American interests and American values.

This ongoing dilemma in foreign policy is not new. The list of unsavory characters the United States historically supported—the Pinochets, Somozas, and Duvaliers—is long. The biographic reporting cables detailing excesses and abuses pose the question: Where to draw the line between American interests and American values? The cables provide plenty of evidence that the United States continued to deal with unsavory characters; there is grim reading about the Mubaraks, Bouteflikas, and others. Embassies dutifully reported on how the dictators behaved toward their own people. Almost invariably, Washington's view was that in spite of problems, American interests were best served by continuing to deal with them.

Whether that was the right decision certainly varies by country. But it is hard to find an example in which embassy reporting on dictators became the foundation for a policy review. Also troubling is the lack of debate. The embassies gave Washington far more information than what was available in the media, but relationships continued— sometimes for decades—with dubious leaders. The cables show that at least sometimes, political pressure works. Aliyev released the donkey bloggers; Richard Boucher ultimately got Tadjibayeva released.

Even more disconcerting are the stories of the saints. While it is important to celebrate the courage of these women, it is appalling that they endured hideous conditions. A photo op with the secretary of state seems a small reward for their pain. Even more disconcerting are the nominations of all the women who endured equal hardships but were not selected for the award.

The focus on the plight of women in Islamic countries stands at odds with many public pronouncements in which U.S. officials pay deep respect to Islamic culture but remain reticent on the status of women. Most disturbing of all is that this well-intentioned award process encourages the notion of women as victims. It reinforces existing impressions instead of changing the debate. An idealist might look forward to the day the Women of Courage Award is phased out— because there is no need of it.

The Havel-Zappa story points to a persistent underappreciation for the role of cultural diplomacy. Chronically underfunded and misunderstood, cultural diplomacy is about far more than sending American performers to remote capitals. Truly effective cultural diplomacy engages a country's intellectuals and artists on a continual basis. This is hard work, requiring not only language skills but a fluency with the world of culture. Many public diplomacy officers have the skills to do this, but without a strong mandate from an ambassador who sees the connections and makes culture a part of the mission, it is often the first program to languish in the face of budget and personnel cuts. If Washington evinces no curiosity about a country's cultural thinking, cultural reporting will fall by the wayside.

The cables also show the risks of drawing too many conclusions from personalities. It is human nature for Americans to assess leaders solely by their attitude toward the United States. The embassy's dismissiveness of Guido Westerwelle was a good example of this. The message to Washington, reinforced with phrases such as "lightweight," "lacks gravitas," and "wild card," was: here's a man who doesn't matter and one who often disagrees with us. The embassy accurately predicted the spectacular decline of his political party after the 2013 election, in which it failed to cross the 5 percent threshold, the minimum percentage of the vote required for a political party to enter parliament. But Westerwelle was still young, had impressive media skills, and, with nearly four years as foreign minister, should not have been counted out. Had he not been sidelined by leukemia, he might well have gone on to a second act. People who disagree with the administration in Washington often are not inconsequential.

One might want to think of foreign policy as an intellectual process grounded in history, founded on principle, and carefully calculated. But there is an inescapable personal aspect to diplomacy. And in some cases, the personal trumps all.

Chapter 6

WILD ANIMALS:
Noble Causes
and Jungle Diplomacy

Recently, a rare endangered Siberian crane was spotted along the banks of the Irrawaddy River. The large bird dancing on the riverbank began to attract large numbers of gazers. Eventually they included the military, who proceeded to shoot the rare bird.

—*U.S. Embassy Rangoon*

THE OFFICER AT THE U.S. CONSULATE IN GUANGZHOU was troubled by a British report on Independent Television Network about people buying tiger meat and drinking tiger "wine" at two Chinese wildlife preserves near Guilin (about 500 kilometers from Guangzhou, in southern China), one of which housed thirteen hundred rare tigers. He decided to make an unofficial visit. Reporting officers sometimes visit public places on their own as a means of avoiding the trappings of protocol and to get a better sense of what an average person would experience.

It was worse than he thought. On arrival, he stumbled onto a circus theater where tigers were made to perform while their human handlers whipped and struck the big cats with metal poles. Tiger cubs in a nursery eagerly greeted visitors bringing treats. The lack of fear made the animals unfit for release into the wild. The souvenir store did indeed offer tiger wine (enriched with tiger bone), ranging in price from $10 to $117, and locals assured him it was possible to purchase tiger skins with advance notice.

The officer painted a grim picture of the wildlife preserves, which seemed geared toward sleazy entertainment, with dirt tracks for camel and horse racing. The theater hawked performances by bears, including a mock marriage with cubs acting as the bride and groom. Some of the two hundred bears on the premises had small patches of hair shaved off their torsos, an indication of surgical removal of valued bear bile, an ingredient in traditional Chinese medicine, as is tiger wine and tiger bone. The bile was available in the gift shop, where it sold for about $52 for 500 milliliters. The officer concluded that the so-called wildlife preserves were heavily dependent on sales of animal products produced in-house that affected the well-being of the animals they were supposed to protect."[1]

The officer belongs to a new generation of diplomats who ditch the black-tie world of receptions and limos to pull on hiking boots, hop into four-wheel drive vehicles, and head for remote regions. They tell tales of species teetering on the edge of extinction, threatened by poachers, big game hunters, and venal officials. These cables aren't front-page foreign policy news and they won't necessarily build careers, but they suggest an important generational shift. No one wrote about wildlife in George Kennan's time. There are no questions on the Foreign Service exam about wildlife, and none of the profession's core competencies, as defined by the State Department, mention a love for rare species. Few officers bring any special expertise to the topic of wildlife management, but their determination to document the plight of wildlife suggests a deep affinity for animals and an understanding of how they fit into the larger environment.

These millennial diplomats, raised on *Animal Planet* and the Discovery Channel, reflect a very Western sense of animals' place in the world. They care.

The volume of their reporting is astounding: WikiLeaks contains several thousand cables on wildlife, hunting, poaching, illicit trade, endangered habitat, and on specific species such as lions, apes, elephants, rhinos, tigers, leopards, cheetahs, and whales. To monitor this Noah's Ark, the State Department's Bureau of Oceans and International Environmental and Scientific Affairs (OES) posts fifty officers to a dozen regional environmental hubs covering multiple countries and issues, aided by a seemingly inexhaustible supply of volunteer embassy officers keen to supplement their regular duties for something off the beaten path.[2]

Since the world's most exotic animals live in some of the world's most corrupt states, there are some disconcerting developed/developing world disconnects. Diplomats found stories so bizarre as to defy belief. They wrote about rhinos caught in the crossfire of Maoist insurgents in Nepal; rare cranes shot by Burmese military for no good reason; and start-up zoos in Thailand where cafeterias offered dishes made from the species of animals on view. They recorded Saudi fatwas against family dogs and countries shipping off scores of large animals in exchange for favorable United Nations votes.

Not all the news was so disheartening. A trip to one of Russia's farthest corners described efforts to save the Amur leopard. A diplomatic observer at a Guangzhou park watched yuppie Chinese and their dogs, commanded in English, sporting matching outfits.

In an earlier age, if a diplomatic officer bothered to report on wildlife at all, he would have visited the relevant ministries—environment, forestry, interior—met with a few national parks officials, and called it a day. Today's officers also stumbled onto the evolving role of international NGOs dedicated to wildlife. In some cases, these well-heeled Western-oriented groups acted in lieu of (or in spite of) national governments, contributing enormous financial resources and making decisions about wildlife without the involvement of the country's political stakeholders. The biggest of these groups dwarf the resources of a small country. For example, the Nature Conservancy had assets of roughly $6 billion, which exceeded the GDPs of countries such as Mali, Burundi, or Niger at the time the cables were written. Top-tier NGOs rely on scores of international lawyers, scientists, environmentalists, and other highly trained staff to spend their funds efficiently, something that cannot always be said of the countries in which they work. They also lobby their home governments to raise wildlife issues at the international level and count on a steady stream of donors who share their commitment.

American diplomats saw reporting on animal welfare in all forms as part of their diplomatic mission. They began with the premise that the way a country treats its animals—in the wild, in zoos, or in private homes, is a fair barometer of its civil society. At their most optimistic, they chronicled steps nations took to recognize the importance of animals and the need to protect them. At their most pessimistic, they observed wildlife losing out to lack of money and competing human-animal interests while corrupt officials hustled endangered animals toward ever-more inevitable extinction.

"PROTECTED" WILDLIFE

Wild animals are big business. The U.S. government estimates that the illicit global trade in poached animals and their hides, tusks, and bones is worth $10 to $20 billion a year, ranking third after arms and drug trafficking.[3] A leopard skin can fetch $20,000; a kilogram of rhino horn goes for more than $65,000. The effort to stop this illegal trade is one of the most challenging areas of diplomacy.

The Convention on International Trade in Endangered Species (CITES) often serves as the policy point of departure for embassy reporting on wildlife. The United States proposed the idea for what became CITES in 1973 and hosted a conference that led to the creation of what is now a 178-member organization.[4] A rare example of modest international organizational success, CITES has achieved a measure of cross-border cooperation to ensure that international trade in wild animals and plants does not threaten their survival. Conservationists would counter that protection of wild animals and plants has a long way to go and charge that CITES has a legacy of mixed messages and an overwillingness to grant exceptions to its rules.

CITES' function is simple: to list and categorize some thirty thousand species on three lists, called appendices, according to their level of endangerment. The member states meet once every two to three years, against a backdrop of furious negotiations, to uplist, downlist, or even delist species to more or less restrictive appendices.

The WikiLeaks cables demonstrate mounting discord within CITES over wildlife policies in the developed and developing worlds. In general (but not always) wealthy countries work to get animals moved onto the most stringent Appendix 1; developing countries, often where the animals actually live, work to get them off Appendix 1. While this international diplomacy plays out at the meetings, the reality for CITES-protected animals illustrates the clash between officials who see wildlife as a revenue resource and those who see it as an endangered treasure. Consider the 2010 efforts of ministers from Zambia and Tanzania to secure Washington's support for legalizing the sale of elephant products (meaning ivory) in advance of an upcoming CITES meeting.

Catherine Namugala, Zambian Minister of Tourism, Environment, and Natural Resources, was in no mood for sentimentality. "We have too many elephants!" she complained to the U.S. ambassador. "They endanger Zambians and prevent children from going to school." She insisted that Zambia should have the right to permit "the legal, regulated killing of elephants," which she saw, at best, as a national resource that could promote development.

The embassy was unpersuaded, commenting that Zambia's track record on wildlife conservation was "not stellar ... only a single rhinoceros remains in the country." Officers noted reports of then-president Rupiah Banda and his entourage on hunting trips in the countryside feasting on Cape buffalo and rare klipspringer antelope, which they also presented as gifts to local chieftains.[5]

Erasmus Tarimo, director of the Wildlife Division of the Tanzania Wildlife Research Institute, tried a different tactic, comparing the ivory ban to failed U.S. Prohibition laws. He said the ban only increased the international price of ivory without deterring poaching, and that Tanzania was helpless against poachers because of its huge land mass, limited resources, and the limitless demand from the Asian market, not to mention international traders who corrupted Tanzanian officials. He told the U.S. ambassador that downlisting the elephant would allow Tanzania to sell its ivory stockpile while ensuring that all of the estimated $20 million in proceeds would be earmarked for antipoaching activities and benefit local communities caught up in human-elephant competition for land. Elephants need an enormous amount of land for grazing and range over a wide area. Agrarian communities that lie in elephant migratory paths can see their crops wiped out by elephant herds.

The embassy questioned whether Tanzania would really devote the entire $20 million to antipoaching efforts, especially during an election year, and doubted Tanzania would agree to third-party custodianship of proceeds from ivory sales.[6]

Despite their lobbying, both Zambia and Tanzania lost their bid to downlist elephants and ivory at the CITES meeting in Doha in March 2010. But the battle was far from over.

HUNTERS AND GATHERERS

In the world of diplomatic reporting, as well as wildlife conservation, not all animals are created equal. Large mammals get far more publicity than their more obscure or less appealing relatives. The popular animals confront conservationists and diplomats with moral dilemmas: Will a controlled sale of ivory reduce the slaughter of elephants? Is it ethical to auction off big game hunting licenses to increase a country's budget for wildlife management? Should we allow the killing of a few animals in order to save a lot more?

Diplomats are sensitive to the age-old economic truth that banned products fetch high prices. By the mid 2000s, rising prosperity in Asia helped bid up sought-after wild animal products such as ivory to levels that would keep the rural families who sell them afloat for years. Yet poachers are not always rural families. There is mounting evidence that international organized crime has found a foothold in poaching and is deploying sophisticated weaponry including AK-47s, rocket-propelled grenades, and helicopters, effectively militarizing large swathes of Africa.[7] Complicating the picture even further are wealthy big game hunters collecting trophies of what they call Africa's Big Five (elephant, lion, Cape buffalo, leopard, and rhino), who will pay hundreds of thousands of dollars for the privilege—attractive revenue few African countries can overlook.

Wildlife preservation costs money. The poorest African countries are outmatched by the Western NGOs who focus their conservation efforts on them. Diplomatic cables chronicle a drama that pits animal-loving citizens of the developed world against the people who actually live with them, where hunting so-called bush meat may be a way of getting scarce protein, protecting precious crops from trampling herds, or saving villages that lie on a herd's migratory path. Inadequacy and lack of will from national governments to protect their resources further stokes the conflict.

Case in Point: Zimbabwe

Zimbabwe is beset by overabundance and scarcity. It is home to one hundred thousand elephants on land meant to support fewer than half that number, and a population of rhinos whose numbers have dwindled to fewer than three hundred. The so-called elephant over-abundance creates opportunities and problems in terms of culling, poaching, and income-generating hunting safaris, while the severe rhino scarcity illustrates the basic law of supply and demand. As sought-after rhino horns become ever scarcer, the rising price makes the risk of obtaining one more attractive to poachers, who sell them to Asian markets where they are valued in traditional medicine.

Zimbabwe, a southern African country slightly larger than the state of Montana, offers a case study in how inseparable wildlife problems are from a country's political, economic, and social problems. U.S. embassy officers, in cable after cable, pounded home the point that the country's chaotic policies governing land usage have so damaged its ecology that Zimbabwe might never again sustain large numbers of wild animals.

Land use policies had over time displaced both people and wildlife. Until 1979, about 70 percent of the country's most fertile land had been owned by fewer than 5 percent of the population—farmers of European origin. Aside from the obvious social inequities, the large plantation-style farms produced foreign exchange–earning export crops and also allowed wild animals to roam on land lying fallow.

Robert Mugabe, who came to power in 1987, made land reform a hallmark of his three-decade tenure. What started as a reasonable land redistribution scheme founded on the premise of willing sellers and buyers changed in 2000 to an aggressive fast-track land reform. With government sanction, war veterans and the rural poor invaded and occupied farms, resulting in the displacement of landowners (some of whom were American) and a full-scale land management disaster. By 2002, the embassy was reporting that Zimbabwe had gone from being the breadbasket of Africa to a country in which nearly half the population was malnourished.[8]

Year by year, the embassy determinedly chronicled an unintended consequence of the land invasions: rampant poaching by both com-

mercial and subsistence hunters who took game illegally from occupied private reserves, conservancies, national parks, and occupied
farms that bordered protected game areas. The results were devastating. Some conservancies lost 60 percent of their animals. One
source reported six to ten elephants were being killed every month;
the rhino death toll in a nine-month period stood at thirty-eight.
A major wildlife conservancy reported that 718 animals of a wide
variety of species had been killed by land occupiers and poachers.
Apart from its irreplaceable wildlife, Zimbabwe was also losing legal
hunting revenue of more than $40 million a year.[9]

The embassy reported that poachers, if caught, were rarely convicted, even in the face of overwhelming evidence. They sold smaller
animals as bush meat but also were part of well-organized networks
smuggling high-value ivory, tusks, horns, and hides to export markets in China and Europe. Zebra hides, for example, were destined
for German furniture markets. And once poaching networks forced
open the gates to national parks, rural villagers soon followed.

> National park boundaries are no longer respected by rural dwell-
> ers, be it for grazing, firewood collection or hunting. Poaching
> has led to widespread destruction of habitat, mainly deforesta-
> tion, but also riparian damage caused by illegal gold mining and
> unmanaged poor farming practices. Ongoing power cuts have led
> more families to rely on burning wood for heating and cooking.
> Deforestation is evident in satellite photos and increases vulner-
> ability to erosion and flooding.[10]

Calling Zimbabwe a dystopia, one diplomat described land occu-
pations in which chaos reigned and productivity had fallen to zero. In
one field, an estimated $80,000 in crops rotted in full sight of people
claiming to be land-hungry farmers. "Two giraffe calves, fit for neither
sport nor table, were killed—one left to rot next to the farmer's drive-
way, the other cut up for meat to feed the poacher's hunting dogs."[11]

Rhinos and the Big Game Hunters

With the triple threat of habitat loss, Asian demand for its horn, and big game hunters seeking a Big Five trophy, it's a miracle that there are any rhinos left. The rare African black rhino's numbers, estimated by the Rhino Resource Center at 70,000 in the late 1960s, had fallen to 2,300 by 1992, despite having been listed on CITES "critically endangered" Appendix 1 since 1977. Ensuring the survival of those rhinos that remain illustrates the dilemma posed by sport hunting. The conflicting positions of CITES, the Namibian government, the U.S. Fish and Wildlife Service, NGOs dedicated to wildlife protection, and wealthy U.S. and European hunters beautifully captures the perverse notion that it makes sense to kill animals in order to save them.

Big game hunting was once the sport of kings, and today it takes a king's ransom to hunt large game. Both South Africa and Namibia were able to convince CITES to allow small quotas of five rhinos per country for sport hunters. But the quotas are of little value unless the hunters can claim and export their trophies. Namibia had long wanted to expand its hunting tourism industry, and the minister of environment and tourism complained to the ambassador that a U.S. ban on imports of black rhino trophies was hampering revenue.[12]

The U.S. Fish and Wildlife Service has the authority to issue import permits for sport-hunted trophies, but since the black rhino is also protected by the U.S. Endangered Species Act, Americans cannot bring their trophies home. Ironically, the meeting between the Namibian minister and ambassador occurred because the embassy was pushing for long-awaited *export* permits for fourteen cheetahs destined for the Smithsonian National Zoo, Cheetah Conservation Fund, and White Oak Conservation Center. The minister introduced a not-too-subtle quid pro quo: lift the ban on black rhino trophies and then we can talk about cheetahs.

The invisible figure behind this conversation was Colorado-based

David K. Reinke, who paid $215,000 to hunt a black rhino in Namibia in 2009, a sum that included a $175,000 fee to the Namibian Game Product Trust Fund.[13] His lawyer argued that he had the right to bring his rhino trophy home, and for the first time in more than thirty years, the U.S. Fish and Wildlife Service finally relented, issuing him a one-time permit for the import of his black rhino trophy in March 2013. Having allowed the unthinkable, Fish and Wildlife Service director Dan Ashe then appeared weeks later on PBS's *Antiques Roadshow* to warn about buying and selling antique rhino horns.

"We want to get the message out on protections for wildlife," he said. "Anything that creates a demand for products made from endangered species can be bad news for survival of the animal in the wild, and that's exactly what's happening to rhinos."[14]

If Ashe missed this apparent double standard, there were plenty of conservationists who did not. The president of the U.S. Humane Society called the decision to allow Reinke to bring home his hunting trophy "more than ridiculous," and the regional director of the International Fund for Animal Welfare called it "perverse, to say the least." The outrage continued as Namibia, working with the Dallas Safari Club, an American outlet whose website bills itself as "the greatest hunter's convention on the planet," auctioned off permits for big game hunts from which it said the proceeds would be used for wildlife preservation.[15] The winning bid for the black rhino permit was $350,000 at a January 2014 auction. According to the *Dallas Morning News*, the Texan who posted the winning bid shot the black rhino in Namibia in May 2015. The 2015 auction featured a chance to kill an African elephant, which the group canceled in the face of protests from numerous wildlife welfare organizations. However, it still included a hunt in Mozambique for a male leopard.

Zimbabwe is also home to a few rhinos—emphasis on few. On the theory that eliminating the horns would deter poachers, in the mid 1990s conservationists had implemented a massive dehorning campaign, but the animals' horns grew back over three years' time.

Small-scale farmers also killed rhinos to defend their crops, using pesticide-laced melons. By 2008, nearly a quarter of all rhinos in Zimbabwe had been killed off, according to a CITES-funded study cited by the embassy, which estimated that 235 rhinos (both black and white) were killed in Zimbabwe between 2006 and 2009.[16] Conservationists told the embassy that Zimbabwe's rhinos were on a path to extinction.

As in Namibia, the greatest hope for Zimbabwe's rhinos seemed to be from organized big game hunting with revenue from hunters—including Americans—funding a substantial part of the park service budget. That kind of hunting requires sophisticated operations, and the embassy intensively followed the fortunes of Save Valley Conservancy (SVC), Africa's largest private wildlife sanctuary, which also held the largest population of black rhinos in Zimbabwe. This unique consortium of two dozen landowners (including Americans and Europeans) pooled their resources to stock the conservancy with elephants, giraffes, black and white rhinos, and other big game. While SVC began as a photographic-only safari, the conservancy found it needed the income from big game hunting to survive.

The embassy had written admiringly of SVC's model of sustainable conservation tourism but by 2009 was warning of SVC's imminent demise.[17] Despite generating revenue for the government, employing forty people full time, and setting up community programs to channel earnings into five neighboring rural districts, SVC endured politically forced partnerships with Mugabe cronies, part of a pattern of dispossessing longtime landowners and rewarding Mugabe supporters. Reports told of unrestrained and irresponsible hunting by the Mugabe set, and the embassy warned, "Wildlife stands to lose."[18]

A continent away, Indian rhinos were at the center of a bizarre example of human-animal interaction when they got caught in a shoot-out between the Nepalese army and a Maoist insurgency. The embassy described a dramatic skirmish near Chitwan National Park, a UNESCO World Heritage Site in south-central Nepal, that broke out as ten rhinos were being relocated under the watchful eyes of the diplomatic corps, which had been invited to this unusual nature outing. The relocation, sponsored by the Nepalese government, the U.S. Fish and Wildlife Service, and the World Wildlife Fund (WWF), was proceeding according to plan when shooting broke out. The insurgents killed two soldiers and forced four trucks carrying rhinos off the road.[19]

Although no rhinos died in the incident, the embassy noted that the insurgents' violent takeover of wildlife preserves was imperiling Nepal's wildlife. As park rangers fled their posts to avoid the fighting, rampant poaching resulted. Officers wrote that the Maoist insurgent activities placed wildlife "under siege," and that poachers had earlier killed thirty-eight rhinos, along with countless endangered species such as musk deer, snow leopards, and Bengal tigers.[20]

Elephants

Perhaps no animal is more beloved and more controversial than the elephant, targeted by poachers and hunters for its ivory; targeted by farmers and villagers for its tendency to trample crops and farmland; and seemingly capable of rebounding from worrisome low numbers to gigantic herds in need of ever-vaster acreage. Embassies ranging from Zimbabwe to Burma chronicled the struggle over elephants among countries, conservationists, and poachers.

CITES has banned the sale of ivory since 1989, but under pressure from conservationists, African nations, and China, it allowed a one-time sale in 2008 of stockpiled African ivory, with proceeds to be earmarked for wildlife conservation. According to conservationists, the sale of some one hundred tons of ivory proved disastrous because such a limited offering merely stoked Chinese demand and opened the floodgates of illegal ivory from African nations.[21]

Ivory is only one aspect of the problem. In Asia, where wild elephants number 25,000 to 35,000, they are also seen as traditional and ideal beasts of burden. India has 20,000, followed by Burma, where the embassy reported that their numbers in the wild dwindled from 5,500 in 1996 to 4,000 in 2009. Elephants in Burma are used in the timber industry as draft animals, and conservationists complain that abuse and overwork result in high mortality, while the logging also destroys elephant habitat.[22]

The Burma state timber company owns 2,500 elephants, and an additional 2,000 are privately owned and rented out to the timber industry. A Burmese wildlife NGO official told the embassy that as the regime uses the timber industry to meet the increasing demand for hard currency—essential for its economic integration and development—there is constant pressure to capture additional wild elephants and use them to fell more trees. Burmese officials defend the practice, saying elephants are more environmentally friendly than heavy machinery. That's one view, but if the combined elephant abuse and loss of trees does not dismay conservationists, there is also the proximity of Burma's border to China with its high demand for ivory.

Sometimes the greatest threat to elephants comes from climate change. Mali's Gourma region, straddling the area between the country's fertile southern savannah and the semi-arid Sahel, somehow supports the northernmost herd of elephants in West Africa and the only elephant group in the Sahel. The survival of the 550 to 700 Gourma elephants hinges on a nomadic migration circuit of six hundred kilometers—the longest annual migration of elephants ever recorded, according to embassy reports.[23] The elephants follow a vast, counterclockwise route punctuated with watering holes and seasonal grasslands, but after centuries of elephant-human harmony, recent trends of reduced rainfall alongside more farms, livestock, and settlements have meant heavier competition for scarce water. Embassy officers reported that NGO groups had used satellite technology and radio collars to identify choke points on the migration corridors, reasoning that any negative human-elephant interaction could increase the already high mortality rate. The NGOs worked alongside the World Bank on a $10 million biodiversity project that relied on local knowledge, leadership, and commitment of the Gourma population, working with tribal chiefs from eighteen communes.

The officers described the difficulties of the collaring expeditions. One older and weaker elephant died from the anesthesia. Three baby elephants died while trapped in a mud hole, despite efforts by rescuers who were only able to help an adult female accompanying the babies. The adult became enraged and injured a worker. Another NGO team barely avoided disaster when the engine of their spotting plane failed, forcing the pilot to glide to safety on a donkey path.[24]

Great Apes

Fewer than three hundred gorillas survive in the border region between the West African countries Nigeria and Cameroon. Ensuring their survival and protecting this important wildlife corridor has involved at least four U.S. government agencies and several wildlife NGOs—and notably not the Nigerian government.

On a visit to assess local conservation projects to help the critically endangered Cross River gorilla, diplomats and NGO officials learned that a USAID-funded program employing nine "eco-guards" to conduct patrols and collect data on the gorillas was not working. They immediately decided to help the local group seek more funds from a variety of U.S. sources ranging from the U.S. Department of Defense's Africa Command Biodiversity Fund to the U.S. Fish and Wildlife Service, which administers the U.S. Great Apes Conservation Fund, which dispensed more than $17 million in U.S. government grants in 2011.[25]

The gorillas' habitat in Cross River State lies in the southeasternmost corner of Nigeria, abutting Cameroon. Cross River governor Donald Duke sadly admitted that his countrymen "do not consider the Cross River Gorilla a national treasure," a fact born out when locals killed three gorillas for raiding crops after severe storms wiped out the animals' usual vegetation source.[26] The governor's solution was to habituate gorillas to humans' presence as a means of boosting tourism, an idea that embassy reporters said alarmed conservationists. Another embassy report underscored this divide. "Most (Nigerian) states see the wildlife reserves primarily as a source of income and do very little to advance conservation," with the predictable result being deteriorating wildlife habitat, increased poaching, and illegal trafficking.[27]

Across the river in Cameroon, the gorillas are losing their habitat to the Lom Pangur dam project. The embassy warned that the need for electrical capacity so far outscaled the need for conservation that the Cameroon government pushed aside environmentally stringent World Bank funding to pursue alternative assistance from European, French, and Chinese sources, all of which would impose looser environmental conditions, and none of which stipulated conservation measures for the gorillas' habitat.[28]

The Big Cats

U.S. diplomats in India give Gujarat, India's westernmost state, high marks for wildlife conservation. The grade may stem in part from the fact that 80 percent of the population is vegetarian. The officers wrote approvingly that "a combination of strong political will, education, and culture has put Gujarat at the forefront of cutting edge wildlife conservation in India."[29] Gujarat's Gir National Park shelters three hundred and fifty of the world's last remaining wild Asiatic lions. But even in this enlightened spot, lions come under threat from poachers, who killed eight in an attempt to pass off lion bone, for which there is no market, as highly prized tiger bone, an ingredient in traditional Chinese medicine. But unlike the lax enforcement seen elsewhere, the perpetrators were prosecuted and given three-year sentences. The state also hired one hundred new forest guards and an additional fifty supervisors, while installing high-tech monitoring equipment and a centralized control room.

Gujarat lies nearly seven hundred kilometers northwest of Mumbai, where the United States maintains a consulate headed by the consul general, who made a visit to Gir National Park to learn firsthand about how well conservation measures were working. The Gujarat park director proudly spoke about what he called a culture of conservation. Officials conduct more than a hundred public awareness workshops each year, and local NGOs promote greater understanding of the lion's role in India's ecosystem. Should a lion kill a villager's livestock, the park director said, "he considers it an offering." Consular officials noted that the forestry department quickly pays compensation to reduce the chance of villager retribution. Although the lions live in close proximity to villages and settlements along the park's perimeter, the director said violent incidents are rare, with a human death occurring once every three to four years.[30]

What could go wrong? The consul's report said human-animal competition led to the creation of nine thousand open irrigation wells ten feet wide and one hundred feet deep, with no rails, boundaries, or markings. The wells would be dangerous to any species (including humans) walking near one at night, and there were some fifty incidents of lions drowning. As a result, the forestry department raised funds to fence in two thousand of these wells.

Inbreeding presented an even more serious threat to Gujarat's lions. One solution would split the population and move at least half to a neighboring state. Gujarat officials vehemently opposed the plan, citing the likelihood of poachers in neighboring states. The Indian government spent $6.4 million preparing for the relocation, but Gujarat state officials dug in. Local Indian NGOs filed litigation on behalf of the lions, and the case went to India's Supreme Court. The court subsequently ruled that the Gujarat government must relocate some of the lions to neighboring state Madhya Pradesh's Kuno-Palpur sanctuary.[31] But in March 2015, Gujarat officials were using other legal arguments to fight the Supreme Court ruling, and the fate of the lions was still undecided.

The year 2010 was the Year of the Tiger, and with a wild population of only thirty-two hundred animals, thirteen tiger-range states convened a series of meetings of the World Bank's Global Tiger Initiative (GTI), a partnership with the Smithsonian, the International Tiger Coalition (a consortium of thirty-nine NGOs), and both the South Asia Wildlife Enforcement Network (SA-WEN) and the U.S.-supported Association of Southeast Asian Nations Wildlife Enforcement Network (ASEAN-WEN). The amount of American diplomatic activity, reporting, and above all funding of these initiatives is all the more remarkable since there are no wild tigers in North America (although there are many in captivity). Adding to the challenge is that some of the thirteen countries in which tigers range—including Bangladesh, Bhutan, Burma, Cambodia, China, India, Indonesia, Laos, Malaysia, Nepal, Russia, Thailand, and Vietnam—have spotty records on tiger conservation efforts.

Embassy officers in Nepal had warned in 2009 that although momentum was building for the GTI through a workshop designed to foster regional cooperation, consensus, and antitrafficking efforts, the momentum alone "will not save the tiger without concrete actions on the ground."[32] And indeed, a follow-on GTI meeting in November 2009 of more than two hundred tiger experts from governments and NGOs ended in a series of sensible recommendations, but not before China proposed legalized trade in tiger parts, a move rejected by all the other states. As described early in the chapter, China allows tiger farming, a controversial practice tiger experts reject as a means of legalizing the sale of products such as pelts and parts, "providing an unacceptable incentive to consumer demand that would give motivation to kill the few tigers remaining in the wild."[33] And at the GTI ministerial, it was China that, consistent with its previous position,

lodged reservations on the final declaration's separate trade section
that banned trade in tigers and tiger parts.[34]

Sometimes tigers clash with other critically endangered species, a
factor the U.S. consulate in Vladivostok, located at the crossroads of
western Russia, China, and North Korea, noted in its all-out reporting efforts on behalf of the Amur leopard, the world's rarest big cat.
Some thirty-five remained in the wild when the cables were written
in 2008; today, according to WWF, their total has almost doubled.
The Amur tiger, also endangered, threatens the much smaller leopard.
Tiger-on-leopard attacks have increased because of reductions in their
hunting habitat, which has pushed tigers into the leopards' range. The
exacerbating factor is the deforestation of trees producing pine nuts,
a staple for wild boar, which is the foundation of both the leopard
and tiger diet. Much of the pine is illegally harvested and exported to
China, ultimately winding up in furniture for various U.S. chains.[35]

Reporting officers had continual contact with the WWF and a
host of Vladivostok-based NGOs. They noted that none of the workers had ever seen a leopard in the wild (all the leopard film footage is captured by hidden cameras). The consulate remained heavily
engaged, organizing films and lectures, chronicling joint efforts of
U.S. and Russian scientists to use radio tracking collars, and bringing
in a big cat expert from the National Institutes of Health to examine
the genetic makeup of the remaining leopards. Heart murmurs and
reproductive problems pointed to inbreeding concerns.[36]

Consulate staff wrote about hiking through leopard territory on
WWF-leased forest in Barabash, across Amurskiy Bay and inland
from Vladivostok, and warned that a planned six-lane highway would
cut through the leopard's remaining habitat. Officers said local conservationists were skeptical of the construction company's promise to
build tunnels for the leopards, citing the Russian proverb, "Promises
don't mean there will be a wedding."

A year later, the consul general reported that the forest mafia,
which had taken enormous illegal harvests of cedar and other rare spe-

cies, had torched the houses of two WWF workers and had declared war on anyone working to protect forests and enforce environmental laws.[37] The illegal logging industry of Russia's far east is run by criminal gangs, sometimes called forest mafia. They filled a vacuum after the fall of the Soviet Union and the collapse of state-supported forest industries, which led to widespread unemployment. Taking advantage of the sparse population and even sparser law enforcement presence, they chop down hardwood species of ash, maple, and oak, destroying habitat for critically endangered species.

This remarkable series of reports on the prospects for the Amur tiger and leopard shows both the reach and the limitations of diplomatic reporting. The consulate wrote passionately about wildlife and detailed the work of NGOs, but at the end of the day, the Russian government has to take action.

Birding Mania

Many species of birds are endangered, and embassies found opportunities to report on migratory and exotic birds, ranging from the parrots of the Amazon to the cranes of Burma. Even in war-wracked Somalia, an officer took time to note the mysterious death of fifty Croatian-tagged white storks in a local village. The storks, native to a village about sixty-four kilometers southeast of Zagreb, were noteworthy, the officer insisted, because they had been tagged and sampled for avian influenza testing at Croatia's Poultry Center Lab with negative results. Storks from Croatia usually migrate to South Africa on a route through Egypt and Sudan, and experts were puzzled as to why they should have flown far off course to Somalia. The local residents in Elbaraf notified vets after they saw the exotic birds unable to fly and walking with difficulty. By the time veterinarians arrived in the village, the carcasses had been piled up and were too decomposed to test. With obvious consternation, the officer reported that the cause of death would remain a mystery.[38]

Diplomats are trained to be nonjudgmental, but sometimes their outrage shows through. One officer visited Kachin State in Burma, which sits on a major migratory bird flight path and attracts bird-watchers from around the world. "Recently, a rare endangered Siberian crane was spotted along the banks of the Irrawaddy River. The large bird dancing on the riverbank began to attract large numbers of gazers. Eventually they included the military, who proceeded to shoot the rare bird."[39]

Defending avian wildlife can be a dangerous business. Brazil's Tinguá Natural Reserve in Nova Iguaçu was the scene of the 2005 murder of a celebrated naturalist who spent fifteen years of his life defending the reserve from illegal trade. The suspect, allegedly hired by a group of poachers, animal traders, and corrupt environmental officials, was a hunter who grew up in the area and sold tropical birds and other animals to local restaurants. The challenge of patrolling Brazil's vast wildlife regions is overwhelming, with one inspector for every ninety-one thousand acres of protected land. Home to dozens of rare and endangered species, wildlife trafficking in birds has reached a critical state. The consulate estimated Brazil accounted for about 10 percent of the world's illegal trade in wild animals, of which nearly half—mostly parrots and other birds—went to Europe and the U.S.[40]

Parrots are also native to Africa. The Cameroon minister for Forests and Wildlife said he was trying to improve governance in the corruption-riddled forestry and wildlife sectors and told the U.S. ambassador that police had intercepted one thousand parrots being smuggled out of Douala.[41] The situation for birds in neighboring Nigeria is even grimmer. Wildlife officials told the embassy that the Hajj- and Umrah-chartered flights for religious pilgrimages were convenient conduits for trafficking in wildlife, particularly parrots.

Trafficking overland is also rampant, and smugglers use empty fuel tankers to export live birds, as well as hides, skins, and ivory.[42]

THE EATERS

While the wildlife preservation movement mainly targets the illegal market in ivory for decorative or medicinal uses, a considerable proportion of poaching is for food. In most of the world, meat of any kind is a luxury, and the most exotic sources are in high demand. The U.S. embassy in Hanoi summed up the problem in a cable titled "We Eat Everything on Four Legs Except the Table." Writers documented Vietnam's voracious consumption of wild animals and concluded that cravings for wild meat trumped wildlife concerns. According to the embassy, demand increased as Vietnamese got wealthier, and most failed to see any link between wild animal products and diseases, despite outbreaks of avian flu and SARS. Forest rangers were shot in the line of duty, and official impunity compounded the problem. A high-level Vietnamese official and war hero was allowed to keep nineteen tigers smuggled in from Cambodia despite the clear violation of CITES regulations. Vietnam is also a transshipment point for animals brought into China by wildlife smuggling networks that the embassy believes are well organized and linked to cross-border drug and counterfeit trading.

Vietnam is home to 10 percent of the world's species, several of which are only found in Vietnam. The embassy related the usual story: the government lacks will and the people lack awareness. NGOs estimate three thousand tons of edible wildlife are traded every year for $67 million. Delicacies, including Malayan sun bears, pangolins, turtles, snakes, lizards, macaques, langurs, leopards, tigers, porcupines, wild pigs, civets, and birds are among the many exotic and endangered animals bound for Vietnamese tables. Nearly half of Hanoi residents consume wild animals, a custom the embassy cynically called Vietnam's version of PETA: People Eating Tasty Animals.[43]

Vietnamese wild game restaurants in Ho Chi Minh City also serve bear products, and the consulate reported that the capital lacks the will to eradicate illegal bear farms "against the backdrop of widespread lack of appreciation for, or commitment to, the protection of wildlife in Vietnam." The officers wrote that bear bile extracted from the gallbladders and paws remains highly prized in Vietnam as an aphrodisiac and health tonic. According to the NGO Animals Asia Foundation, three thousand to four thousand bears are caged throughout Vietnam, often in wretched conditions.[44]

ZOOS

Since the dawn of diplomacy, countries have been giving each other exotic animals as gifts. Over time, zoos replaced royal menageries, and common people gazed at exotic animals brought from distant corners of the empire as a symbol of a nation's imperialism.[45] Perhaps no zoo animal is more iconic than the panda, which came to symbolize China and its efforts to emerge through "panda diplomacy" from decades of isolation. The Chinese have successfully managed to "own" pandas, retaining exclusive rights in a way that no other country has managed with any other animal. To meet incessant demand (and take advantage of a lucrative export), China has developed panda breeding centers and worked to master the difficult feat of reproduction of pandas in captivity. The U.S. consulate in Chengdu was surprised by the high survival rate of the Ya'an Panda Breeding Center's panda twins. All twins born in 2009 survived as the staff became adept at switching them back and forth so the mother would feed both of them. The cable noted that offspring born to pandas lent to foreign zoos also belong to China under the terms of the standard panda agreement.[46]

Embassy officers see zoos as a barometer of a country's humanitarian values and civility. The plight of zoo animals in war-torn or impoverished countries is not difficult to imagine. The 2009 inauguration of President Obama sparked a photo contest in Albania called "A Day of Change," which one photographer marked by taking photos at the zoo. "No one needs greater change in Tirana than these poor animals living in this decrepit zoo," he declared.[47]

For entirely different reasons, the Baghdad Zoo, one of the largest in the Middle East, became an early symbol of poor planning when many animals died in the chaos that followed the U.S.-led invasion in 2003. A few years later, embassy officers were surprised to discover that the local zoo had become the most popular destination for family outings in postwar Baghdad. Attendance doubled between 2006 and 2008 along with revenues, allowing the zoo to hire one hundred workers and fourteen veterinarians. The embassy noted special features unique to Baghdad, including the daily slaughter of two donkeys to feed the lions, and exotic fish with the image of the old Iraqi flag etched permanently into their scales. With the old flag outlawed, zoo officials were uncertain whether they would subject the fish to laser surgery to remove the illegal version.

Another big draw are the exotic animals formerly possessed by Saddam Hussein and his family, including his son Uday's cheetah, now tame enough for petting, and the growing pride begun by two of Saddam's lions. The zoo also exhibits some "disheveled looking brown bears, reportedly plied with arak" (an alcoholic beverage), and Saddam's former stallion, billed as "the most famous horse in Iraq." The embassy suspected the zoo's large public garden and proximity to the relatively safe international zone, commonly called the Green Zone and filled with international organizations, embassies, and the security forces to protect all of them, might have been partially responsible for its popularity.[48]

A newer and far more troubled zoo was Chiang Mai's Night Safari, a pet project of deposed Thai prime minister Thaksin Shinawatra, who built it in his native city after seeing a similar zoo in Singapore. The embassy and consulate sent Washington five cables between 2005 and 2008 dissecting the development as a litmus test for animal rights, environmental protection, and political corruption.

The Night Safari story is a comedy of errors in which each unwise action is compounded. To begin with, the government imported 175 nonnative large animals from Kenya, ostensibly as a gift, or, as the cables darkly suggest, as pawns in exchange for Thai votes backing Kenya's bid for a seat on the United Nations Security Council. Wildlife NGOs predicted a high mortality rate during a mass move of such a great distance. Upon arrival, the animals were confronted with cages that were too small, inadequate sunlight, and insufficient roaming space.[49]

Night Safari also planned to bring in rare species of white rhino, leopards, and spotted hyenas, all of which are protected under CITES. Its website advertises a Safari Zone with nonnative animals, including white rhinos, hyenas, lions, cheetahs, wildebeests, giraffes, ostriches, zebras, water buffalos, kangaroos, dingos, and emus; and a Predator Prowl Zone populated with tigers, lions, African hunting dogs, vultures, wolves, white tigers, Canadian wolves, Asiatic black bears, and crocodiles. Somewhat disconcertingly, the website reassures guests: "Don't worry, all the nasty animals are well fenced in."[50]

All this was merely backdrop to the jaw-dropping suggestion of Night Safari's director to serve dishes made with exotic animals in one of the zoo's restaurants. The director planned to offer set meals of zebra, lion, and crocodile, prepared by prominent chefs, for $112 dollars a plate. Digging in, he insisted that the animals on the menu were not endangered species, a fact that did little to pacify animal lovers. Even local monks objected, and the director was forced to concede. Only locally raised crocodile and ostrich would be served. The embassy noted the dining plan was particularly appalling given Thailand's bid to be a leader in regional wildlife conservation. At the time, it was about to host the launch of the ASEAN Wildlife

Enforcement Network (WEN), which aims to reduced illegal wild-life trafficking.[51]

Six months later, Night Safari was in trouble again. The U.S. consulate in Chiang Mai reported that an alliance of NGOs had filed a case in the Supreme Administrative Court, accusing the government-appointed tourism administration of "illegally encroaching on the Suthep-Pui National Park" to create Night Safari. The cable stated that the Love Chiang Mai Alliance "charged that Thaksin's ideas for tourism development are poorly conceived, environmentally harmful, not transparent and lacking in community input." Although the park is still up and running, which means that the NGOs lost, it is significant that an alliance of NGOs actually tried to take the government to court in the first place.

Public relations disasters multiplied. An escaped (nonnative) wolf prowled the area, eating villagers' chickens. Then Night Safari road construction was blamed for flooding. Finally, Thaksin's plans for a large elephant park with tourist lodgings put him at odds not only with villagers but with the military, given that a road for the park would go through a Thai army training area.[52]

Thaksin's cavalier approach to wildlife earned him more opprobrium when he focused on orangutans. Perhaps no single species of zoo animal faces a more precarious existence, even though they enjoy full protection under CITES, which bans their trade. Originally native to Indonesia and Malaysia, they are now found only in the wild in remoter parts of Borneo and Sumatra. Embassy Bangkok officers recounted "Orangutan Odysseys," which painstakingly detailed the trek and ultimate fate of a now-you-see-them-now-you-don't group of fifty-seven illegally trafficked orangutans through Vietnam, Thailand, Cambodia, and Indonesia.

Thai animal parks—this time Safari World in Bangkok—played a prominent role in the scheme. The story began when Thai authorities took custody of fifty-seven orangutans from Safari World. The owner first insisted the orangutans were offspring of parents acquired before Thailand's accession to CITES back in 1994. He later changed his story to say they had been given to Safari World by pet owners who no longer wanted to keep them and that Safari World was "performing a public service." Ultimately, he admitted to having obtained the animals illegally.

Custody passed to the Thai Department of National Parks until officials repatriated the animals—forty-eight of them at least—to Indonesia at some considerable cost, requiring the use of an Indonesian Air Force C-130 and eight veterinarians. The orangutans were welcomed by Indonesia's first lady and several ministers. But five of the fifty-seven original orangutans were not repatriated because they were on loan to perform at—where else?—the Chiang Mai Night Safari. Under mounting pressure, the five "performing" orangutans were relocated to a Thai wildlife preserve as they awaited relocation to Indonesia. According to the embassy, which was tenacious in following the story, "The Director [of the Department of National Parks] expressed incredulity, as well as irritation, at the U.S. government's interest in the matter."[53]

Yet another orangutan odyssey began when a European couple vacationing in Vietnam noticed two young orangutans in their hotel's private zoo. They called an animal protection hotline run by a local NGO. Vietnamese government officials raided the hotel, confiscated the orangutans, and notified Indonesia, where they believed the orangutans had originated. The animals were flown to Jakarta, where they were to spend a thirty-three-day quarantine in a local zoo. Four months later they were still at the zoo, which advertised "entertaining and educational animal shows highlighting orangutans and other animals."

In neighboring Cambodia, a local version of Safari World paid $57,000 in fines for illegally importing thirty-six orangutans from Thailand. Despite the fine, the zoo owner was able to keep the animals. Zoo patrons paid to see them perform in kick-boxing, skateboarding, and bicycle-riding skits. Officials suspected the orangutans came from Safari World in Bangkok. "As evidence, they cited the fact that Thai police first raided Bangkok's Safari World and found 110 orangutans. In a subsequent raid they found only 69. Safari officials claimed 41 apes had died and their bodies had been cremated. Wildlife smugglers seldom go to court and rarely go to jail," the cable ruefully noted.

THERE'S A FATWA ON YOUR DOG

Perhaps nothing illustrates the cultural division between American diplomats and the world they report from more than the concept of pets. Most foreign service officers grow up in middle-class families and share a common experience of Fido or Fluffy. Implicit in the Western idea of pets is the availability of pet food, veterinary care, and a market for pet care accessories. In this vision, socially conscious people adopt their pets from no-kill shelters, and all responsible pet owners have their animals spayed or neutered. For some diplomats, it comes as a shock to work in countries where pets are an unheard-of luxury, where there may be religious or governmental bans on them, or where they find themselves on someone's dinner table. In the developing world, strays lead violent and disease-ridden lives. Diplomats argued in reporting cables that tolerance of pets and transparency about regulations is a fair barometer of a country's economic rise and a test of its civic engagement. Having the family dog confiscated by Beijing police is heartbreaking, as is waking up in Riyadh to find there is a religious fatwa against him.

Pets require care, and one major obstacle to keeping one is that not all countries embrace the concept of private veterinary services. In formerly communist and agriculturally oriented Turkmenistan, a private veterinarian is unheard of. State Veterinary Service is responsible for all animal care in the country, maintaining healthy livestock, preventing the spread of contagious diseases, and certifying the quality of meat. But the underfunded service has difficulty caring for the country's farm animals, let alone pets. Many vets are more than willing to work independently (off the books), but without private clinics they have no equipment or access to medicines. Simple surgeries are performed in the pet's home.[54]

Dogs in Moscow have long been caught in the country's transition away from communism. On the negative end Moscow is home to some forty thousand stray dogs, described as fixtures outside almost every metro station. Strays suffer from inhumane treatment, and roaming packs of dogs are a common sight. But the embassy cited new hope for strays, thanks to an NGO that set up a stray cat and dog clinic, the opening of which drew eighty guests, including veterinarians, journalists, and government officials. The reporting officer said Muscovites have always been dog lovers, noting wryly, "The smaller the apartment, the larger the dog." The growing number of pet owners in the city reflects a growing middle class, while the new clinic reflects "the ongoing importance of [the NGOs'] civic education and community outreach efforts."[55]

A pet's experience in China, another country with a rapidly growing middle class, is proportionate to its size. Unsurprisingly, a country known until recently for its one-child policy also has a one-pet policy. The U.S. embassy in Beijing reported outrage over new rules in 2006 limiting households to one dog and outlawing "big and dangerous breeds." The crackdown touched off street demonstrations and led to eighteen arrests and heated exchanges in Internet chat rooms. One source told the embassy that the controversial dog policy reflects "the poor state of China's civil society. The lack of transparency surrounding regulations affecting people's lives provokes suspicion and frustration."

The rules caused headaches for police as well, who had to house confiscated dogs in precinct basements. The embassy saw the policy as symptomatic of press freedom limitations, noting that reporters are not allowed to criticize the policy, compare the policy to that of other countries, or write about the harmonious shared existence of people and animals.

"The controversy reflects the underdevelopment of China's civil society. No one knows the origin of Beijing's new directive, leaving ample space for rumors and speculation. Middle class families pay fines (or bribes) to keep their dogs. The directive includes a hotline so the public can call in to report scofflaws. Official encouragement to inform on others is uncomfortably reminiscent of the Cultural Revolution."[56]

The situation in Guangzhou was much the same, according to the consulate, and police cracked down on violators by conducting house-to-house searches, confiscating unregistered pets from parks and veterinary clinics, and ultimately killing some fourteen thousand dogs. Despite the grim figures, the consulate noted that pet ownership is on the rise, with 7 percent of Chinese households caring for a pet, and sales of dog and cat food up 13 percent year on year.

Owners seemed keen to display their dogs. Consulate officers walking through parks at Er Sha Island and Shenzhen saw dog social club meetings with breeds ranging from golden retrievers, English sheepdogs, King Charles spaniels, and Pekinese—with their yuppie owners. "Many of the dogs sported doggie outfits and one of them was even dressed to match its owner. An organizer soon arrived, checked off names from a list, and handed out matching yellow hats. Soon after, dogs and owners departed on buses for an outing. Asked why he was speaking English to his dog, one owner replied that naturally, dogs understood English."

The consulate noted that dogs have come a long way from a few decades ago, when pets were seen as a bourgeois decadence. Throughout the late 1970s, regular dog extermination programs were carried out; dogs were seen as a threat to public hygiene and possible carriers of SARS (although they were also served in restaurants as a delicacy).

In a telling comment on Chinese society, the writer editorialized that as more Chinese raise dogs, they might also come to care more about their fellow citizens. "In the best case scenario, today's pet owners will come to see their neighbors as worthy of at least the same care and attention as Fido, and thus their concern of their own species may increase as well."[57]

Dogs face a different problem in some Muslim countries, where there is debate over whether they are unclean. Two Saudi governors—one in Riyadh and another in Makkah—both decided to ban sales of cats and dogs and prohibit walking them in public places, following fatwas from religious police, known by their initials as CPVPV.

Embassy diplomats were fascinated by the risky debate that followed these rulings and duly reported conversations with many Saudis who saw the decision as an example of "religious police run amuk." English-language press had a field day: "Cats, Dogs, the new threat to morality," and "once again the CPVPV misses its goals." Arabic-language websites joined in: "We live in a strange racist society, even against pets." Some noted the likely inequality of enforcement: "What about the dogs and cats of their royal highnesses?" And still others thought the triviality was telling: "Aren't there more important matters to issue fatwas on than selling dogs and cats? The CPVPV is even interfering in dogs and cats. Goodness!"[58]

One embassy diplomat provided a thoughtful analysis of the relationship between pets and Islam, arguing that rules on pets create a paradox within Saudi culture: institutionalized interpretations of the Qur'an and conservatism have collided with exposure to Western ideas and progressive thinking. Past experience with similar bans suggests enforcement is unlikely to be effective. The writer argued that the Qur'an is full of examples showing that kindness to animals is an important aspect of the Islamic creed, and that pets are in fact permitted.

The embassy also noted that some Saudis disapprove of exorbitant spending on pets while poor families suffer from hunger, disease, and homelessness. "They do not see the care given to dogs and cats as a sign of kindness and mercy, but rather as a lack of humanity."

Despite the two arguments—that dogs are anti-Islamic and that the keeping of one is decadent—embassy analysts point to Internet chat room conversations as evidence that many Saudis aren't buying either line. (Those chat rooms are increasingly part of diplomatic reporting, as social media gains traction in countries where more public dissent might be dangerous. Just as older diplomats scanned local papers before drafting their reports, a new generation checks the mood of the public on a constantly changing array of social media.) They concluded that frivolous fatwas expose a divide between religious leaders and the general public. "This is a struggle between old and new. Some will say the field of action for the more conservative elements in Saudi society is constricting, therefore, an increased emphasis on the more inane issues, such as banning pets and Pokemon videos."[59]

NGOS: THE GAME CHANGERS

The officers' underlying contention in many of these cables is that treatment of animals is a bellwether for the health of civil societies. Where animals are seen as an exploitable resource, they get entangled in endemic corruption. Where animals are caught in a country's impulse to modernize, they create friction over changing social values. In highly regulated societies, rules governing their care and interaction with humans is a test of transparency. And in places where they struggle for humane treatment, they reflect the growing role of NGOs that are local, Western-based, or global.

Increasingly, these NGOs are well-established international players in their own right. A new generation of environmentally savvy diplomats seeks out NGO colleagues who are better funded, better staffed, and readier to take action, often with decades of considerable on-site expertise. Reporting officers see them as valuable contacts, authoritative sources, and potential partners. On the plus side, Western-based NGOs have deepened their in-country roots, and their staffs often include local people. American diplomats can engage with these local staff, accompany them on journeys to rural backwaters, and rely on their professionalism. Given the usual two- or three-year diplomatic tours, that's a level of depth no peripatetic diplomat can match.

In addition to the wealth of reporting on wildlife, the WikiLeaks cables reveal the increasing capacity of NGOs to find substantial funding, expertise, and long-term commitment by highly trained experts to travel within countries and reside—sometimes for years— in remote locations, all of which has made them relatively new players on the international stage. By offering diplomats their expertise as full partners, they heighten the odds that their views will be heard in Washington, giving them a wider audience and increasing cachet with policymakers and, of course, potential donors.

But the cables unwittingly reveal how some Western-based wildlife NGOs have effectively done a workaround to manage national governments that are corrupt, inefficient, uncommitted, or simply too distracted by more pressing issues. Aiding this disconnect is the fact that wildlife habitats tend to be in remote regions, far from national capitals. The fact that good conservation work happens without the involvement of national governments should give us pause. Conservation efforts without the active engagement of key players sets up rifts and robs permanent stakeholders of the opportunity to take charge of their own fate. NGOs would argue that many animal populations face such imminent danger of extinction there is no time to wait for national authorities and that repeated prior efforts to engage governments resulted in failure. Saving the animals now means leaving a species intact for a better day when better governments can take on the stewardship themselves. It's one subtext of the message diplomats are sending Washington.

Chapter 7

CORRUPTION:
Immunity, Impunity, and Impudence

Corrupt, compromised, and even recently incarcerated candidates appear poised to enter parliament in this summer's national elections.

—*U.S. Embassy Sofia*
June 18, 2009

BULGARIA IS A CULTURE SO THOROUGHLY PERMEATED by corruption it is difficult for outsiders to conceptualize it—even with vivid examples provided by the embassy. Technically part of Europe but spiritually entrenched in the Balkan region, it is surrounded by Turkey, Greece, Macedonia, Serbia, Romania, and the Black Sea. A cable entitled "Sofia's Mean Streets" linked the crumbling (and stinking) urban landscape to the *mutri* culture of criminal thugs.

Once a traveler hits the airport access road . . . drab, decrepit Soviet-style blocks rise up, in stark juxtaposition to the Porsche dealership . . . Crumbling streets with unevenly patched pavement, potholes that can pass for tank traps, and sidewalks crammed with parked cars are routine. A years-long garbage mess has gotten worse over a contract dispute with the collection companies, and refuse is both scattered and piled high. Packs of wild dogs roam widely.

Bad as that is, the organized crime situation is ugly as well . . . Organized criminals and their no-neck, black-leather-clad bodyguards flaunt and disobey the law; big black SUVs are the rage, barreling down streets ignoring traffic and parking regulations. Seeing no force to control them, many ordinary Bulgarians have followed suit, running lights, passing against oncoming city traffic . . . young people find "mutri"—cool guys above the law with money and status—an attractive role model.[1]

Local journalism is no help. "Reporters and editors accept bribes to cover stories, to print propaganda articles as though they were news, and to not print information that sponsors do not approve. The media's cooption obviously limits its ability to serve as a voice for civil society."[2]

Not even soccer is exempt. Most teams in the country are owned or controlled by organized crime figures, who use them as fronts for money laundering and tax evasion. The last three presidents of the team Lokomotiv Plovdiv were all assassinated. Years of blatant match fixing has disgusted fans, who now stay away, no small thing in a country whose defeat of Germany in the 1994 World Cup advanced it to the semifinals: "many Bulgarians only half-jokingly refer to this as the country's greatest accomplishment since the fall of communism."[3]

The justice system offers little help. The embassy's portrayal of organized crime bosses is reminiscent of cartoon characters. The brothers Krasimir "Big Margin" Marinov and Nikolay "Small Margin" Marinov made a mockery of Bulgaria's courts when they were arrested and then released on bail, despite their spiderweb syndicate involving drugs, fraud, car thefts, smuggling, extortion, racketeering, and prostitution. The embassy wrote that the Marinov case, postponed four times, "has become symbolic of the inability of the Bulgarian courts to bring about swift justice." Other infamous gangsters have included drug kingpin Zlatomir "the Beret" Ivanov, Nikola "the Beaver" Ivanov, and Vasil Krumov Bozhkov, aka "the Skull." The embassy illustrated the government's complicity in this network in a cable that described Todor "Borat" Batkov, who officers said served as a frontman for local businesses and interests of the infamous Russian-Israeli businessman Michael Cherney, aka Mikhail Chorny. While the Bulgarian government labeled Chorny a national security risk and banned him from entering Bulgaria, the embassy reported that Batkov received Bulgaria's highest honor for his donations to ill children, orphanages, emergency rooms, and local universities. He also gave eleven cars to the Ministry of Interior.[4]

Things looked up, briefly, when the police arrested Aleksi "the Tractor" Petrov, considered one of the most untouchable organized crime figures. He was nabbed in Operation Octopus in February 2010 in a sting that raided twenty strip clubs and other illicit businesses. Petrov was charged with extortion, forceful debt collection, prostitution, trafficking, fraud, and money laundering.[5] But months later he was released from jail to house arrest, and then released from house arrest to reappear on the streets. He promptly announced he'd be running for president.[6]

Lest this 1920s Chicago-of-the-Balkans seem like an outlier, the leaked cables offer overwhelming evidence that U.S. embassies in dozens of countries were seized with the problem of corruption and wrote about it voluminously. The heading "corruption" turns up in 24,182 leaked cables, "organized crime" is mentioned in 6,905, and "bribery" in another 1,870. Corruption was the theme of 1,054 cables from Iraq, 953 from Afghanistan, and 903 from Nigeria.

When it comes to corruption, Bulgaria is far from the worst. In 2015 the country ranked sixty-ninth—less than halfway down Transparency International's Corruption Perceptions Index for 2015, where it is tied with Jamaica. The annually published rankings are a composite index based on a combination of surveys and assessments of how people view a country's public sector. Of course, the United States itself does not come with clean hands. It ranked sixteenth in 2015, tied with Austria in this 168-country index. The Scandinavian countries vie for first place; Afghanistan, Somalia, and North Korea bring up the rear.[7]

Why does it matter? Corruption is a barrier to economic development and foreign investment. It is expensive—in some cases consuming a sizable percentage of a country's GDP. Public works projects offer telling illustrations of this type of corruption-driven inflation. A World Bank report estimates that it costs three to six times as much to build a road on the Russian side of the border than on the Finnish side, despite a similar climate.[8] In 2007, Russian president Vladimir Putin announced the upcoming Sochi Winter Olympics would cost $12 billion. But at the 2014 event, the reported cost of $50 billion got almost as much ink as the athletes.[9]

Corruption ought to matter to the U.S. government because it robs U.S. businesses of public tenders from around the world for everything from fighter jets to nuclear power plants—projects that they might otherwise win on merit. In countries struggling to forge a civil society, it undermines public confidence in democracy. Respect for public officials and institutions plummets. The rule of law founders under the weight of corrupt police and court systems. As criminals muscle in, space opens for organized crime, and the possibility of meaningful partnerships with governments grows remote. Trafficking in drugs, weapons, and people pits the United States against potential allies. Given increasingly global connections, organized crime and money laundering funds more mischief and, occasionally, even terrorism. The coopted country stalls out.

The cables suggest that embassies believed corruption was a major impediment to American foreign policy initiatives. Yet it is unclear that policymakers focused on terrorism understood how thoroughly

corruption thwarted cooperation. Corruption is an old story, and globalization has brought its economic and political consequences to the
United States in ways that Washington leadership is only beginning
to understand. Despite the number of embassy cables, policymakers
did relatively little to confront the issue.

While corruption can suffuse all aspects of life, embassy reporting centered on three areas: elections—no surprise given the United
States' long-standing commitment to supporting democracy;
procurement—especially important when U.S. firms are competing
for public tenders; and organized crime—a clear threat to U.S. security, given the reach of illicit global networks. Officers also found
time to highlight the ways a lack of good governance touches ordinary
citizens—everything from a phony law degree in Pilsen to a Potemkin village in Turkmenistan.

YOUR VOTE COUNTS! (MAYBE)

Americans place great stock in elections as indicators of democracy
and are heavily invested in seeing that other countries carry out
elections that are free and fair. That finely resonating phrase has a
meaning in the United States that doesn't always translate overseas.
The U.S. government, along with the international community and
many NGOs, helps fund the cost of elections and training for local
poll workers. The taxpayer-funded National Democratic Institute for
International Affairs and its counterpart, the International Republican Institute, frequently serve overseas as election observers, and the
Carter Center is only the best known among many NGOs that have
made a reputation monitoring elections in struggling countries. They
join a flotilla of international organizations, ranging from the Organization for Security and Co-operation in Europe to the Organization of American States to the African Union, all of whom attempt
to monitor this most basic aspect of democracy. Observers only enter

countries that want their presence, but most countries have a strong incentive to have their elections observed and characterized positively by international monitors. One might wonder how it is even possible to pull off electoral fraud, given all those international observers, modern technology, and social media.

Embassy personnel play a crucial role in elections. Their sustained presence in a country allows officers to build long-term contacts among various political parties and candidates. Their familiarity with local people, languages, and regions builds trust and provides perspective. Embassy officers frequently serve as on-the-ground election monitors. Occasionally their reporting offers eye-popping examples of the gap between Washington's ideal of "free and fair" elections and what actually happens.

Embassy reporting on the 2010 Ukraine election (which brought Viktor Yanukovych to power) shows the dangers of attaching too much meaning to voting. The winner was deposed in 2014 after a six-month opposition campaign attracted worldwide attention (including that of Russian president Vladimir Putin). Given the disastrous aftermath of the coup, which led to civil war, a Russian invasion, loss of the Crimea, and continued unrest in the eastern part of the country, not to mention economic free fall, Ukraine offers a cautionary tale: elections in fundamentally nondemocratic places cannot be a measure of democracy.

Although the U.S. embassy in Kyiv clearly saw that the main issue in the election turned on whether Ukraine would cast its lot with Europe or Russia, reporting officers could not have realized how high the stakes would become. Yanukovych, born in the eastern Donetsk region and advocate of a pro-Russia policy, won against Yulia Tymoshenko, then prime minister and advocate of a closer relationship with the European Union. Tymoshenko lost 45.5 percent to 49 percent and alleged election fraud—charges that went nowhere. She was ultimately jailed for corruption by her rival Yanukovych while the EU negotiated behind the scenes for her release.

Yanukovych reneged on signing an EU association agreement in November 2014, an act that unleashed the Euromaidan, called the largest pro-European demonstration in the history of the European Union. The protests, which continued through February, were remarkable for the persistence of people willing to endure freezing weather, for the large turnout, and for the ensuing military intervention by Russia, which led to the loss of Crimea and the ongoing military skirmishes in the eastern part of Ukraine. As crowds gathered daily in Independence Square in Kyiv, the violent government reprisals resulted in the killings of hundreds of protestors and led to Yanukovych's removal from office. The events have only heightened the urgency of the question of whether Ukraine belongs in the West or the East.

Such a dark future seemed unthinkable given the hopeful tenor of election day reporting in February 2010. Embassy officers painted colorful scenes, describing some voters traveling to precincts in horse-drawn sleighs. One woman slipped on ice outside the polling station and broke her leg. After a trip to the hospital and a cast, she sent her husband back to the precinct to ask for a mobile ballot box, throwing local election officials into confusion over how to accommodate her.[10]

Embassy reporters were warmly welcomed at the precincts. "Anxious PEC (Precinct Election Commission) members sometimes sought our reassurance that they were doing everything correctly; PEC members, domestic observers, and ordinary voters often asked how we thought the whole process was going." However, officers also described devious ways in which fraud was perpetrated. The idea of planting pens filled with slowly disappearing ink—a stunt worthy of *Mad* magazine—was not beneath both sides, evidently.

> The idea of disappearing ink occurred to both camps. In Bila Tserkva, where Yulia Tymoshenko took 69 percent of the vote, the problem of disappearing ink was not discovered at one precinct until the counting stage, when one-quarter of the ballots turned out to be blank. Embassy observers were treated to a Flor-

ida 2000 exercise in which grannies on the PEC held ballots up to the light trying to discern voter intent from indentations left by the pens with the disappearing ink. Local observers illuminating ballots with cigarette lighters barely avoided setting some of them on fire.[11]

In Georgia, election task force members in 2008 also worried about hijinks with the voting pens, along with a nasty fight over stuffing ballot boxes and voter intimidation with slogans such as "To the Grave with Saakashvili," and by "promoting tension by spreading propaganda about disappearing ink, taking photos of ballots, and waving around suspect protocols in front of the media."[12]

In Uzbekistan, elections in 2009 were so obviously unfree that the OSCE opted not to deploy a full election observation mission. The embassy used the opportunity to sketch the political climate in the country.

The GOU [government of Uzbekistan] approach is characterized by the paternalistic assumption that ordinary Uzbek citizens are not ready for real, "no holds barred" democracy. Accordingly, the parliamentary elections are a type of semi-democratic exercise wherein the government strictly limits the "variables" and then allows the elections themselves to proceed with little apparent interference. After first vetting very narrow parameters for candidacy and virtually guaranteeing that eventual parliamentarians will fully support the executive branch (if not completely agree with each other), the GOU made the elections themselves as technically correct as possible.

Although the GOU seems to miss the point of the most essential aspects of a democratic society, particularly a free press and robust political dialogue with opposing viewpoints, it tries to make up for its democratic shortcomings by focusing on minute details during the elections themselves. For example, our teams noted each polling station had a first aid room staffed by medical professionals, and a "mother and child" room stocked with toys, so that parents can comfortably vote without worrying about childcare. . . . Polling station officials generally appeared to be conscientious and committed if not downright enthusiastic. (One poloff noticed an election chairman removing his own eyeglasses and lending them to an elderly gentleman who was unable to read the ballot.)

The most obvious technical weakness on election day was the widespread practice of allowing a single family member to cast proxy ballots for all of the eligible voters in the family. Evidence of this practice was noted in every polling station that embassy observers visited. In many polling stations, there was not even an attempt to conceal this "family voting." In full view of embassy teams, a single voter would present multiple passports at the registration point and receive multiple ballots in return. One team observed a single voter stuffing an estimated 30 ballots into the ballot box. In other polling stations, particularly those where most people had already voted, observers looked over the registration lists and noted long series of identical signatures, indicating that a single person had "signed out" numerous ballots. Only in a few polling places did election officials attempt to conceal the evidence of proxy voting by refusing to issue multiple ballots while the embassy's observers were clearly watching. (COMMENT: Emboffs thought that the voters presenting multiple passports appeared visibly upset not to receive all of "their" ballots, and believe that election officials probably told those voters to come back after the embassy team left. End Comment.) Evidence of proxy voting was still apparent on the registration lists, though election officials at those locations tried to convince embassy observers that very similar handwriting "runs in the family."

And then culture intervenes.

For many (particularly in the rural areas), election day seemed
to be a social occasion and a welcome break from their routine.
Several of the polling stations were playing loud, festive music;
one of our teams saw a number of people dancing . . . prominent
members of the community were seen to cast their ballots and
then nip off for a cup of tea, a plate of plov (rice pilaf), or a bowl
of stew with members of the election commission.

Welcoming 18-year-olds seemed to be a source of pride. Several
of the election commissions had planned a special acknowledge-
ment for first-time voters upon registration. One polling station
even had small gifts for all young people casting ballots for the
first time.[13]

The bonhomie in Uzbekistan contrasts with elections that are outright nasty, violent, and underhanded. In Slovakia, a middle school
teacher who pursued public office to improve the quality of the
public schools began questioning some of the district mayor's sweet-
heart deals with local mobsters. Shortly after a warning phone call,
he awoke to find his car engulfed in flames outside his apartment.[14]
Elsewhere, ruling parties ensure their entrenchment by writing (or
rewriting) the rules, moving the goalposts, and otherwise making it
impossible for any opposition to run a real campaign.

In Russia, frustrated opposition candidates in the city of Ryazan
(about two hundred kilometers southeast of Moscow) detailed the
ways elections were rigged by United Russia, the ruling political party
of Vladimir Putin and Dmitry Medvedev. Municipal officials allowed
United Russia to place huge billboards in government-owned bus
stops but told opposition groups that there was no bus stop space
available or dramatically inflated the advertising rates.

United Russia also had candidates stand outside popular shopping centers and large grocery stores handing out shots of vodka
to passersby . . . a sure way to attract the homeless, alcoholics, and

the lower class to vote in favor of United Russia . . . One opposition candidate said city employees who voted for other parties would be harassed at their workplaces or even fired. The candidate alleged that local government even targeted the sick at hospitals and clinics, denying them medical services and medication if they did not vote for United Russia.[15]

Voters aren't fools. If they suspect fraud they simply stay home, as was the case in Bashkortostan, the most populous Russian republic, situated alongside the Ural Mountains. "No one we talked to bothers to vote because, they say, the results are pre-ordained," the embassy reported. "Several people commented on the 2005 elections when voter turnout was alleged to be 80 percent although people in the cities do not vote. It turned out that thousands of fake ballots were printed; activists protested and provided evidence of the fraud to Moscow.[16]

Embassies cataloged almost unlimited ways to throw an election. For example, the presence of outside observers hardly guarantees that elections will be aboveboard. It all depends on who is invited. Zimbabwe's longtime dictator Robert Mugabe reached out only to those nations that had never voted against Zimbabwe in the UN—Venezuela, China, Iran, Russia, and Brazil. Perhaps unsurprisingly, Brazil's envoy declared that the 2008 elections had been, in his words, "exemplary."[17]

Having a system in place is no guarantee against fraud. In many places, institutions ostensibly set up to ensure free elections are shams designed to do the opposite. In Nicaragua, the Supreme Electoral Council used the Orwellian tactic of protecting electoral integrity by severely restricting election observation and threatening to disqualify opposition candidates.[18] In Cameroon, after months of tussling over the biased rules of the election agency ELECAM, the United States sent a message of disapproval by boycotting the public swearing-in of the leadership—a move that was joined by the British, Dutch, Canadian, and EU chiefs of mission.[19]

Elsewhere, technology has enhanced the old-fashioned practice of vote buying. In the Bahamas, the embassy found that votes were worth anywhere from $250 to $2,000 in three constituencies. "Workers allegedly offered cash in return for cell-phone camera pictures of PLP (Progressive Liberal Party) ballots, causing the parliamentary registrar in charge of voting to ban cell phones from polling stations."[20] And if those in power are still uncertain of victory, they can always postpone elections. In Angola, the National Assembly sat for sixteen years before a new election was called, despite constitutional provisions for elections every four years.[21]

Why would a seat in parliament be worth such high-risk (and high-cost) gambits? In a word, immunity. Most parliaments offer sitting members immunity from prosecution. To illustrate the lengths to which the concept is taken, we'll let the U.S. embassy in Bulgaria have the last word. Reporting on the consequences of a court decision that allowed gangsters to go free on bail to run for parliament, where their position would gain them immunity from prosecution, the embassy wrote that amid a climate of opaque financing and shadowy political parties, "There is a strong stench of malevolent manipulation of the electoral system by entrenched and unscrupulous interests."[22]

BUY AMERICAN! PROCUREMENT, BRIBERY, AND SWEETHEART DEALS

In 1976, the U.S. Congress passed the Foreign Corrupt Practices Act in response to revelations that U.S. companies bribed foreign officials to gain contracts. Enacted in 1977, the statute makes it illegal for a citizen or corporation of the United States to influence, bribe, or seek an advantage from a public official of another country.[23] "Everyone else is doing it" would no longer suffice as an excuse. The act was amended in 1998 to conform to the Organization for Economic Cooperation and Development's Convention on Combating Bribery of Foreign

Public Officials in International Business Transactions.[24] To date, the thirty-four OECD members and seven nonmember states have signed the convention, a small proportion when contrasted with the much larger number of countries that have not signed.

Public tenders, in which billions of dollars are often at stake, are especially vulnerable to opaque decision-making processes. Former Communist countries, no matter how bright other aspects of their transition to the free market, failed repeatedly when it came to transparent tenders. Even those in Central Europe that were among the first to incorporate themselves into the European Union, the OECD, and NATO struggled to overcome a legacy of cronyism, kickbacks, and bribes.

In Slovakia, the embassy scoffed at the firing of the minister of environment over a public procurement scandal, calling it no more than politics as usual. The case involved an €85 million public tender for the disposal of coal ash. The minister awarded the contract to a company that bid €27 million, almost 33 percent higher than the nearest competitor. Prime Minister Robert Fico had by then fired no fewer than nine ministers in the three-party coalition government, mostly over corruption. Still, the embassy was unimpressed. "The SNS (Slovak National Party) is the most egregiously corrupt and self-serving of the three coalition partners, and what Fico appears to object to is not so much the fact of SNS ministers' cronyism as their sheer ham-fisted clumsiness, which rarely leaves more than a week's respite between banner headlines."[25]

In the neighboring Czech Republic,[26] Ministry of Defense (MOD) procurements were a mechanism of corruption, with successive governments using contracts "as a way to reward themselves and their political supporters with lucrative business deals, cheap asset sales, and kickbacks . . . Politicians appear able to manipulate the procurement process by utilizing single source tenders, requiring the use of preferred intermediaries, and paying higher prices than other countries for similar items."[27]

To paraphrase bank robber Willie Sutton, corrupt politicians target the MOD because that's where the money is. With the second-largest budget in the Czech government, more than a quarter of the MOD's funds in the late 2000s went to construction and procurement as it upgraded its Soviet-era equipment to meet NATO commitments in Iraq, Afghanistan, and the Balkans. The shopping list expanded alongside the MOD's addiction to shady deals, from parachutes that didn't open to secondhand airplanes that kept breaking down. The embassy wrote that the 2008 purchase of 19 IVECO light multi-role vehicles (called Dingo 2s) epitomized the MOD's procurement problems. Done as a sole-source purchase without a public tender, the Czechs paid $2 million for each vehicle. In contrast, the Norwegians paid only $385,000 for the same vehicle, and the thrifty Belgians paid only $220,000 each.[28]

The procurement scandals of the Czech Republic were closely tracked by the embassy in part because of the involvement of American-owned firms. One featured the dramatic arrest and prosecution of a former defense minister, the arrest of the American head of a renowned Czech truck company, and the in-court testimony of a former American ambassador. How did things get so out of hand? Two purchases—one for armored personnel carriers and another for army trucks—illustrate perfectly the endemic corruption.

The first deal involved a billion-dollar contract between the U.S. General Dynamics' Austrian subsidiary Steyr and the Czech MOD for armored personnel carriers (APCs). A multi-year trail of venality began openly enough in 2004, when the center-left government approved a plan to replace Soviet-era vehicles with 240 new APCs (called Pandurs). The following year, a tender for 199 vehicles was let, and in 2006 the center-left government awarded the contract to Steyr. (The company's subsidiary relationship with General Dynamics meant the U.S. embassy could advocate for the company as the only U.S. firm competing among seven others for the tender.) When the center-right party took control of the government in 2007, it repudiated the entire contract. General Dynamics threatened to take the case to international arbitration, and after intense negotiation, the government agreed to buy 107 Pandurs, subject to successful field testing and at a revised cost of $700 million, down from the original $1 billion original deal in 2006. The Czech army took delivery of the first 17 Pandurs in September 2009.[29]

The Czech press blew the whistle, charging that 6 percent of the Pandur contract was earmarked for payoffs to both political parties and implicating current and past government ministers. The embassy had reported in March 2009 that a General Dynamics/Steyr representative alleged that then–deputy defense minister Martin Barták had engineered an opportunity for a personal friend of the prime minister to solicit a bribe from Steyr in exchange for getting the contract issues sorted. The embassy felt it was important enough to warrant mention in another cable nearly a year later, noting that "although Embassy Prague is unable to confirm any allegations against Barták, the circumstantial evidence is considerable."[30]

Barták surfaced frequently in embassy reporting cables. A trained physician, he gravitated to the military and served as deputy defense minister under Vlasta Parkanová from 2006 to 2009, where he was seen as an adept manager, happy to run the day-to-day details for his less-experienced boss. (Parkanová later became a member of the Czech parliament, but in July 2012 the parliament stripped her of her parliamentary immunity to enable her to be prosecuted for corruption in connection with the purchase. She has not yet been charged.) Barták thrived at the ministry and finally got the top job under the caretaker government of Jan Fischer in 2009. A political survivor, he resurfaced in August 2010 for a third act as the deputy finance minister under Miroslav Kalousek.

The embassy's reporting was only part of the story. Barták was later accused of bribery in a second deal, worth $150 million, for the purchase of several hundred heavy trucks from Tatra, a Czech company owned at that time by the U.S. firm Terex. Tatra was run by the American CEO Ron Adams, who also served as the president of the American Chamber of Commerce. A key member of the Tatra supervisory board was William Cabaniss, former U.S. ambassador to the Czech Republic from 2004 to 2006. The Tatra truck deal ran into trouble when Praga, one of its suppliers, failed to provide parts for the large military order.

William Cabaniss created a media sensation in November 2010 when he went public, accusing Barták of soliciting a bribe in February 2008 at the Bull Run Public Shooting Center firing range in Centreville, Virginia. He told the same story in a Czech court on March 17, 2014, asserting that Barták said the problems Tatra was having with Praga could be fixed.[31]

"At some point in the conversation, [Barták] said: 'For a certain amount of money'—I don't remember the exact amount—'the problems between Tatra and Praga can be solved.' I didn't respond, I thought it was a very unusual and out-of-order conversation for someone at the Defence Ministry, and I walked away and had no further conversation with him."[32]

Barták, perhaps sensing that the noose was tightening, played hardball. In August 2010, Tatra CEO Ron Adams was briefly arrested by Czech police on charges of bribery—charges allegedly brought by Barták. Adams was later released and charges were dropped.[33]

The 2014 trial of Barták brought out other allegations, including offers to arrange personal meetings—for a price—with the then–prime minister. The scandals swirling around him failed to scuttle an earlier Barták visit to the Pentagon for a meeting with Defense Secretary Robert Gates in September 2009. The United States had announced a month earlier that it was unilaterally canceling plans to install a missile defense program in the Czech Republic and Poland. The United States seemed eager, despite its knowledge of the defense procurement scandals, to secure continued Czech military involvement in Afghanistan and elsewhere.

The years-long scandal ended, at least for Barták, in May 2014 when he was acquitted of all charges. CEO Ron Adams, also acquitted, left Tatra. The company fell into bankruptcy and was sold to Czech investors. The embassy, trying to explain what it acknowledged was "a mind-numbing number of corruption scandals," despaired of any political consensus on how to end them, saying politicians thought the proposed cures were worse than the disease. Giving the police more power through witness protection programs, the use of undercover agents, and wiretapping were all tactics painted by critics as "a step backward . . . a clear effort to associate [reforms] to the excesses of the former Communist regime," an objection that might well be true for many other post-Communist countries.[34]

ORGANIZED CRIME

"If it were not part of Italy, Calabria would be a failed state."[35] Thus began a cable describing the last-place locale of Italy, located on the foot of the Italian boot, a region in thrall to the 'Ndrangheta, Western Europe's largest and most powerful crime syndicate. The consul general, traveling through the region, described a bleak wasteland in which inhabitants had lost all hope.

And it seemed true not only for Calabria but for much of southern Italy. The consulate quoted a report from the Roman think tank Censis that called organized crime "a true national emergency" and asserted that 95 percent of the Naples population coexisted with active organized crime gangs, the highest percentage of any province in the country. The results were frequently fatal. Naples's murder rate was more than thirteen times the national average: 2.6 per 100 residents in Naples, as compared to 0.2 for the country as a whole. Naples also had the highest rates of extortion, arson, and loansharking.[36]

The United States has a substantial presence in Italy, with a large embassy in Rome supplemented by consulates in Milan, Florence, and

Naples. It also has a permanent mission in Vatican City and another to the UN agencies in Rome. There are several military installations, including the Naval Air Station Sigonella in Sicily, and thousands of accompanying family members. In addition, centuries-long immigration patterns have created countless Italo-American familial connections and an American awareness of (and fondness for) Italy that other countries envy. In a remarkable effort, the Naples consulate, covering everything from Naples southward all the way to Sicily, chronicled organized crime's grip on Italian society. Over and over again, the consulate made connections between organized crime in Italy and security interests in the United States and articulated why the United States should be concerned and involved.

The Naples consulate described a criminal society with global tentacles. The three main players—Sicily's Cosa Nostra, Calabria's 'Ndrangheta, and Campania's Camorra clans—did business with Chinese, Turkish, and Balkan syndicates. According to a Calabrian-based anti-Mafia prosecutor, "The 'Ndrangheta is far more sophisticated and international than most people believe, maintaining bank accounts in Monte Carlo and Milan, and transporting operatives to Colombia, Spain, Germany, the Balkans, Canada and Australia."[37] They had ties with Colombia's FARC (Revolutionary Armed Forces of Colombia), a leftist guerrilla group trading drugs for arms. The Italian parliament's anti-Mafia committee characterized the 'Ndrangheta as "having an international structure similar to that of Al-Qaeda."[38] In a public statement, Italy's national anti-Mafia prosecutor identified links between Islamic militant groups and the Camorra, declaring that the evidence implicated the Camorra in an exchange of weapons for drugs with Islamic terrorist groups."[39]

FBI statements bolstered that viewpoint, noting numerous instances of "opportunistic interactions" between the Italian mobs and Islamic extremists, all of whom have members and/or affiliates in the United States.[40] The post quoted an FBI intelligence assessment that "criminal interaction between Italian organized crime and

Islamic extremist groups provides potential terrorists with access to funding and logistical support from criminal organizations with established smuggling routes and an entrenched presence in the United States."[41]

The consulate described the high costs of organized crime, which deters investment and leaves the formal economy in shambles, with unemployment rates in southern Italy of more than 20 percent and a GDP per capita of only half of the northern Italian regions. Criminal activities lead to higher costs for the government, business owners, and consumers, and it is harder to measure lost opportunities for foreign investment, environmental and health effects, losses due to corruption and inefficiency, and social costs related to higher rates of drug dependency and drug-related crime. Accounting for an estimated 7 percent of Italy's GDP, organized crime is the single biggest sector of the Italian economy. The three biggest syndicates earned more than €57 billion a year tax-free, an amount that was equal at that time to Slovakia's GDP.[42]

The consulate reported that the syndicates earned this income through protection rackets, drug trafficking, rigging of government contracts, trafficking in persons, loansharking, arms deals, illegal construction, distribution of pirated and counterfeit products, illegal waste disposal, and money laundering for all of the above.

Not even food is sacred. The post reported that the Camorra ran two thousand illegal bakeries

> using expired flour and ovens which emit toxic fumes (the wood is often old doors covered in paint). Caserta, right in the heart of Italy's cheese country, has illegal cheese factories which mix buffalo milk with powdered milk from Bolivia, cutting real mozzarella costs by a third; they also use lime [from limestone] to help ricotta keep longer. According to a commander of Naples' Carabinieri, the most flourishing business is recycling expired products. The Camorra also passed off low quality imports with

made-in-Campania labels, from pesticide-laden Moldovan apples
to E.coli infested Moroccan industrial salt [as table salt].[43]

Even more repugnant is the Mafia's waste disposal racket. Naples
is infamous for its periodic garbage problems, and understanding
why citizens would tolerate meter-high stacks of rotting garbage in
a metropolitan area dense with more than four million is a lesson in
how organized crime can bring a city to its knees.[44] The post described
how three "lacks" converged: lack of space in local landfills, lack of
modern high-capacity incinerators, and lack of political will. "Particularly hard hit by the crisis is suburban Pozzuoli, just west of Naples,
where garbage piles stretch as long as 200 meters. At one site, Roma
children picked through a five foot high heap; at another, noxious
smoke billowed from a massive pile."[45]

The consulate described how the Mafia became part of the problem decades earlier, when it learned there was money in toxic waste
disposal—especially when done illegally. The Camorra earned $6
billion in two years by buying farmland at distressed prices and
transforming it into illegal dumping grounds. "The type of garbage
dumped includes everything: barrels of paint, printer toner, human
skeletons, cloths used for cleaning cow udders, zinc, arsenic, and the
residue of industrial chemicals . . . One dump was brimming with
hospital waste, including used syringes, thousands of vials of blood
samples and a human embryo." Concerns abound about the garbage's
long-term effects on the underground water supply and aquifers for
nearby crops, as well as more direct consequences on public health.
The World Health Organization found cancer rates outside Naples
were 12 percent higher than the national average.[46]

Organized crime has wormed its way into local politics, undermin-
ing any hope of a legislative fix. The cost of a vote was a $75 cell phone
(to offer proof of a "correctly" marked ballot) until the Italian parliament banned the use of cell phones and cameras in voting booths.
Considering that throwing an election in a multiparty system can hang

on small percentages, the power of organized crime seems even greater. In interviews with numerous Italian pollsters and political observers, the post learned that the Camorra clan can move 10 percent of the vote in Naples province. The Cosa Nostra controls about 150,000 votes in Sicily, enough to determine whether a party crosses the 8 percent threshold required for a Senate seat. In some areas of Calabria, the 'Ndrangheta controls up to 20 percent of the vote. "By deciding who holds elected office, the mob creates a web of dependencies to ensure election victories for inept politicians that are guaranteed to produce policies favorable to organized crime." The post continued, "It is clear from our meetings with elected officials in Calabria that they are a step down in quality from those in other parts of Southern Italy; some are so devoid of energy and charisma that it is hard to imagine them mounting—let alone surviving—a real electoral campaign."[47]

The United States has a further security interest in the region. Calabria is home to Gioia Tauro, Europe's busiest transshipment port, where Department of Homeland Security employees work as part of the Container Security Initiative. The consulate offered many accounts of corruption at the port and 'Ndrangheta intimidation of both Italians and foreigners in the local communities. "The 'Ndrangheta controls the legal and illegal activities of the port, earning a commission on every container and controlling the hiring of personnel (even the guy who operates the access gate)."[48]

The region hosts only a few American business interests and is losing opportunities for tourism. One cable noted that "the savvy general manager of one of the best hotels in the region has spent two years and over one million euros to obtain authorizations for a five star Marriott resort on the Tyrrhenian coast, but is still waiting for a ministry in Rome to move the necessary paper." Infrastructure is missing too—the consulate reported in 2009 that the infamous Salerno–Reggio Calabria highway was still a construction mess twenty years after the project began, and the more ambitious Strait of Messina bridge to Sicily had once again been canceled.

The visiting consul general found the inhabitants enveloped in pessimism, disinterest, and resignation. Asked why the region had not adopted the anti-Mafia strategy of nearby Sicily, the regional president of Calabria responded, "We are the real island." Asked why no one had made an effort to contact tour operators who were now bringing cruise ships to Sicily, the president of the province of Reggio Calabria asked, "What's a tour operator?"[49]

Antonio Lombardo, chief prosecutor of Catanzaro, the regional capital of Calabria, explained that the 'Ndrangheta's family-based structure and lack of informants makes it nearly impossible to penetrate. Organized crime in Italy is not considered an emergency, he said, but rather "a stable factor in our country. We are accustomed to losing part of our GDP to organized crime and we factor it into our economic planning." Adding a chilling note to the overwhelming sense of despair, the reporting officer wrote that the provincial president never spoke above a whisper.

Inevitably, comments from the citizenry led the consul general to broach the idea of complicity. How can organized crime maintain such a chokehold on business and political activities without the compliance of the wider society? One answer described a vicious cycle—in the absence of the state, the Mafia becomes the only alternative for services, employment, and protection. Another important institution, the Catholic Church, has come under criticism for decades, if not centuries, for looking the other way. But there are signs that things are changing. One bishop was under police escort in 2008 for refusing to preside at funerals for mafiosi.

The consul general interviewed a few brave souls willing to stand up to the 'Ndrangheta. Calabria's senior anti-Mafia prosecutor, Nicola Gratteri, under constant police protection, said what made him effective is that he realized he is "not afraid to die." At the time of the interview, his investigations had led to the capture of one hundred and eighty mafia members, and he had eighty ongoing investigations. A few civil society groups have organized, including Addiopizzo

("Good-bye pizzo," the Italian word for extortion payments). They put up fliers all over Palermo stating, "An entire people that pays the pizzo is a people without dignity." Another group, Ammazzateci Tutti ("Kill us all"), is also run by fed-up young people, one of whom told the consul general that the group's name is a message that expresses both hope and challenge, saying, in effect, "See if you have enough lead to kill us all."[50]

On the economic side, the consulate predicted that as citizens lose their tolerance for the fact that the price of a bottle of olive oil, a jar of tomato sauce, a bottle of wine—the staples of Italian life—has been inflated by organized crime, or the products have been adulterated by the same sources, their disgust with "the system" may take more tangible form. Culture matters too, and change will mean "breaking the culture of illegality that is so rampant in Southern Italy, that is, the blatant disregard for the law by average citizens and the lack of a sense of civic responsibility. The Naples chief prosecutor suggested—while lighting a cigar in a no-smoking office to underscore his point—that Neapolitans have 'something in their DNA' that causes them to react to any law by breaking it."[51] Prosecutor Gratteri, despite his bravery, ended on a pessimistic note, saying, "As long as the human race exists, the 'Ndrangheta will exist."[52]

From New Jersey to Naples, from Spain to Sarajevo, organized crime is every bit as dangerous as terrorism. The pattern is similar, no matter the place. Criminal activities initially focus on businesses, but they soon leach into civic life. Mobsters buy corrupt politicians; they buy corrupt voters; and they finally buy elections. Losing patience with the time and effort needed to buy influence, they soon find it is simpler and more cost-effective to enter politics themselves, tapping unlimited campaign finance chests funded by their extortion and racketeering practices, completing a truly vicious cycle.

When this happens in Russia, it sets the stage for a country in which no amount of "resets" will make a difference. When this happens in transitioning countries such as Bosnia-Herzegovina, it impedes progress and wastes precious assistance funds. But when it happens in one of America's closest allies, such as Italy, it is disastrous. Lest policymakers think such problems can be confined to Italy's borders, reports from law enforcement suggest otherwise. Globalization has increased connections between markets. The 'Ndrangheta and its ilk are not coming to a town near you soon. Likely, they are already there.

GOOD (AND BAD) GOVERNANCE

While not every embassy or consulate took the enormous all-out reporting initiative of the Naples consulate, many invested time and effort translating corruption's effects on the small, day-to-day actions of normal citizens, trying to convey to Washington the helplessness of an individual in a corrupt system.

When the Tajikistan government inaugurated sales of shares for its megaproject hydroelectric dam known as Roghun, there was nothing voluntary about citizens' purchases. The embassy in Dushanbe reported that employers ordered staff to buy shares at rates that far exceeded their monthly salaries or risk dismissal.

National television larded the airwaves with footage of Tajik citizens clambering over each other to give their money to the bank. Happy stock owners recited poems about Roghun to the cameras as they proudly grasped their stock certificates. State media followed up with music video paeans to the dam, heroic images of Roghun builders, and aerial footage of a column of trucks on route to the construction site as if off to war. Images were straight out of Soviet central casting, including footage of President Rahmon in deep conversation with Roghun craftsmen, apparently discussing details about the masonry. Once could almost hear him exhorting, "Comrades, this grout must be thicker!"[53]

The top-down approach included targeted amounts for everyone in Tajik society. At the bottom were students, forced to "volunteer" to buy 100 somoni worth of shares (roughly $20). Professors warned students that failure to present a share certificate bearing their full name would bar them from their exams. "As an added incentive, students could present their stock certificate for better grades. A certificate for 300 somoni in shares reportedly buys a '3' (a passing grade roughly equivalent to a 'C' in the American system), while 400 somoni yields a '4,' or 'B.' A student told us her professor told her not even to bother showing up at the exam; her 500 somoni contribution had already won her a '5.'"[54]

Higher education figures frequently in corruption tales. A law school in Plzeň, in the Czech Republic, began awarding degrees on a fast-track basis, challenging even the most liberal diploma mills in the United States. A joke made the rounds: "What are you doing this weekend? Answer: Getting a law degree." The post reported that the story had all the ingredients of a classic corruption case: "potentially undue influence on state tenders, lack of transparency in school procedures, politicians and other well-placed individuals receiving special treatment, and allegations of involvement by organized crime."

The story began when a student noticed that a vice dean had plagiarized a number of pages in his dissertation. The press quickly discovered that many politicians, police, and other officials and members of Mafia families had obtained law degrees without completing the five-year program. In some cases, degrees were awarded in just two months. Dozens of dissertations were "missing" from the law library (or were, in fact, never written). Embarrassed Czech alumni, several of whom held office, could not produce their dissertations and could not remember the names of their faculty advisors or professors. The president of the Czech university accreditation commission told the embassy she believed organized crime set up the entire system with the goal of controlling or blackmailing officials who had bogus degrees. To substantiate this allegation, she pointed to an analysis written by the law school's vice dean and signed by the dean for an institute that provides expert legal advice to the government, which recommended that a $6.5 billion environmental cleanup project be treated as a concession and not as a more transparent public tender. This decision would have allowed the government to award the contract without opening it to public bidding. [55]

Elsewhere, embassy officers tried to describe the frustration for the average citizens living in societies where corruption is the rule and bribery is not confined to public tenders and megaprojects. "Turkmen routinely pay bribes when obtaining a driver's license, during stops by the traffic police, registering children for school or university, and registering a business.[56] Turkmen doctors and nurses, forced by law to make house calls without the means to do so, pay bribes to the deputy heads of the clinics where they work to avoid paying stiff penalties. The heads, in turn, use the money to bribe health inspectors to make sure their reports are favorable. Laboratory workers also pay bribes, as do many hospital workers.[57] This entrenched system stifles competition and public confidence, not to mention degrading the quality of health care. But nothing beats the surreal tale of one Turkmen village.

When Turkmenistan president Gurbanguly Berdimuhamedov opened a model village in fall 2009, there was plenty of hoopla at the brand-new school, hospital, mayor's office, market, and apartment building. "Medical staff waved balloons and flags outside the hospital. Inside, they scurried around the halls and populated various offices. Berdimuhamedov toured the apartment housing and visited a family living in their brand new, well-appointed home."

The embassy described the Potemkin aspect as follows:

One of the diplomats, who had accompanied the president on this visit, stopped by the village the following day when all the officials had left. She found a ghost town. The schools, mayor's office, and most of the other buildings, including the apartment building where the family that hosted the president supposedly lived, were empty. The family was nowhere to be seen and their furniture was gone. The hospital director told the diplomat that his hospital was not really open, because he had no staff. The people, whom the diplomat had seen the day before, had come from other areas to play the part of hospital workers.[58]

It might be easy to dismiss corruption in out-of-the-way places, but Moscow, Europe's largest city with almost twelve million inhabitants, makes other examples seem like child's play. The embassy characterized former Moscow mayor Yuri Luzhkov as the personification of an out-of-control spoils system. Luzhkov's uniquely Russian brand of conservatism grabbed international media attention when he banned gay pride parades, calling them "satanic," and plastered the city with posters of Stalin, refusing to be "an apologist" for a leader he admired.

Luzhkov, the embassy wrote, had "a national reputation as the man who governs the ungovernable, who cleans the streets, keeps the Metro running and maintains order. As a loyal founding member of the political party United Russia, he can also deliver the votes." But, the embassy noted, Muscovites increasingly questioned their mayor's links to organized crime. Some called the city "dysfunctional, operating more as a kleptocracy than a government." The embassy described the intricate *krysha* (roof or protection) system that links organized crime, business owners, and several crucial public agencies: the police, the federal security services (FSB), Ministry of Internal Affairs (MVD), and the prosecutor's office.

Getting much of their information from Russian journalists, the embassy officers contended that Moscow's elaborate three-tiered structure placed Mayor Luzhkov at the top, the FSB, MVD, and militia at the middle, and ordinary criminals and corrupt inspectors at the bottom. Apart from its illegality, they characterized it as a highly inefficient system in which criminal groups filled voids in areas where the city did not provide services.

"Luzhkov oversees a system in which it is apparent that almost everyone at every level is involved in some form of corruption or criminal behavior," the officers wrote. An investigative reporter said that having received enormous sums in protection money, Luzhkov, in turn, paid off key insiders in the Kremlin, ensuring his eighteen-year tenure, which began in 1992. "People often witness officials going into the Kremlin with large suitcases and bodyguards."[59]

While Luzhkov as a corrupt leader is hardly unique, the embassy described a complex structure of interlocking bribes that is uniquely Russian. The system runs through all sectors of society, including government, where most members of the Russian parliament buy their seats but quickly recoup their investment. "The lawless criminal climate makes it difficult for businesses to survive without being defended by some type of protection. According to that Transparency International's 2009 survey, bribery costs Russia $300 billion a year, or about 18 percent of its gross domestic product."[60]

A Russian reporter told the officer how the system worked:

A cafe owner pays the local police chief via cash through a courier. He needs to pay a certain negotiated amount over a certain profit. The high prices of goods in Moscow cover these hidden costs. Sometimes people receive "bad protection" in the sense that the *krysha* extorts an excessive amount of money. As a result, they cannot make enough of a profit to maintain their businesses. Yet, if people forgo protection, they will instantly be shut down. For example, officials from the fire or sanitation service will appear at the business and invent a violation.

Everyone has bought into the idea of protection in Moscow, so it has become the norm . . . Business owners understand that it is best to get protection from the MVD and FSB (rather than organized crime groups) since they not only have more guns, resources and power than criminal groups, but they are also protected by the law.

The division of spoils has police and MVD collecting from small businesses while the FSB collects from the larger ones. "Despite paying for protection, nobody is immune; even rich people who think they are protected get arrested. The *krysha* system has led to an erosion of police internal discipline. Young police officers spend their money buying luxury vehicles that a normal worker could never afford."[61]

What seems extraordinary about corrupt systems is the symbiotic relationship between organized crime and officialdom. In the Russian case, the government officials maintain their own separate (but equally corrupt) identity. In contrast to the Italian protection rackets, official Moscow seems to have clear supremacy over the criminal element, which is relegated to lower-level functions.

Embassy officials wondered at what point Luzhkov and the system he personified would become a bigger liability than an asset. The cable noted mounting evidence that corruption had metastasized to a point that even those who benefited most could no longer defend it, and fate ultimately dealt with Luzhkov. The embassy began noticing numerous signs that his days were numbered, reporting that ultra-nationalist Vladimir Zhirinovskiy had called for Luzhkov's resignation, saying his city government was "the most criminal in Russian history." Such a remarkable denunciation, carried on state TV flagship Channel 1, was widely seen as an indirect Kremlin rebuke. Journalists and others willing to talk to the embassy agreed that Luzhkov was on his way out, one way or another. That day finally arrived on his seventy-fourth birthday. He was summarily fired by President Dmitry Medvedev, via long-distance decree, while Medvedev was visiting China.

Systemic problems require systemic changes, however. No single person, however corrupt, can be responsible for all the evils in a complicit system. Thus Medvedev also decided to take on the MVD, proposing a 20 percent cut in positions, higher salaries for those remaining, rotation of senior leadership, and a review of hiring and promotion practices. Like Luzhkov, the MVD had possibly exceeded the number of allowable scandals, with its leadership confessing to a shooting spree resulting in the murders of local residents, the torture death of a prominent lawyer while in pretrial detention, and YouTube postings by a former police officer chronicling widespread corruption in the ranks. The U.S. post noted that Medvedev was savvy in using these crises to manipulate public opinion against the Ministry of Internal Affairs. "The reputation of the police forces in Russia has been low for years, with Russian polling results depicting that more than two thirds of Russians distrust the police. It would probably take major reforms sustained over years before public opinion toward Russia's police officers significantly improved.[62]

Of course, American businesses working in corrupt climates are not exempt from shakedowns. Any business that is slow or falls into arrears with any kind of payments can encounter trouble. This became a growing problem in southern China during the global financial crisis, when orders slowed and businesses of all kinds had difficulty making ends meet. The Guangzhou consulate reported an increasing number of cases in which American citizens were forcibly detained for owing money. The caseload peaked during trade fairs, when the numbers of foreign businesspeople in the country swelled.

"Extra-legal, strong-arm tactics are long established methods of resolving business disputes in southern China . . . Frequently the victim is threatened with violence by hired thugs and detained at a factory, hotel, or private residence until payment is received." The consulate illustrated the lengths to which perpetrators will go. "Two Amcits [American citizens] and their Taiwanese business partner were forced from the road in Dongguan, a major manufacturing center in Guangdong's Pearl River Delta. The victims were driven to a rural location and threatened with torture and death unless $4 million was transferred to a bank account in China. The suppliers transferred the money and the hostages were released the next day.

We learned of the incident after the Amcit victims returned safely to the U.S. Their lawyer notified us that he had asked DOJ [Department of Justice]/FBI to help him work with Chinese authorities to investigate and prosecute the case."[63]

Two other cases offer clear examples of extortion. In one, an American citizen was detained by a group of men and threatened with violence at his factory in Xiamen. The victim was convinced his interlocutors were affiliated with organized crime and insisted that he had no connection with them. In a separate case, an American was held in his home until money was paid for his release. In both cases, local authorities assisted the American citizens in escaping only after telephone calls were made from the consulate. No arrests were made.

The consulate saw a clear link to globalization, noting that old customs die hard but will be increasingly exposed as China continues to court international investment. As foreign entrepreneurs pour into the country, there will be cultural clashes over their expectations of acceptable business conduct. The consulate also linked extortion to the global economic crisis. "As economic conditions deteriorate, business owners and factory employees grow more fearful that expected income will fall through. Weak enforcement of contract law was already a problem in China's legal system; the economic downturn has worsened the situation. Under these conditions, it appears that the use of vigilante tactics to collect on debts is growing."[64]

While examples of corruption in Italy, Russia, and China are easy to envision, there are cases in smaller places that stretch credulity—both for their security implications and that they could have happened in the first place. One of the era's sillier cases of corruption—but one with alarming possibilities—involved Slovakia's Border and Alien Police and its senior officer at the Ukrainian border. An airport officer working a bomb detection exercise with sniffer dogs hid live explosives in the luggage of a Slovak who worked in Ireland. Incredibly, the officer failed to retrieve the package after the exercise. Through a series of errors the luggage made it to Dublin, where three days later the Irish police were able to track it down. The uproar spurred a secondary scandal in which the regional chief in charge of eight hundred and eighty police at the country's most sensitive border—and a key embassy contact—was accused of accepting a bribe and abusing his public office. The post commented, "It would be surprising if an officer of [his] length of service just decided to begin a life of corruption now, given the well-known and lucrative smuggling of cigarettes and other contraband over the border from Ukraine. One newspaper reported that on the Ukrainian side, officers pay EUR 10,000 to secure a job on the border, which they swiftly make back."[65]

In a chapter full of incredible stories of other people and places, it seems appropriate to end with the most mind-boggling—an American private citizen's impersonation of a U.S. member of Congress—a bit of mischief perpetrated on the unsuspecting country of The Gambia, a tiny West African nation. Business consultant Richard T. Hines, lobbying for World Air Leasing, which hoped to run transatlantic and subregional flights out of the capital, Banjul, hoodwinked the Gambian president into believing he was a member of Congress.

When the chargé d'affaires attended a large celebration for President Yahya Jammeh, she was shocked to see Hines sitting next to the president at the head table. Hines awarded the president a pin from the 82nd Airborne Division that he "happened to have with him at the time." The Gambia's newspaper of record carried a banner headline the next day stating "President Jammeh Receives U.S. Award for Fight against Terrorism."

The embassy's account of what it called a "surreal episode" is blistering in its condemnation of Hines's "charade." The chargé read Hines the riot act at breakfast the following day, and Hines and the World Air Leasing CEO left. The chargé then had to explain Hines's ruse to the permanent secretary at the president's office. The post reported that the official was grateful for the information but said he would not be advising President Jammeh of the problem—at least not right away. Passing the buck, he said that since the Gambian embassy in Washington had organized the trip, it would be up to the Gambian ambassador to write a letter to the Gambian government explaining what had happened. Perhaps wisely, he said he would only discuss the problem with the president after receipt of the letter."[66] The 2004 episode came to light when the post (by then staffed with new personnel) was asked in 2007 to confirm the accuracy of a *New York Times* story that mentioned the Hines escapade.

CORRUPTION AS A SECURITY THREAT

For citizens in Western democracies, it is hard to imagine endemic corruption. While the U.S. has had some spectacular scandals (Enron, Madoff, etc.), most Americans still believe they can go to the post office and mail a package, reasonably confident that their money will not end up in the postal worker's pocket. Most Americans get driver's licenses, register their vehicles, and pay taxes with confidence that the various fees will be collected and credited. Students engaged in the annual rite of university applications are fairly sure that stuffing the envelope with extra cash will not enhance their chances. No one pays to be hired by the Department of Homeland Security thinking they will earn back ten times more through bribes.

The intensity of embassy reporting about how things work elsewhere did not seem to be matched by an intensity of interest on the Washington side. The Pentagon's willingness to welcome the very tainted Czech minister of defense suggests an "unfortunate but inevitable" attitude, or a willingness to subordinate procurement irregularities to the higher priorities of keeping the Czech military committed to coalition activities in Iraq and Afghanistan. Other stakeholders, including Congress, missed opportunities to engage the countries the United States most wanted to work with, including allies like Italy. They didn't see how corruption made unreliable partners. And they clearly did not see how it posed a grave security risk to the United States. In countries where cooperation is for sale, promises mean nothing and vaunted partnerships are phony.

The rigidity of entrenched corruption kills the promise of possibility—of progress, investment, and justice. In the words of a Saudi interlocutor, "The lack of transparency, nepotism, tribalism all exist. I have no doubt that a corrupt official is just as much a terrorist as those that blow things up, considering the damage they inflict upon society." He pointed to the Saudi justice system as a source of much discontent. "If I don't feel my rights will be addressed in a system that is free of corruption there is something wrong."[67]

- - - - - - - - - - - - - -

Chapter 8

IRAQ:
Diplomacy in a
War Zone

- - - - - - - - - - - - - -

*We have nearly the same number of State Department per-
sonnel in Germany, a country of 82 million people, that we
have in India, a country of one billion people.*

—*Secretary Condoleezza Rice*
January 18, 2006

- - - - - - - - - - - - - -

THE WASHINGTON ROOM WAS THRUMMING WITH
negativity. The civility implicit in the phrase "town hall meeting"
belied what had turned into a nasty no-confidence vote from foreign
service rank and file on the George W. Bush administration's effort to
staff a diplomatic offensive in Iraq four years after coalition forces had
removed Saddam Hussein from power. Officers angrily challenged
Harry K. Thomas Jr., the director general of the foreign service, on
the threat to use the tactic of directed, or forced, assignments.

At issue was the immediate need to fill forty-eight positions in
Iraq, but, as is often true in quarrels, much more was in play. The State
Department had determined it needed 250 foreign service officers in

Iraq by summer of 2008, and at the time of the town hall meeting on October 31, 2007, it had filled only 202. In an e-mail notice to officers around the world, Thomas said the department would begin directed assignments to fill the anticipated shortfall. Additional messages were sent to about 250 officers who were told they had been selected as "highly qualified" for the vacant positions. If enough of them did not volunteer, the letters said, some would be ordered to serve in Iraq.

By tradition, officers have always volunteered for postings. They are "worldwide available" and routinely go to some of the most challenging countries in the world. But until Thomas's directive, the only time the State Department had ever resorted to directed assignments was in the Vietnam era. Technically, the State Department has the right to send its diplomats anywhere. Officers agree to be worldwide available when they join the foreign service.

Posts are classified as nonhardship, hardship, and greater hardship according to a complex scale weighing danger, health, and living standards. There are rules governing "fair share assignments," ensuring that officers cannot hop from Paris to London to Rome. In reality, ambitious officers often avoid those cushy and touristy spots. It's hard to make an impact, and the mostly routine kinds of issues the United States manages in Western European embassies are unlikely to earn promotions. At the meeting in 2007, the point of contention was really over hardship and greater hardship posts. The latter are sometimes unaccompanied assignments, meaning married officers must leave spouses and children behind. The rise in the number of unaccompanied posts caught officers by surprise. Many had made a life in Africa or Latin America, exposing their children to international schools, foreign languages, and a deep dive into foreign cultures. For some, the idea of leaving family behind was unthinkable.

The meeting reverberated like an earthquake and revealed a wide rift between the State Department's leadership and the officers, unusual in an organization that values tradition and collegiality. A poll taken by the American Foreign Service Association, a professional group that is the exclusive bargaining agent for the foreign service and perhaps best known for its *Foreign Service Journal* publication, revealed that only 12 percent of FSOs believed Secretary of State Condoleezza Rice was fighting for them. She had followed the highly popular Colin Powell, whom many officers felt had taken a hit for the White House after he told the United Nations in 2003 that Iraq had weapons of mass destruction. Some felt Rice was too close to President Bush and lacked sufficient independence and managerial experience to run the building. The anger at the town hall, if nothing else, exposed a simmering communications problem between Rice and her FSOs.

Objections to Iraq service came down to three factors: proportion, preparation, and purpose. Some officers charged that the size of the Baghdad embassy, vaunted as the world's largest, was Bush administration hubris at its worst. Why, they argued, should it be bigger than the U.S. embassy in China? Within the Middle East, how could it compare with America's long-standing relationship with Israel, or with the strategic importance of Egypt or Saudi Arabia?

The number of diplomatic positions in Iraq had increased every year since the new embassy opened in 2004, and the expansion of Provincial Reconstruction Teams (PRTs) outside Baghdad—from ten to twenty-five—required still more foreign service officers. Each PRT was a multi-agency unit comprised of military officers, diplomats, and reconstruction experts with skills ranging from medical, electrical, water, agriculture, and more. The PRTs, led by the State Department, were meant to serve as a counterinsurgency bulwark by taking resources far outside the capital and shoring up provincial and municipal civil society. The staffing requirements were rapidly creating an unsustainable demand, especially as these twelve-month assignments meant the State Department was dealing with near-constant turnover in-country. Officers argued that simple arithmetic made it impossible to fill Iraq slots, given an officer corps of fewer than seven thousand and nearly two hundred diplomatic missions worldwide.

Preparation was also a divisive issue. At the time of the town hall, most officers were getting only a few weeks of training before departure, clearly inadequate for a post with so many challenges. Typically, training would last several months and include at least courtesy-level language lessons and area studies, but need dictated that nearly all officers were sent without knowledge of Arabic. This runs contrary to foreign service culture, in which acquiring a language is often an indispensable part of the job. Officers invest years working on hard languages such as Arabic, Mandarin, Japanese, or Korean, and most assume they will serve multiple tours and become regional specialists, building political and economic knowledge to go with the language. Forcing, for example, East Asian language speakers to do tours in Iraq seemed to devalue their expertise and place them in a region for which they had no preparation. Longtime Latin American and African hands felt the same way.

The biggest objection concerned the purpose and goals of the United States' mission in Iraq. Having heard the domestic political debate over the futility and distaste for nation-building, the U.S. embassy in Iraq symbolized nation-building on a grand scale, and in 2006–2007 the military clearly had the lead role. This was a significant shift for many diplomats, whose work with military personnel began and ended with the routine presence of a defense attaché office at embassies. Foreign service officers were uncertain about what they would be allowed to do, what would be safe to do, and to whom they would report. Who was the *real* chief of mission—was it the ambassador, Ryan Crocker, or the general, David Petraeus?

This was not a silly question. Former Iraq ambassador Christopher Hill, who succeeded Ryan Crocker and served in Iraq from 2009 to 2010, analyzed the pressure points between the diplomatic and military presence at some length. "U.S. goals in Iraq, increasingly economic ones, were often set by senior U.S. officials, including senior military generals, who had neither the expertise nor the patience to slog through the no-man's land of economic development projects and capacity building. The military had become the largest dispenser of foreign aid in Iraq for programs whose primary and more sober purpose was to convince the Iraqis not to shoot at our soldiers."[1] Hill said the embassy had "a reputation for being supersized" out of a misplaced need to keep pace with the military. "Story after story came back from Iraq of people having little to do, of sitting around in endless meetings and writing telegrams that no one wanted to read."[2]

Apart from the tension between diplomats and the military, there was mounting evidence that the State Department had not adequately prepared for the consequences of Iraq service. The department's medical unit had yet to ramp up to assist officers with war-related ailments such as posttraumatic stress, and support for officers' families staying behind was minimal. FSOs had an overall sense that despite lofty talk at the top, the department was just as unprepared as its officers, asking something it had not fully thought through, and which it had certainly not communicated to them.

A small resident press corps works out of the State Department building, and to the everlasting woe of the foreign service, the disastrous town hall was covered by reporters whose subsequent stories portrayed foreign service officers as shallow, spoiled, and selfish.[3] What might have been a valuable opportunity for State Department leadership to explain the idea behind a new "expeditionary" foreign service degenerated into a scene in which management looked arrogant and FSOs looked whiny, especially in comparison to troops who served multiple tours without complaint. While the news stories mentioned legitimate problems, such as a recently returned Iraq officer who said the State Department would not authorize her medical treatment for posttraumatic stress disorder, other comments were less helpful, ranging from the much-publicized complaint that Iraq service is "a potential death sentence," to "who will care for our children?"[4]

It was a bad day for the foreign service. No amount of blogs, op-eds, or letters to the editor from FSOs enthusiastically serving in Iraq could undo the damage. A little-known fact is that fifteen hundred diplomats had already served in Iraq from 2002 until the day of the meeting in late 2007. Many officers disagreed with those who had been most vocal. By the end of the day, fifteen more had volunteered for the forty-eight unfilled positions, and soon all forty-eight had been quietly filled with no need for directed assignments.

The real story is that many FSOs went to Iraq because they wanted to serve there and were intrigued by the policy challenges and attracted by the resources at their disposal. In an organizational culture in which promotion is predicated on an ability to manage people and money, Iraq service offered plenty of opportunities. Many of those who served were enthusiastic about their stints, and some went back for more. Hill's memoir supports the notion that many officers were glad to go, and he described his office colleagues volunteering and his phone ringing with offers from FSOs who wanted to serve with him in Iraq even before his ambassadorial nomination had been made public.

Of course some officers were attracted by the danger and hardship pay, which allowed them to double their salaries. Hill noted that the bureaucratic pressure to fill Iraq slots had begun to have unintended consequences.

> The people who served repeated tours in Iraq as opposed to those who simply wanted to check that box, were often seen as those who could not get jobs elsewhere, or who viewed Iraq as a place to go to line up a next assignment to a cozy job in Europe. The State Department's personnel system had been skewed as a result of Iraq, with those who had returned being offered jobs ahead of everyone else ... Iraq, it was said, had also become a kind of French Foreign Legion, where after a particularly unsuccessful assignment somewhere, a person could wipe the slate clean and start afresh.[5]

The era of the "expeditionary" foreign service seemed to have arrived almost overnight.

Hill's predecessor in Iraq, Ryan Crocker, who served from 2007 to 2009, had exerted enormous pressure on the State Department, Congress, and anyone who would listen for more resources, especially in the form of FSOs. Crocker served as the Iraq surge began in 2007 and was determined to ramp up the embassy's capacity to match the military. This meant staffing twenty-five PRTs as well as the large embassy. The cables he sent reveal exasperation with a bureaucracy that was overwhelmed by personnel demands and slow to meet his needs. All ambassadors try to be advocates for their posts and seek more resources from Washington on the theory that it never hurts to ask, but Crocker was unique in having the world's largest embassy along with Washington's affirmation that staffing Iraq was a policy priority. That didn't mean it always worked well.

Crocker's desire for more officers embraced nation-building at its most fundamental level. "The success or failure of the Iraqi government will depend in large part on its ability to function well and to deliver services to Iraqi citizens. That makes ministerial capacity building an essential part of our strategy," he wrote in 2007, following up with a torrent of numbers explaining and describing the work of some 214 officers he said were essential—just to work on ministerial capacity building.[6]

In another cable, he excoriated the State Department's personnel system for its failure to meet a staffing deadline. Crocker took this issue so seriously that he ordered his embassy's Office of Provincial Affairs (OPA) to update the staffing document twice a day. His enumeration of the problems illustrates the bureaucratic challenges of such ambitious staffing goals. Crocker was incensed to learn that PRT team leaders were rejecting a significant number of candidates, sometimes because of qualifications and sometimes because they lacked the facilities to support them (billeting, transportation, security, etc.). "Under no circumstances will a position not be filled or diverted without the express permission of the ambassador," he wrote. He fulminated over bureaucratic snafus. "Furthermore, various offices in Iraq and Washington were keeping their own tallies of surge staffing that were often inconsistent and resulted in confusion. To address this problem OPA now has a single transparent manning instrument that is maintained by one person, with a back-up, and accounts for the status of each position in each phase."[7]

But as an illustration of how quickly personnel needs can shift, just two years later Embassy Baghdad was describing to Washington how it would handle a drawdown from sixteen PRTs to only five, and a reduction of some seventy officers. Three of the PRTs—Basrah, Erbil, and Kirkuk—became full-fledged U.S. consulates. Drawing from President Obama's February 27, 2009, speech at Camp Lejeune, the embassy focused on timing, coordination, pace, and sequence. In a prescient observation, it noted, "It has become clear that security issues (and related costs) are going to be among the most difficult. If, in 2012 and beyond, we assess that diplomats require a security footprint as heavy as is required in 2009 (but without military support) we will need to annually reassess the viability of some of the enduring presence posts."[8]

WORKING IN A WAR ZONE

Against the contentious backdrop of staffing, security, and the vagaries of Washington politics, the leaked cables provide day-to-day details about the actual experience of serving in Iraq. They demonstrate that it was indeed possible to perform traditional diplomacy along with diplomatic outreach work—meeting diverse groups of contacts and running programs. Timing helped. Iraqis had been coping with multinational forces since the initial invasion in 2003, and many yearned to form a more normal relationship that would exchange boots for books. By 2008, they were about to get their wish.

The Iraq cables paint a complex but surprisingly upbeat picture. Officers clearly found plenty to do, and their reports offer an eloquent rebuttal to some of the more outlandish statements at the town hall meeting. Iraq service, while of course dangerous, was full of meaningful opportunities to do what many officers hope for when joining the foreign service—to make an impact and a difference. For officers who had spent much of their careers competing for scarce programming resources, Iraq represented a bonanza—more than enough. Even rarely funded cultural programming was encouraged.

Public diplomacy officers faced a great challenge, since they were tasked with creating and running programs designed to reach the people of Iraq, rather than the government. The success of their work depended on access to students and professors, journalists, think tanks, democracy-building NGOs, and communities of artists and intelligentsia. The security situation complicated many aspects of their work, as hazards fluctuated from one month to the next and from one part of Iraq to another. Multiple cables reflect officers' frustration at canceling, postponing, or circumscribing programs solely for security concerns. They clearly wanted to do more. Yet just as often, their cables reported successful events in which U.S. experts spoke to a wide range of audiences or offered artistic productions that resonated with all kinds of Iraqis.

In the province of Wasit, south of Baghdad, the PRT sponsored a comedic play performed by actors from the Iraqi television sitcom *Mud House* in a municipal auditorium with a seating capacity of eight hundred. The Iraqi police estimated more than forty-five hundred people showed up, and they somehow crammed fifteen hundred into the hall. When the PRT public affairs officer and the PRT commander walked onstage to open the show, the crowd "erupted with wild and unexpected applause . . . that mirrored the way Iraqis receive their soccer stars." The officers described the play as a comedy set in agrarian Iraq in the 1950s, as seen through the characters in a family headed for the city of Baghdad. The actors performed a second night to accommodate those who had been turned away. In a cable, the post celebrated the success, writing that "no PRT member that attended has ever seen so many Iraqis smiling and laughing."[9] This tentative foray into the world of theater marked a new opening for imaginative officers, who began using Iraqi theatrical troupes to perform plays that were recorded for broadcast and mass media distribution.

The Wasit play was hardly a one-off. Another cable describes, in hilarious detail, the PRT's valiant effort to provide musical entertainment in the multicultural town of Ain Sifni, in Ninewa province in northern Iraq. Hoping to hook readers back in Washington, the post asks rhetorically:

> What do you get when a US Army band plays an Eastern Orthodox wedding hall in a Yezidi town with Arabs, Christians, and Kurdish musicians under the watchful gaze of the Barzani patriarch, a crucifix, and the Iraqi flag, plus a banner celebrating the anniversary of an anti-Saddam uprising?
>
> The presence of five wonderful American ambassadors—on tuba, trombone, French horn, and trumpets—made this gathering possible and helped it morph into a pinkie-dancing conga line to a caterwauling beat—a fleetingly inclusive Kurd-a-palooza in which we clearly danced to another's tune.

The cable describes in giddy detail the PRT's first-ever attempt at performing arts diplomacy and the lengths officers had to go to to overcome all manner of problems—both silly and serious. The stage, set for a variety show for local musicians, provided an irresistible platform for smuggled Kurdish flags. The public affairs officer solved the problem by ordering the town scoured for an Iraqi flag, "from whence it came we may never know." The performance hall was "a barn-like venue with a lousy sound system and 250 people who would have been arrested in the Kennedy Center." The PAO resolved the sound system distortion by having the PRT team turn off the electronic countermeasures employed against remote-detonated IEDS. The lack of signal meant no phone service, a by-product of which was an undistracted audience.

The writer described the town's complex cultural crossroads, with competing Orthodox and Catholic churches, tombs of two prominent Islamic scholars, and security provided by Kurdish Peshmerga. The PRT leader met with nervous members of varying minority groups, all of which looked to the United States to guarantee their safety, a prescient request from the Yezidis, who came under horrific attack from Islamic State five years later and were driven to a mountaintop. The cable ended on a sober note, reminding readers that the Yezidi, a minority in a heavily Kurdish region that is itself a minority in Iraq, are "a group of people whose continued daily existence in a twice hostile world is their daily accomplishment. The power of our instruments . . . can quiet the crowd when we are all in harmony, but it cannot long overpower the indigenous noise of this place."[10]

Another important aspect of engagement involved bringing American scholars to Iraq. Professor Mike Hannahan, director of the Civic Initiative program at the University of Massachusetts at Amherst, went to the Kurdistan region to discuss the American electoral system with more than 1,100 Iraqis at universities, ministries, and in the media. He hosted an election-themed video teleconference in English between his own students in Amherst and those at the University of Kurdistan–Hawker (UK-H), causing a faculty member to marvel, "I've never seen the students so excited about something." At another regional university, students sat in the aisles once the auditorium seats were filled. The embassy told Washington to bring on more speakers. "Hannahan's host institutions and the KRG (Kurdistan Regional Government's) Ministry of Higher Education have a simple message for the USG: thank you for making the visit possible and please send more professors!" The embassy was eager to dispel security concerns and pleaded for longer visits. "The success of Professor Hannahan's program demonstrates that American academics can and should come to Northern Iraq for extended periods for the purpose of building stronger ties between Iraqi and American institutions."[11]

Six months later, the University of Kansas Political Science Department chair Burdett Loomis had an equally successful visit to several universities in the Kurdistan region, discussing political transition issues for the new Obama administration. The post described unheard-of access for an academic, with Loomis invited to meetings with the regional governor, a luncheon hosted by the Minister of Education, media interviews and a rock star reception from deans, faculty, and students at several universities.[12]

Despite these triumphs, security trumped all other factors. The embassy outlined a three-day program request for Bard College's Walter Russell Mead, with an ambitious schedule of meetings ranging from the Ministry of Foreign Affairs, dinner with Iraqi authors, meetings with faculty and students at the University of Baghdad, events with Baghdad-based NGOs, and media interviews. Mead was no stranger to hot spots, having traveled previously as an embassy speaker to places such as Turkey, Jordan, Egypt, and Saudi Arabia. The officers were frustrated. "Post has attempted to bring Walter Russell Mead to Iraq two times previously but security considerations have prevented the implementation of the trip . . . post believes it is time to engage Iraqis with high-level discussion on these matters with a well-regarded, *non-Embassy source*" (emphasis added).[13]

The embassy had made a point well known to State Department insiders. There is only so much talking and representing that diplomats can do. For decades, the State Department has turned to America's best-selling writers, academics, journalists, former high-level officials, and even Supreme Court justices to engage foreign publics through lectures, workshops, and seminars. This classic illustration of soft power connects illustrious Americans with their foreign counterparts. They willingly travel to tough destinations and forgo their usual speaker fees for the chance to represent the United States in a unique way. The State Department has featured musicians such as Wynton Marsalis and Yo-Yo Ma, who have performed concerts and offered master classes; writers such as Tom Wolfe and Frank McCourt; athletes such as Kareem Abdul-Jabbar and figure skater Michelle Kwan; dancer and choreographer Debbie Allen; architect Daniel Libeskind; photographer Joel Meyerowitz, and many more.

These cultural and intellectual ambassadors are an invaluable part of the State Department's outreach. Embassies have learned that speakers can make an impact, but only if they are part of an overall strategy of engagement that includes the less exciting work of building audiences and laying groundwork. A famous cultural figure doesn't just show up—the visit is the culmination of months of work by cultural affairs officers who cultivate audiences through frequent contact, demonstrating genuine interest in their art, and occasionally through small grant support when the art links to a higher purpose such as multiculturalism or promotes the values of civil society. While much lip service is paid to the goal of "mutual understanding," showing interest and respect for the artistic endeavors of other cultures is a way in which diplomats actually fulfill that mission.

Such strategic planning happens as a matter of course in most embassies, but in Iraq, nothing was routine. The embassy was in need of a framework through which the work of diplomacy—including cultural and educational exchanges—could be institutionalized. The November 2008 signature of the Strategic Framework Agreement (SFA) was a watershed, the single most important document for how U.S.–Iraqi relations would be managed. After five years of operating under UN Security Council Resolution 1790 (which extended the mandate of the Multi-National Force–Iraq until 2008, the third such extension of the original mandate from 2004), the SFA was meant to normalize the bilateral U.S.–Iraqi relationship into one in which two fully sovereign and equal states would cooperate.

The SFA was built on seven key areas, including a pillar for cultural and educational cooperation. It offered public diplomacy officers an opportunity to think strategically about all the programming tools available—the cultural and academic speakers but also academic and nonacademic exchanges, English language teaching, and cultural programming. Officers were tantalized by the promise of making public diplomacy programming part of the routine work of the embassy, and in July 2008 newly arrived Public Affairs Officer Adam Ereli wrote to Assistant Secretary Goli Ameri, who headed the State Department's ECA Bureau (Educational and Cultural Affairs), passionately calling for a higher level of programming and investment.

Ereli, an Arabic speaker and public diplomacy officer who had previously served as U.S. ambassador in Bahrain, saw the SFA as an important crossroads.

> To Iraqis, this means that they are getting their country back and joining the community of nations as a full and respected equal . . . One of the prime minister's inner circle said to me recently, "We want to be like any other country. Instead of American soldiers and checkpoints, we want to see American doctors and professors and students." ECA programs are the peace dividend that Iraqis for so long have been waiting.[14]

In his cable, Ereli outlined ambitious possibilities for the Iraqi Fulbright program, calling for a ten-fold increase in the number of scholarships, already a hefty thirty-five per year. He asked for a Fulbright binational commission, a full range of other academic and citizen exchanges, English language teaching, and arts and cultural heritage programs, arguing that military engagement must be replaced with public diplomacy.

The Fulbright program is often seen as the jewel in the crown of academic exchanges. It was founded in 1946 by Senator J. William Fulbright, and over the years some 325,000 people—Americans and foreigners—have received grants. Each year the program awards about four thousand grants to foreign students and about an equal number to American students, scholars, teachers, and professionals. Embassies play a critical role in administering the program. They liaise closely with Fulbright binational commissions, and in countries where no commission exists, they administer the programs themselves through their public diplomacy offices. Talent spotting is a point of pride. As of this writing fifty-three alumni from thirteen countries are Nobel laureates; thirty-one are heads of state or government. This is enlightened self-interest—a Fulbright alum in a position of power or influence speaks English and has had years of living in the United States as a graduate student. That familiarity (and hopefully fondness) for American society and culture pays dividends when the person is sitting across the table in a high-level negotiating session.

Ameri came to Iraq three months later, bringing a delegation of key State Department ECA officials to meet with the deputy prime minister, minister of Higher Education and Scientific Research, and several Iraqi university presidents. The deputy prime minister offered to match U.S.-funded Fulbright scholarships one-for-one, doubling the Fulbright program. The president of an Iraqi university told Ameri and her delegation that student and faculty exchanges were crucial to democracy. "Students need to see democracy to believe it," he said. An important subtheme, reiterated in many cables, was that Iraqi officials were not asking for a handout. They were prepared to pay for their part of these exchange programs.[15] The expansion of the flagship Fulbright program became real in a ceremony announcing Iraq's $2.5 million contribution. Ambassador Christopher Hill and Deputy Prime Minister Barham Salih signed an agreement doubling the number of student grants from thirty-five to seventy.[16]

Public diplomacy officers seemed to be on a roll from 2008 to 2010, describing in cable after cable triumphant programs, first-ever accomplishments, and standing-room-only audiences of all kinds. A workshop for English-language teachers would normally be a routine part of the job, but thirty years of academic isolation "has left Iraqi English teaching professionals starved for contact and resources. The level of English language ability is generally dismal." The post rhapsodized that the participants committed to resurrecting English language learning and that distribution of the State Department's *English Teaching Forum* magazine was "riotous," while a returned Fulbright Language Teaching Assistantship (FLTA) alumna, "mesmerized the conference" with tales of her Fulbright experience. "We believe there is a pool of excellent qualified candidates in Iraq for the FLTA." The desperate tone in the reporting reflected that, inexplicably, Washington had dropped Embassy Baghdad from the program, and the post ended the cable strongly requesting Iraq's immediate reinstatement.[17]

By 2009, Embassy Baghdad was proudly enumerating a catalog of exchanges and programs that would be the envy of any U.S. embassy, including the largest International Visitor Leadership Program in the world with one hundred and seventy participants; the largest Fulbright program in the region; a Young Leaders Exchange program, which sent more than two hundred Iraqi high school and university students to the United States each summer to focus on leadership, conflict resolution, and team building; the MEPI student leaders program, sponsored by the U.S.–Middle East Partnership Initiative; plus English-language teaching, student advising, and much more.

The embassy supported Iraq's cultural heritage through a program for twelve Iraqi archaeologists and conservators who attended a six-month workshop on conservation techniques at Chicago's Field Museum. The United States also provided funding for the Future of Babylon Project, where experts from the World Monuments Fund and the Iraq State Board of Antiquities and Heritage collaborated to develop a site management and conservation plan for the ancient site of Babylon.[18] This was no doubt motivated in part to make amends for the fact that Iraqi antiquities were poorly protected in the 2003 invasion and were subject to damage, vandalism, and theft.

All these great exchanges would be for naught, Ambassador Crocker warned in early 2009, if the United States did not improve visa processing time for Iraqis seeking to visit the United States.

Crocker railed against the 120- to 150-day waiting period required for most Iraqi visa applicants. "The SFA's Joint Coordinating Committees are off and running. For example, this week seven Presidents of Iraqi universities arrived in Washington for meetings with U.S. counterparts to create educational partnerships. In January, representatives of 25 American universities came to Iraq to recruit students. This fall, the first several hundred of an eventual 6–7,000 Iraqis per year will come to U.S. universities on government scholarships." He went on to lambaste the process of requiring a Security Advisory Opinion, the cause of the long delays. "We have the opportunity to bring thousands of young Iraqis every year for university degrees in the U.S. and in doing so, build the long term partnership we have never had with Iraq. We risk losing that opportunity due to our visa regulations."[19]

FIGHTING THE WAR OF IDEAS

In a key allusion, Crocker mentioned "the relationship we never had," and the cables offer evidence that FSOs were eager to meet ordinary Iraqis and build a foundation for mutual understanding. Learning another culture is a long-term endeavor, but officers wanted to take the first step and, one conversation at a time, deepen and broaden America's knowledge of a country that everyone had heard of but few knew.

A cable from Erbil profiles Kurdistan's so-called 1991 Generation, those born after the March–April uprising of that year, which followed the Gulf War and nearly succeeded in toppling Saddam Hussein, thanks to a rough alliance between Kurds and Shi'a forces. When the tide turned, Saddam's reprisals against both the Kurds and Shi'a were heavy. In the Kurdistan region, the median age was twenty, with more than 50 percent of its population under the age of twenty-five, and officers believed this demographic was the key to

its future. Through interviews with the education minister, several
university presidents, faculty, business leaders, and students, they
found a Facebook-savvy generation frustrated with limited higher
educational opportunities and even fewer career options.

They reported that educational institutions lacked adequate labs,
computers, and other tools of educational technology. One frustrated
student asked, "How can I learn biology from a book?" A greater
problem was lack of opportunities for graduates, most of whom used
to go into government service for lack of alternatives. But government jobs are no longer the sinecure they once were, and students
felt caught in a world in which old ways had withered without being
supplanted by newer and more exciting options. "Students have been
told since they were small to work hard, go to university, and plan
to get a nice, secure government job. They are unable to think of a
world in which that might not happen," explained the chairman of a
local Chamber of Commerce. University leaders who profited from
Fulbright grants or other academic exchanges said the answer lay
in curriculum reform and expanded vocational training. "We are
not training students to perform different types of work that have
to be done here. We are training students to get degrees," said one
university president, "and they have no idea how they will use what
they have learned."

In higher educational systems with such limited opportunities,
study abroad takes on added importance. While the cable enthuses
about the intense interest among young people to study in the United
States, it also notes competition from other countries. Even students
with full scholarships from the Iraqi government were having a hard
time deciphering the U.S. system and deciding where to study. "Con-
versely, for students looking to study in the UK, a very large and
active British Council office in Erbil provides first-rate advising services."[20] Thanks, perhaps, to cables such as this one, Iraqi students
soon benefited from State Department–sponsored EducationUSA
advising centers in Baghdad and Erbil, with trained advisors walking

students through the many steps of the American college application and selection process.

Another 1991 Generation—this one in Dhi Qar, a province in the Shi'a heartland of southeastern Iraq between Wasit and Basrah—fared far worse, educationally. PRT officers found that young people were less likely to be literate than their parents. Post believed the illiteracy rate was a legacy of Saddam's reprisals targeted at southern Shi'a provinces that had also taken part in the 1991 uprising. They found that dropping out of school was a growing trend. About 20 percent of primary school students stayed away as poverty forced children to work, security risks and tribal disputes dampened attendance, and administrators lacked the legal authority to compel schooling. The cables described schools that were often overcrowded, with shabby facilities, incompetent teachers, and corporal punishment.

Coalition forces had built many new schools in the province and refurbished others, but the PRT got a unique opportunity to address the problem when the Iraqi Army administered literacy tests and 50 percent of its soldiers in one division failed—a cause for dismissal. The division's general asked for help, and two Iraqi-American PRT staff members volunteered their time and soon had a class of forty.

"The PRT literacy effort, designed to prevent twenty-something soldiers from joining the swelling ranks of Dhi Qar's unemployed, was done on a shoestring, with photocopied articles for the more advanced and photocopies of three dog-eared adult literacy books for beginners." As word of the class got out, the ranks swelled to sixty. Then one day, only two students showed up for their lesson. "Basim, one of the hardest working students, reported that his brigade was moving to Amara, and everyone else was packing up to go. But he packed early so he would not miss class. His teacher didn't bat an eye. He taught Basim and the one other student for an hour and a half."

Pride in being able to help suffuses the cable, but so does incomprehension at why the province leadership was not more committed and engaged in the literacy problem. "The PRT program to reach young men at risk of being kicked out of the army is aimed at a critical group that could potentially feed insurgent or militia troops . . . Iraqis blame educational institutions and facilities for poor education, but many poorer countries with worse facilities do better at educating pupils."[21]

The thirst for improved education at all levels was nationwide, and the need in Iraq was so great that embassy officers could have easily filled their calendars with nothing but visits to schools and universities. While they were surprised at the high levels of illiteracy, they also had opportunities to interact with well-educated university students. Political officers visiting Baghdad University's political science department found their encounter with students and professors challenging. They heard some frank views and what they described as "hard versus soft" power issues: in the Iraqi context, it meant students advocated for a reduced U.S. military presence and more cultural and educational initiatives.

The cable set the scene: Baghdad University is Iraq's leading institution of higher learning and one of the largest universities in the Arab world. The deputy president recalled the dark days of sectarian violence that were recent (2006–2007) and real—seventy of its three hundred and thirty faculty were murdered. "Classes continued to be held in order to keep the university alive; the studying never stopped."

Students questioned U.S. involvement in Iraq, touching on sectarianism, the long-term role of the United States, and its commitment to repair environmental damage caused by the invasion. One of the professors referred to former Coalition Provisional Authority administrator Paul Bremer's book *My Year in Iraq,* in which the former American official conceded he knew little about Iraq. The professor argued, "Americans would only really understand Iraq by talking to its poor and ordinary people," a comment that was met with loud applause by the assembled students.

The officers commented, "Our two hour engagement with the animated gathering of political science students showed that while most had seen a lot of American hard power since our 2003 invasion, not enough had experienced (or received answers to tough questions) our soft power and overall policy objectives."[22]

Not all outreach was academic in nature. PRT Najaf members attended an Expo Najaf business promotion event organized by the Small Business Development Center, a partnership between USAID and the Najaf Chamber of Commerce. The idea behind the event was to diversify Iraq's economy away from oil, encourage expatriate Iraqi businesspeople to return home, and build a foundation for a thriving and diversified private sector. Iraqi business had struggled under years of international economic sanctions targeting the Saddam regime along with a dangerous security environment and lack of connections to overseas markets.

In the way of things in Iraq, the event was organized with the explicit support of the national spiritual leader, Grand Ayatollah Bashir Al-Najafi. An internal tug-of-war over the guest list led to an invitation for the PRT leaders, followed by one faction's move to disinvite them. That decision was overruled by the head of the Chamber of Commerce, who had recently returned from a Najaf-Minneapolis sister-city program and insisted on U.S. participation. Sister Cities International was started in 1956 by President Dwight Eisenhower to encourage people-to-people diplomacy. It works by pairing an American city with an overseas counterpart. The partnership is meant to promote mutual understanding and foster economic development, culture, education, and humanitarian assistance. Najaf is one of eleven sister cities paired with Minneapolis, part of a global program with 2,100 partnerships in 145 countries. The power of citizen diplomacy is easy to see in the case of the Najaf Expo. The trip to Minneapolis gave the head of the Chamber of Commerce the insight to see that U.S. support for the Najaf business community could be enormously helpful. In the end, the keynote speakers publicly praised the PRT and USAID's support for the business community.[23]

To understand why a business promotion event might need the blessing of a grand ayatollah, a cable from Najaf provided extraordinary background on all four grand ayatollahs, referred to collectively as the maraji. For Americans used to separation between church and state, the description of how these religious leaders flowed seamlessly between religious and public life was a revelation. One was deeply concerned with economic development and was the biggest supporter of an international airport in Najaf. Another was outspoken on electricity shortages and anticorruption efforts. Still another asserted that while clerics should not be politicians themselves, they should communicate important messages to politicians. Given the description of the constant stream of visitors to the ayatollahs and the media's willingness to grasp at any hint or rumor of their pronouncements on laws or proposed reforms, this seems an easy task. Such a nuanced account suggests that here, too, FSOs were making steady and valuable inroads in their understanding of the complexities of Iraqi society.[24]

Not every effort was instantly successful. A report covering summer 2010 (just after the end date of the leaked cables) disclosed the embassy's embarrassingly inadequate outreach efforts through social media, especially Facebook and YouTube. After an initial burst of interest with "friends" and "likes," the number of active users plummeted from a peak of four thousand in February 2010 to just over one thousand six months later. The author cited problems with English versus Arabic, embassy efforts to control what was posted, and, worst of all—Facebook management by committee. With careful neutrality, the author noted that the Public Affairs Section required the committee's clearance for every item, twenty-four hours before posting.[25]

Eventually the embassy learned from its errors and banished the Orwellian Facebook committee, broadened the content to include non–U.S. government material, increased the frequency of postings, and, perhaps most important of all, expanded Arabic language content. Instead of nameless administrator posts, the Facebook page used first names and pictures of the administrators—a challenge in a high-turnover post with high security threats. The embassy also began making better use of its YouTube site, posting films of cultural events. Hits went up when the embassy revamped its postings into Arabic and called them "Window into the Embassy." In both cases, the embassy regrouped quickly and took (for government) breathtaking risks to get the approach right.

Of course, not all public diplomacy efforts engage the soft side. Officers also worked to combat violent extremism. In a 2008 cable enumerating a depressing number of violent and deadly attacks on different ethnic groups, the embassy argued, "The pattern of violence demonstrates that Al Qaeda in Iraq (AQI) has absorbed the blow of the surge, adapted its tactics and introduced a new phase to its continuing campaign to undermine public order. We have initiated an information campaign to highlight this threat, including television spots, op-eds, interviews and talk shows. The message is simple: Al Qaeda remains a ruthless, relentless enemy that can change its tactics but will stop at nothing to destroy those who oppose it . . . Virtually the only significant ethnic-sectarian violence in Iraq today is that perpetrated by Al Qaeda itself."

The cable posed three questions:

How do you break these extremists and their apparatuses throughout the region? How do we talk about Al Qaeda's setbacks, how they have responded and what this says about their continuing capabilities and intentions? What are we and others doing (and need to do) to stay one step ahead of the enemy? The answers to these questions—and how we and our partners talk about them—lie at the intersection between the operational and public diplomacy communities. To do this right will require some creative thinking and coordination between operators and communicators.[26]

A second cable discussed how the United States might help to extricate Iraq from its vicious cycle of extremist violence.

Public Diplomacy can do its part through programs that promote strong, enduring linkages between Iraqi and U.S. institutions . . . There is no shortage of credible, persuasive Iraqis, who speak out publicly against extremist violence.

At the largest embassy in the world, many different offices and agencies support programs to identify, support, train, equip, and empower voices for moderation and tolerance . . . There is always more that can be done. Our national leadership has called this struggle "the long war" which means that we have to take a long-term approach to the problem. For most of its modern history as a state, and certainly since 1958, Iraq has defined itself in opposition to, if not open hostility with, its neighbors and the West. We have now an opportunity to change history and reorient Iraq.[27]

THE COSTS

The cables make clear that the work in Iraq was absorbing and all-consuming, but it was also dangerous and occasionally cost lives. One of the more poignant personal stories is that of Paula Wikle, an office management specialist who had been serving in Guatemala. Long before the town hall meeting, she answered the State Department's call in 2003 for volunteers to go to Iraq. In her first few days on the ground she thrived in the intensive environment, efficiently handling more tasks in a day than most people would complete in a week. Early in the morning of October 26, 2003, a rocket tore through the Rashid Hotel where she had been staying. She nearly lost her arm and would endure dozens of reconstructive surgeries. After recovering enough from her injury to work again, she went on to become a public diplomacy officer and continues to serve both at overseas postings and in Washington, DC.

Others were not so lucky. For example, the name of Terrence Barnich, deputy director of the transition assistance team and co-chair of the New Electricity Projects Working Group, surfaces in many cables that detail the crucial effort to bring power to all parts of Iraq. Sadly, Barnich was killed in a bomb attack on May 25, 2009.

Iraq is a challenging operational environment in many ways, and not every Iraqi is a charming and earnest future Fulbrighter, anxious to learn all about the United States. Every idealistic embassy officer proud to meet the challenges of rebuilding Iraq soon confronted a staggering level of corruption among venal officials. These unsavory characters were quick to take advantage of the U.S. presence. Their behavior, along with a pervasive culture of corruption that long predated the Iraq War, could dampen the morale of even the most gung-ho officers.

A cable from PRT Muthanna, in the southernmost part of Iraq, reveals officers getting wise to the ways of Southern Iraqi tribal sheikhs, men who wield power and influence in a social structure in which loyalty is based on families and clans, rather than given to elected officials. One who had returned from a visit to Iran scolded the Americans for failing to purchase his loyalty. After he and other tribal sheikhs visited the White House and met President Bush in 2008, he expected to benefit financially but was disappointed that Americans had "done nothing" for him.

By contrast, he described how Iran had catered to his needs. Ostensibly there for a medical checkup, he told the PRT's local political advisor that it was really a pleasure trip with short-term "marriages" with state-sanctioned prostitutes among the entertainment. He said other tribal leaders had enjoyed similar privileges while guests of the Iranian regime.

The post commented acidly, "Southern Iraqi sheikhs are well known for shifting their loyalties based on financial considerations. PM Maliki's Isnad/Tribal Support Councils are particularly noteworthy in this regard. Susceptible sheikhs will trade their influence for financial support especially if the sheikh is not independently wealthy. In turn the sheikh can mobilize supporters when needed. The influence, however, is rented and not bought. If the financial contributions suddenly stop, much of the support may also cease. The PRT considers this true for Iranian influence in the region as well. If Iran continues to pay for support among influential sheikhs, the Islamic Republic will likely increase its influence. If and when the money dries up, so will the cooperation among these rented sheiks."[28]

Between 2006 and 2010 more than a thousand cables described the various aspects or impacts of corruption. Some focused on election politics and coalition building; others dealt with the judiciary and rule of law; still others described how corruption tainted various administrative tasks inherent in running a modern state. A cable on efforts to secure Iraq's borders predicted that the U.S. military drawdown, completed at the end of 2011, would decrease U.S. visibility on progress, noting that the borders "are clearly porous, and the administration of borders is clumsy (multiple agencies are unable to coordinate) and riddled with corruption."[29]

These cables are especially telling given the collapse of Iraq in 2014, the rise of the Islamic State, and former prime minister Nouri al-Maliki's troubled era. While U.S. political leaders focused on a military exit strategy, few imagined that such a massive investment could be undone so quickly and the earnest work of thousands of Americans and coalition partners would leave so little lasting impact. Within the United States, there was confusion over the role of the military (short-term) and the role of nation-building through State, USAID, and countless other agencies (long-term). Cable after cable describes the Iraqi people's disgust with their own officials and their distrust of the system. While U.S. policymakers in Washington were certainly aware of the corruption, they were perhaps too willing to accept it as inevitable without understanding that it was in fact a fatal flaw that would undermine every effort to move Iraq to a functional democratic and multiethnic state.

SOFT, SMART, OR TRANSFORMATIONAL?
WHICH KIND OF DIPLOMACY?

The on-the-ground realities for American diplomats serving in Iraq played out against a swirling intellectual debate in the foreign policy community on whether post 9/11 America should embrace soft power, smart power, transformational diplomacy, or some combination of the above. Joseph Nye's 2004 refinement of his earlier soft power concept argued that the United States could accomplish more through attraction or persuasion than coercion.[30] The term *soft power* had morphed by the time the Obama administration came into office to the new phrase *smart power,* also used by Nye to mean combining the tools of both hard and soft power."[31] Hillary Clinton used the term *smart power* throughout her tenure as secretary of state, beginning at her confirmation hearing on January 13, 2009.

"We must use what has been called 'smart power,' the full range of tools at our disposal—diplomatic, economic, military, political, legal, and cultural—picking the right tool, or combination of tools, for each situation. With smart power, diplomacy will be the vanguard of foreign policy."[32]

In between soft and smart power came Condoleezza Rice's contribution to the discussion in 2006, when she coined the term *transformational diplomacy.* All three ideas aimed to redefine America's position in the world in light of challenges such as globalization and violent extremism. Each notion in turn assumed that a new world order would require diplomats to take on unconventional roles and think in different ways about the intersections of diplomacy, development assistance, and military power. This would be a lengthy conversation—Rice thought it would be "the work of a generation."

As secretary of state, Rice gave two speeches on transformational diplomacy, both at Georgetown University, two years apart. Her first speech in 2006 focused on new threats to the United States that were emerging within states rather than between them. "It is impossible to draw neat clear lines between our security interests, our development interests and our democratic ideas. American diplomacy must integrate and advance all of these goals together."

But the headline grabber was the case she made for a global repositioning.

> To advance transformational diplomacy, we must change our diplomatic posture. In the 21st century, emerging nations like India and China and Brazil and Egypt and Indonesia and South Africa are increasingly shaping the course of history . . . Our current global posture does not really reflect that fact. For instance, we have nearly the same number of State Department personnel in Germany, a country of 82 million people that we have in India, a country of one billion people. It is clear today that America must begin to reposition our diplomatic forces around the world, so over the next few years the United States will begin to shift several hundred of our diplomatic positions to new critical posts for the 21st century.[33]

Yet the most controversial aspect of her speech, at least in retrospect, was her willingness to join diplomacy to the work of the military. Rice outlined her vision of future diplomats working alongside military officers, citing a need to work at the "intersections of diplomacy, democracy promotion, economic reconstruction and military security." She foresaw what she called a "jointness" between soldiers and civilians.

Rice's second speech about transformational diplomacy, in 2008, offered a darker worldview in which the United States was buffeted by the chaos of failed states.

Globalization is revealing the weaknesses of many states, their inability to govern effectively and to create opportunities for their people. Many of these states are falling behind. Others are simply failing. And when they do they create holes in the fabric of the international system where terrorists can arm and train to kill the innocent, where criminal networks can traffic in drugs and people and weapons of mass destruction, and where civil conflict can fester and spread and spill over to affect entire regions.[34]

Here too is a foreshadowing of the precarious state of Iraq and its vulnerability to the ensuing chaos that was brought by ISIS and other rival factions.

Rice made a reference to the town hall meeting in Foggy Bottom and spoke approvingly of how the Foreign Service had responded. "To staff our positions in Iraq, we have had to transform our personnel system and that is working. We now have some of the most senior and outstanding members of our Foreign Service leading out efforts in Baghdad, including four ambassador-rank officers. And most importantly, our diplomats in Iraq have answered the call to serve voluntarily and I thank them for that." Her use of the word *voluntary* hinted that the threat of directed assignments probably was a heavy-handed and unnecessary approach.

All good officers read the boss's speeches, and not surprisingly, many embassy cables began connecting the phrase "transformational diplomacy," to their reporting efforts. Lacking any context beyond the hot spots mentioned by Rice, posts began using the term *transformational diplomacy* to cover a multitude of concerns, ranging from outreach to the Lebanese diaspora in Brazil, to a post visit of the USS *Cowpens* Navy cruiser in Vladivostok, to a funding gap for a U.S. pavilion at the Shanghai Expo. At its worst, "transformational diplomacy" became a catchall term to justify costs or staff for new programs.

A test of any policy is whether it outlives the incumbent who first articulated it. By this standard, Rice's initiative indeed made an impact, although whether she would agree with all that is being done in the name of transformational diplomacy remains an open question. In retrospect, all the speeches, articles, and debates in Washington and the foreign policy think tanks about whether U.S. foreign policy should be soft, smart, or transformational seem almost irrelevant when set against the incredible challenges diplomats faced in many of the countries mentioned.

Rice's second speech made a revealing point about the tentativeness and uncertainty in charting a new course. "There are no precedents or playbooks for this work. We are trying to do things, quite literally, that have never been done before." She referred to earlier periods of international upheaval, quoting Dean Acheson, who wrote, "The significance of events was shrouded in ambiguity. We groped after interpretations of them, sometimes reversed lines of action based on earlier views, and hesitated long before grasping what now seems obvious."[35]

Given the intellectual honesty of that admission, Rice seemed curiously eager to buy into a new scenario in which diplomats would work alongside the military, as she tried in the Georgetown speeches to provide the intellectual underpinnings for why that might be a good idea. What's missing from her speeches is any sense that she had taken the pulse of the field. Diplomats had been serving alongside the military in Iraq since 2003. There should have been ample institutional memory available to her of what worked and what didn't. In general, the conversations among foreign policy luminaries failed to connect to the concerns of real-life diplomats, many of whom were still asking a legitimate question: How will America's diplomats work in war zones?

Iraq was only one of the critical threat posts—officers wrote equally compelling cables about Afghanistan and Pakistan. The Iraq cables from 2006 to 2010—some 6,651 in total—are not the output of officers triumphantly crowing that they had it figured out. They would be the first to insist they did not. The multiplicity of ethnicities within these countries would take a lifetime to decipher, not to mention fluency in more than one of the many languages spoken in the region.

What makes the Iraq cables noteworthy, and newly relevant given the subsequent unraveling of Iraq in 2014, are the stories they tell of officers, often ill prepared, gamely trying and making the most of the skills they had and experiencing the small victories that come from connecting with people, however fleetingly. They wrote cables because they wanted to let it be known to Washington that they had shown up and done their best in tough circumstances, reason enough to write home.

- - - - - - - - - - - - - - -

Chapter 9

HILLARY CLINTON:
The Good Enough Secretary

- - - - - - - - - - - - - - -

Our challenge is to be clear-eyed about the world as it is while never losing sight of the world as we want it to become. That's why I don't mind that I've been called both an idealist and realist over the years. I prefer being considered a hybrid, perhaps an idealistic realist. Because I, like our country, embody both tendencies.

—*Hillary Rodham Clinton*
Hard Choices

- - - - - - - - - - - - - - -

SECRETARY OF STATE HILLARY CLINTON RECEIVED tens of thousands of cables from American embassies and consulates around the world. Although relatively few would make it to her desk, one of her greatest assets going into the job was the foreign service officers and locally employed staff who could give her unvarnished reports from the field. The cables carried analyses, contradictory viewpoints, and occasionally pleas. They revealed the fault lines between Washington's worldview, by turns both overly neat and overly calamitous, and the minefields American diplomats walk through each day.

These cables matter, because Clinton's record as secretary of state says a good deal about how she would manage foreign policy as president. Her willingness to consider and act upon messages from American officers on the front lines of diplomacy is of direct relevance, especially when those messages diverged from her own views or contradicted conventional wisdom. She is running on her record, which is a fair predictor of her foreign policy priorities. Should she win, she will carry her recent experiences as secretary of state into the White House, and they will influence the kind of candidate she will pick for her old job, secretary of state, along with the many other appointees who will form her foreign policy team. Counterpoised against her own track record, the leaked cables provide clues about how she might structure her foreign policy apparatus.

As it happens, the WikiLeaks cables are not the only behind-the-scenes lens through which to judge Clinton's performance as secretary. Her still-jelling legacy was shaken in March 2015 when mainstream media reported that she had exclusively used a personal email account to conduct business as secretary of state and had some 55,000 pages of emails on a personal server. While the emails—usually quick exchanges between Clinton and senior staffers—serve a different purpose than reporting cables, they do offer additional insight into tone, priorities, and managerial style. They tend to confirm a sense that Clinton, whose term as secretary was generally seen as successful, was not a strategic foreign policy thinker and that she and her overseas missions saw the world from different optics. She offers a contrast with some of her predecessors, particularly Condoleezza Rice and Madeleine Albright, who came to the job with doctoral degrees in foreign policy–related fields, as did George Shultz (with a PhD in economics). Colin Powell brought a worldview informed by military service, Warren Christopher was a distinguished attorney, and James Baker had held high-level posts in the departments of commerce and the treasury and in the White House. Clinton was different, coming to the job primarily as a politician. She is one of a handful of modern-era senators to serve as secretary of state and the only first lady to have done so. More than her predecessors, Clinton often used the secretaryship as a means of translating her domestic policy agenda. She played to her strengths, many of which served her well. But few would assess her tenure as brilliant.

In general, Clinton was admired by the foreign service. She traveled hard, worked harder, and brought can-do energy to the job. She came in as a known entity with a worldwide reputation, and she benefited from a global mood swing. The transition from George W. Bush to Barack Obama brought with it a long-needed lift in America's world standing, and in the first part of her tenure, the giddy enthusiasm overseas for the Obama-Clinton foreign policy team was palpable. America's international approval ratings surged, with foreign ministry doors swinging open and heads of state clamoring for visits. Most foreign service officers credited Clinton as a key part of that change and were proud to be on her team.

The Washington foreign policy establishment was less kind in its assessment of her tenure. Deputy National Security Advisor Denis McDonough's 2010 characterization, "She's really the principal implementer," was interpreted as a barely polite way of saying that she was never really part of Obama's inner circle.[1] In some ways that distance has stood her in good stead. Many of the Obama administration foreign policy failures, some of which came to light after her departure, cannot stick to her. On the other hand, the vaunted Russian "reset," an attempt to improve the long-souring bilateral relationship, is dead; the Islamic State has negated American advances in Iraq; and the Arab Spring's initial promise was eclipsed by violence, instability, and less, rather than more, democracy. The Burma rapprochement is tainted by human rights violations against the Rohingya people; there has been no progress on the Israeli-Palestinian conflict; and the situation in Syria has disintegrated further.

More troubling is the relatively few successes she can claim. Clinton universally gets points for being a stand-up secretary. As *Washington Post* columnist David Ignatius put it, "She is willing to go anywhere, meet anyone, travel to the most remote, god-awful conferences, and press the global flesh," while Brookings vice president and former senior State Department official Martin Indyk noted peevishly that she was "turning up for a president who prefers to remain as aloof as possible in a world that demands engagement."[2] Clinton proved to be good at engaging. She readily grasped the logic of reaching beyond the cloistered world of foreign ministries and connected with the global public. She had good strategic instincts at home, too, forging an alliance with former Defense Secretary Robert Gates—a telling move that underscored the fact that they were both Obama administration outsiders.

Unfortunately, that's where the good news stops. The list of accomplishments seems fairly short for a secretary of her stature, especially when weighed against her successor's opening to Cuba and achievement of an Iran nuclear deal. Clinton had a penchant for racking up second tier wins: renewed relations in Burma; the Asian "pivot," an attempt to recognize the growing economic and political importance of that region when the explosive Middle East allowed any time for it; and the Internet freedom agenda, promoting freedom of speech in hopes that it would lead to democracy. Clinton would no doubt add the State Department's first-ever Quadrennial Diplomacy and Development Review, a blueprint for managerial planning and accountability, but such a bureaucratic triumph is hardly a recruitment poster for the next generation of adventure-seeking diplomats.

The embassy cables rebut some of the nastiest Washington criticism, but they document a troubling disconnect between Clinton and her embassies on the question of how to advance the lot of women. Second, they expose a "yes, but" rebuttal to key Washington initiatives such as the Russian reset. And occasionally, they reveal opportunities that called for a bolder, nontraditional approach that a risk-averse Clinton was either unable or unwilling to take.

Finally, they reflect an absence of meaningful conversation about how to implement transformational diplomacy. Clinton, by all accounts a better manager than Rice, might have initiated a dialogue on at least some of the elements her predecessor had announced— particularly the global repositioning of the foreign service and the ongoing and controversial collaboration with the military. As secretary of state, Clinton proved to be more doer than thinker, more tactician than strategist. Her reputation guaranteed access to the greatest minds of the American foreign policy establishment, but when she built her team she leaned toward trusted operatives and loyalists. Many of these hires were competent people, but few were leading thinkers in diplomacy, which was also a new field for Clinton. The emails underscore the access of inner circle acolytes such as Cheryl Mills, Huma Abedin, and Phillippe Reines.

Her speeches eschewed the theoretical and intellectual aspects of policymaking in favor of sweeping statements and broad-brush pronouncements. She frequently spoke of smart power and her aim to integrate diplomacy, development assistance, and military force "while also tapping the energy and ideas of the private sector and empowering citizens, especially the activists, organizers, and problem solvers we call civil society."[3] What she didn't say was *how* she would go about it, especially in a world where most foreign ministries still operate within the confines of traditional diplomacy. Transformational diplomacy was meant to be a process, and some of its more revolutionary aspects would require check-ins and refinements along the way. What is missing, along with a vision, is dialogue with practitioners in the field. While the WikiLeaks cables showed they had plenty to say, the Clinton emails suggest a reason for the lack of impact: her inner circle was often distracted, already positioning for the run for the White House. The emails reveal a sometimes fawning group of acolytes intensively monitoring Clinton's image. These range from the innocuous "you look cute" comment from Cheryl Mills on the soon-to-be iconic photo of a determined-looking Clinton texting on her BlackBerry to an analysis of her *Meet the Press* appearance from then-spokesman Philippe Reines. The appearance was apparently orchestrated to push back on a comment from Vice President Biden in July 2009 that Russia was a "withering" nation, but Reines was clearly reaching for new ways to praise his boss. "Whenever you do something big on TV we all hear from lots of folks saying you did great. But this time is noticeably different . . . You were definitely on your game. You either threw a perfect game—or at least a no hitter. So this couldn't have gone better, achieved everything we needed to times 10, and comes on the heels of a great 10 days . . ."[4]

The emails show the inner circle forwarding promises of future political support from George Soros and making disparaging remarks about the Obama team. Sidney Blumenthal conveyed a recommendation from former ambassador John Kornblum that Clinton should cultivate a relationship with German chancellor Angela Merkel, who evidently did not like "the atmospherics surrounding the Obama phenomenon." He also had withering comments about senior Obama advisers David Axelrod and Robert Gibbs, calling their appearance on Sunday talk shows "rock bottom performances exposing utter political vacuity."[5]

Former adviser Neera Tanden, in answer to a question on domestic health policy reform, wrote, "The president's policy instincts are to do good and decent things, but the rest of the Administration is just, well, beyond complicated. It's a bit too much for email." And in a discussion about an article assessing the Obama administration's Asian "pivot," Clinton asked aide Jake Sullivan about the term: "Didn't we, not the WH, first use the 'pivot'?" It's fair to note that any secretary of state has to rely on a team of mere mortals to handle the boring and routine stuff, which evidently included complex charts on who gets to ride with her in the limousine. But in 55,000 pages of emails, one would expect to see more focus on foreign policy, strategy, and vision.

THE "DAMN EMAILS"

Like the phases of grief, those on the receiving end of a serious political scandal pass through several stages: confusion, denial, obfuscation, arrogance, and at long last, contrition.

As the 55,000 pages of emails came to light, Clinton tried an initial strategy of lighthearted jokes and dismissiveness. She was aided by content that showed her struggling to operate a secure fax machine and searching for emoticons on her new BlackBerry, a good way to humanize a woman to all those who have ever struggled with a new piece of technology. Other emails are inane—her search for the show *Homeland*, reactions to how she arranged her hair, and enthusiastic comments about her appearance from sycophantic staff.

But for her critics, her handling of the situation revealed a tone deafness to an issue on which she is increasingly vulnerable—the idea of being above the rules. Her explanations that it was "more convenient" and that carrying two phones made her handbag too heavy were unpersuasive.

Clinton staffers contributed to the problem in several ways: when getting wind of a possible investigation, they deleted emails deemed to be "personal," a unilateral decision that later had to be walked back, causing Clinton further embarrassment. They then sent the emails to the State Department as printed hard copies, which meant the department spent several months retyping the messages electronically, prolonging a news story that should have been put to rest quickly.

The State Department's decision to release the emails as they were read and classified on a monthly basis gave the story very long legs. The media seized on each new release looking for revelations, leading in turn to new headlines and new questions which, to the annoyance of Clinton and her supporters, distracted the public from her presidential campaign.

For some, the most concerning aspect was her inability to deal with the problem and put it behind her. Six months into the scandal Democratic elected officials, many of them Clinton supporters, were willing to go on the record, exasperated that she had allowed the situation to run on and on.[6] Clinton's supporters turned their focus on the State Department, overwhelmed by flurries of Freedom of Information Act (FOIA) requests from media and watchdog organizations. Senior department officials, under pressure from federal judges to speed up the process, explained that while they hoped to hire fifty more staffers to handle the volume, they had made offers to only a few dozen applicants, and only three had started working by mid-October.[7] The department had fallen behind by the end of 2015, further prolonging the story.

Clinton got help from an unexpected quarter at the October 2015 Democratic presidential debate when rival Senator Bernie Sanders (I-VT), with evident exasperation, said, "The American people are sick and tired of hearing about your damn emails!" The line got laughs and applause, but not everyone was happy.

Defenders point out ambiguities in the laws at the time—detractors would call them loopholes. Others say the problem is symptomatic of big data and that the entire U.S. government is drowning under the weight of emails that must be archived for the public record. The State Department alone produces 2 billion emails a year. Agencies are required to classify the information, which inevitably leads to the painstaking job of declassifying it, a job requiring reading, analysis, substantive knowledge, and subjective judgment—all of which takes time and money.[8]

As in many aspects of Clinton's tenure, it is the small things that matter. The emails revealed the enormous power and close relationships she has with a handful of carefully selected staff. The emails revealed that two of them, Chief of Staff Cheryl Mills and Deputy Chief of Staff Huma Abedin, argued over a staffing change in Clinton's protective detail. This is a telling exchange. Career officers follow a strict "needs of the service" assignment policy that, as was discussed in chapter 8, sends them to some of the toughest places in the world, occasionally unaccompanied by family. The "needs of the service" imperative is the most frequently heard phrase for officers and supervisors alike come transfer season. But this exchange between Abedin and Mills showed that the needs of Clinton threatened to trump the needs of the service.

Abedin was upset that a trusted security agent was about to be transferred, and she argued that he had given them wider leeway—an unsubtle indication that rules don't apply. "[Redacted] just filled me in on your conversations. I would have appreciated a chance to discuss this before it was finalized," Abedin wrote Mills. The person, she continued, "has been a HUGE asset protecting our interests and balancing usss [U.S. Secret Service] politics. He has gone above and beyond in every way and anyone more stringent will make our life and travel more complicated. Starting from scratch with someone else is going to be challenging."

Protective details are all about being stringent—even when it makes life and travel more complicated. That's their job. Starting from scratch is a normal part of the foreign service, where tours are seldom longer than two or three years.

Mills took the high road stating that the transfer would offer "an opportunity for career growth and development for [redacted] something I know you support . . . We should embrace and reward that, even when it means we have to make new adjustments . . . This is rotation time and while I am sure if asked he would stay, he would miss the chance to manage the security at the [redacted]."[9]

In such trivia lie larger truths. In this instance at least, the emails support the notion that in the Clinton State Department expedience sometimes prevailed over following the rules.

WOMEN'S RIGHTS ARE
HUMAN RIGHTS

Clinton owns the women's rights issue like no one else in Washington. At a watershed speech at the Fourth World Conference on Women in Beijing in 1995, she had told the world that "human rights are women's rights and women's rights are human rights," and she has never looked back. "The message of Beijing and the lifetime of work it represented had become so much a part of my identity it was practically written into my DNA," she wrote in her memoirs.[10]

Following the Beijing speech, she, former secretary of state Madeleine Albright, and then-ambassador Swanee Hunt laid the groundwork in Vienna in 1997 for an organization to promote the empowerment of women. The Vital Voices Democracy Initiative was launched with funds from the U.S. government, along with the United Nations, the European Union, the Nordic Council of Ministers, the World Bank, and the Inter-American Development Bank. By 2000, the organization had evolved into the Vital Voices Global Partnership, a nonprofit, nongovernmental organization, the purpose of which is to "identify, invest in and bring visibility to extraordinary women around the world by unleashing their leadership potential to transform lives and accelerate peace and prosperity in their communities."[11]

No one argues with the goals of Vital Voices. Embassy officers have seen firsthand and reported on how women in many parts of the world face violence, abuse, and stultifying poverty; are denied education and the tools of economic betterment such as lines of credit and bank accounts; and are shut out of participation in government. Apart from being unfair, holding women back holds societies back.

The problem, at least in the early years, was that a very American message about enabling women to become "agents of change" was entangled with cultural hubris. The United States has a history of missteps in this field. As we saw in the discussion on anti-Americanism, Bush administration under secretary Karen Hughes's gaffes to all-female audiences in Turkey, Egypt, and Saudi Arabia were heavily reported, as was her audiences' anger at her presumptuous characterization of their lives. American foreign service officers living overseas were more likely to understand such cultural nuances but were rarely asked their opinion on how to address women's issues outside the United States. There is no indication that Clinton's team had any inkling how tricky the initiative might be.

Vital Voices' privileged pedigree gave it traction with ambassadors and embassies, but it didn't always translate locally. Cultural differences sometimes contrasted with the very American can-do image the organization promoted. For example, women in post-Communist countries were suspicious, recalling how the Communist party exploited women's issues for propaganda purposes. There was sometimes a naive assumption that the goals of Vital Voices were so universal that every woman in every country and society must embrace them.

Vital Voices' outreach overseas proved awkward. Washington staffers relied heavily on help from embassies to run its seminars, programs, and training sessions. This led to demands made on behalf of well-connected big names in Washington and left local embassy staff scrambling to accommodate them. Training sessions were often funded through already strained embassy public diplomacy budgets and representational funds (earmarked for embassy receptions), diverting resources from other post-designed programs that had been calibrated to address unique local issues, which ranged from Muslim outreach to indigenous rights to environmental protection, among other themes. Vital Voices staffers didn't always listen to public affairs officers, and their stubborn insistence on doing it their way led to a canned approach, consisting of a reliance on blockbuster conferences but little follow-through. For embassies already straining to staff reporting requirements for human rights, religious freedom, trafficking in persons, and setting up programs for congressional delegations, Vital Voices became just one more Washington-mandated chore.

The big names swept in and swept out, leaving embassies to sweep up. A week after a conference it was hard to see any impact. The organization's political clout in Washington ensured a virtuous circle of triumphal reporting cables, and embassies found it easier to claim victory than take the fall. There is no analysis, no frank discussion of the organization's limitations. Of the sixty-some WikiLeaks cables mentioning Vital Voices, the organization frequently comes in for a mention only when a post was asked to enumerate a laundry list of women's outreach efforts or in debriefings of participants returning from conferences. Everyone is always "energized, empowered, and excited." Reporting on measurable results is vague. The danger of such perfunctory reporting was that it perpetuated more programs in more countries.

The Vital Voices experience suggests the limits of relying on embassies for advancing agendas. The lack of follow-up with conference participants does not reflect indifference but rather the limitations of embassies already tasked with advocating for so many policies with limited time and resources. As Vital Voices gained experience, it shifted away from embassies and began working directly with local NGOs. Removing the embassy as middleman was probably a good move—allowing Vital Voices an opportunity to invest in sustained contact with women leaders who embraced its goals and could work directly with the organization. No one argues that Vital Voices as it exists today hasn't benefited tens of thousands of women, but its early days show what can happen when programming in the field is directed by Washington.

Clinton's use of the State Department as a platform for advancing women's issues goes back a long way. At one time the women's agenda was the purview of State's Bureau of Democracy, Human Rights, and Labor, but the first Clinton administration created a new office, the Senior Coordinator for International Women's Issues, authorized by Congress in 1994. That entity evolved into the current Office of

Global Women's Issues, which ensures that the rights of women and girls are fully integrated into the formulation and conduct of U.S. foreign policy.[12]

Keeping a focus on women throughout the U.S. government required interagency coordination, so in 1995 President Clinton created the President's Interagency Council on Women, headed by Hillary Clinton as honorary chair and Madeleine Albright as council chair. The body was initially charged with seeing that gains made at the Beijing conference would be implemented throughout the federal government, and the Council headed U.S. activities around the Beijing Plus Five, a special session of the UN General Assembly to review implementation of the Beijing Platform for Action, a comprehensive document enumerating how women and girls are affected by global issues such as poverty, education, health, violence and armed conflict, economic development, governmental leadership roles, human rights, media, and environment.

The council lasted until 2003, when it was disbanded by President Bush, an indication, perhaps, that the government's role in global women's issues is not without controversy. The experience offered Clinton a cautionary tale: presidentially created entities could be dismantled. A decade later she ensured that the position she created for the ambassador-at-large for women's issues would have better long-term prospects, convincing President Obama to sign a memorandum making it permanent and ensuring that the position reported to the secretary of state. The first appointee, Melanne Verveer, came from the Vital Voices operation and had the access and the profile to make a big splash.

Clinton as secretary of state had no patience for stragglers on women's issues and insisted on their priority. As she recalled in *Hard Choices*, "Women's issues had long been relegated to the margins of U.S. foreign policy and international diplomacy, considered at best a nice thing to work on but hardly a necessity . . . We had to push tradition-bound bureaus and agencies to think differently about the

role of women in conflicts and peacemaking, economic and democratic development, public health, and more."[13] She went on to say:

> Even at home in Washington our work on behalf of women was
> often seen as a parenthetical exercise, somehow separate from the
> important work of foreign policy. In one *Washington Post* arti-
> cle about our efforts with women in Afghanistan, an unnamed
> administration official sniffed, "Gender issues are going to have
> to take a backseat to other priorities ... There's no way we can be
> successful if we maintain every special interest and pet project.
> All those pet rocks in our rucksack were taking us down." I have
> to admit, I got tired of watching otherwise thoughtful people
> just smile and nod when I brought up the concerns of women
> and girls.[14]

An alternative interpretation of the quote that so troubled Clinton
might be fatigue and exasperation with Washington's habit of chas-
ing too many priorities with too few dollars. Single-issue advocacy
of the latest policy trend can make those tasked with implementing
new directives feel as though they are operating with no overarching
strategy. Clinton's impatience also revealed a lack of political space
for nuanced points of view on women's issues. It should not be heresy
to suggest that in some countries at certain moments, women's issues,
vital though they are, might need to take a back seat. Clinton might
have done better to consider why the person quoted believed this to
be true. She would have heard that cultural complexities—especially
in war-torn places like Afghanistan—were getting trampled under
the relentless march of multiple Washington directives from multiple
agencies.

Several factors combined to suggest a communications problem
over women's issues, and American diplomats were an audience Clinton needed to reach. As one example, at a time when many were
still redefining their roles in the age of transformational diplomacy,

female foreign service officers were battling low promotion rates and low representation at the highest ranks. Some had been advised to focus on hardcore policy issues such as trade, economics, and arms control and to avoid career-slowing backwaters such as women's issues. Scores of foreign service women had in some cases put off marriages and pregnancies to be "all in" for the rigors of a job that now featured unaccompanied assignments to Iraq, Afghanistan, and Pakistan, service in countries requiring mefloquine and other anti-malarial prophylaxes with side effects, and postings in which the best treatment for any medical complication might be the next flight out. This, too, was part of transformational diplomacy.

A second factor was the knowledge gap. As gender studies have matured, there is an ever-growing body of specialized knowledge, literature, and scholarly thought leaders. Being a woman in an embassy hardly qualified one as an expert on global women's issues. Few officers had the background to be authoritative advocates, and not every female foreign service officer shares an innate passion for women's issues.

A third factor was that some American women in the diplomatic corps were uncomfortable working on women's issues when the United States suffered in comparison to countries with more family-friendly policies. Women in Western Europe have access to paid maternity leave for months and sometimes years, child care is heavily subsidized, and working hours are more family friendly. As one foreign service officer put it, "How am I supposed to advocate for women's issues when my own country won't even give me time off for breast-feeding?" That only changed relatively recently with the Affordable Care Act of 2010. For nursing mothers, the State Department headquarters building offered many reminders that diplomacy had long been a male domain. Bathrooms featured outmoded toilets, and for years there was no private place for nursing mothers who wanted to pump breast milk. Overseas, embassies had even fewer facilities.

Finally, there is the definitional problem of what constitutes global women's issues. Clinton's tendency to focus on women in the developing world meant she missed (or ignored) conversations in the developed world. In many embassies, women were not talking about honor killings in Pakistan but about Sheryl Sandberg's book *Lean In*, Marissa Mayer's chances of success as CEO of Yahoo, and Anne-Marie Slaughter's frustration as evinced in her *Atlantic* article "Why Women Still Can't Have It All," the most-read article in the history of the magazine, and one uniquely relevant to Clinton's State Department, given Slaughter's position.

Clinton's reply to Slaughter's "manifesto" unfortunately got mangled in a quote to a reporter from the magazine *Marie Claire*, in which the secretary seemed to be saying, stop your whining. In the wave of media interest that followed, the State Department released a transcript that made it clear that the "whining" remark was in response to the interviewer's tangential question on the character of Holden Caulfield from the book *Catcher in the Rye*. That helped somewhat, but Clinton's annoyed tone was still troubling.

The reporter wrote,

When I asked Clinton about Slaughter's claim that "juggling high-level governmental work with the needs of two teenage boys was not possible," Clinton's disapproval was palpable. She reminded me that she has spent her career advocating on behalf of women, that she is committed to the idea that "it's important for our workplaces . . . to be more flexible and creative in enabling women to continue to do high-stress jobs while caring for not only children, but (also) aging parents." But, she said, Slaughter's problems were her own. "Some women are not comfortable working at the pace and intensity you have to work at in these jobs . . . Other women don't break a sweat. They have four or five, six kids. They're highly organized, they have very supportive networks."[15]

The Clinton emails reveal another angle—Anne-Marie Slaughter's shock over her boss's reaction to her article. She emailed Mills and Abedin under the subject line "I am really devastated," and asked, "Is she really talking about me? I have been 500 percent supportive and loyal in every possible way I can be? Can I at least talk to her?" Abedin reassured her that Clinton's comments were not accurate. "There is a lot going on here and philippe has been pushing back hard." Subsequent emails show Slaughter did get a chance to talk with Clinton, but Clinton never enlarged the dialogue with other women at the State Department. In other emails Slaughter nudged Clinton to leave for the holidays on December 21 (so that others might also do so) and praised her for working from home on a snow day. Clinton's perfunctory replies suggest bafflement at best or tone deafness at worst over work-life balance issues.[16]

Clinton had missed an opportunity to weigh in on a new direction in the debate on women in the workplace—and link it to similar debates taking place beyond U.S. borders. This issue is never as simple as being highly organized and having supportive networks. It resonates for women in public life as well as those in ordinary jobs. In 2014, Michèle Flournoy took herself out of the running to replace Chuck Hagel as secretary of defense on family grounds.[17]

Another example of Clinton's rigidity on women's issues was continuance of the annual Women of Courage Awards begun under Secretary Rice. A case could be made that it was time to review this practice. The annual ritual of seeking out women who qualify for the adjective of "courageous" often meant embassies nominated women who suffered violent physical abuse, perpetuating the notion of women as victims, as was recounted in the "Frenemies" chapter. That view spilled over into other aspects of reporting, with embassies supplying depressing quantities of examples. The leaked cables offer 13,619 reports on trafficking (mostly concerning women), 3,002 on rape, and nearly a thousand more on other forms of violence against women.

There are other ways to celebrate women in countries undergoing change: as innovators, entrepreneurs, researchers, and leaders. In response to Clinton's request to integrate women's issues into the broader work of the State Department, embassy reporting became more interesting. The USEU Mission reported that the "EU was looking for guidance and increased cooperation and participation . . . ensuring issues affecting women continue to be a focus of EU foreign policy in a way that supports U.S. interests."[18] The U.S. embassy in London wrote about its outreach to minority communities and its sophisticated partnership with British government agencies.[19]

Embassy Kabul, surely on the front lines of women's issues, described a dramatic meeting between the Afghan Women's Network, an umbrella group of seventy women's NGOs and the government's lead official on reintegration and reconciliation efforts. This was a major effort, overseen and encouraged by the United States, to bring together multiple facets of Afghan society, including insurgents. The cable reported that the women pressed the official on concerns that the government would focus on the south, further tipping the balance of development resources and efforts away from the safer provinces in the central and northern regions. In a stunningly patronizing display, the official asked the women for a two-page paper on this complex topic. The embassy commented that the women "are unlikely to accept that submitting a two-page paper on their views suffices; rather they rightfully expect women to be involved in the negotiating process."[20]

Embassy New Delhi's EST (Environment, Science, and Technology) officer noted a troubling absence of Indian women scientists from conferences, laboratories, and universities and hosted a workshop to better understand the hurdles they had to leap to be successful in their society. The women said that caste, the rural versus urban divide, and social customs in which they are expected to place family considerations first were largely to blame.

The Indian scientific establishment tends to be rigidly stove-piped with scientists often spending their entire careers climbing the ladder within a single institution. This organizational structure offers little or no consideration for work-life balance. Those who take time off for family often find they are not welcome back in the workplace, and there are no opportunities for part-time work, flexible hours or work-based childcare facilities to accommodate family demands.[21]

The search for a work-life balance became a drumbeat in reporting everywhere from Malta—where a conference on female entrepreneurship considered best practices for a work-life balance—to Malaysia, where the embassy said the women's minister cited work-life balance as one of what she called four adversities affecting women.[22]

Embassy Warsaw wrote that even though women run a third of all companies in Poland, "Polish women find it difficult to balance an active professional career with family life."[23] In Shanghai, the Women's Federation hosted a meeting of women mayors that focused on Shanghai's economic development but also looked at how to maintain a healthy work life.[24] In Japan, the minister of state for Consumer Affairs, Food Safety, Social Affairs and Gender Equality, when asked about ways in which the United States and Japan could cooperate on empowering women, said, "We need to find ways of improving the work-life balance."[25]

MISSILE DEFENSE AND THE RUSSIAN RESET

Woody Allen once said that 80 percent of life is showing up, an adage that could well serve as a motto for diplomacy's many ceremonial tasks.[26] There are wreath layings, national days, inaugurations, receptions, commemorations, and state funerals. While there is usually no substance in these, there is great symbolic value in showing the flag and having productive conversations with other world leaders on the margins of the main event.

The presence of the United States can catapult a ceremony to the A list, and the question of who will lead the U.S. delegation is watched intensely. Jokes aside, vice presidents do, in fact, attend a lot of funerals, but some are so important that the president himself will go. Obama attended Nelson Mandela's memorial service in 2013 and would have attended Polish president Lech Kaczynski's funeral in 2010 had it not been for a cloud of volcanic ash that spread across northern Europe, closing Polish airspace to all flights. Obama caught flak from conservatives for skipping Margaret Thatcher's funeral in 2013, which only rated two former secretaries of state from previous administrations, yet the death of Václav Havel in 2011 brought Secretary of State Clinton, former president Clinton, and former secretary of state Madeleine Albright.

Sometimes a purely ceremonial event becomes more than the sum of its parts. This was surely the case for the Polish seventieth anniversary commemoration of the beginning of World War II. The Poles always meant for it to be a big deal, and the date, commemorating events that included the Holocaust, the deaths of millions, and an all-out U.S. military engagement, could hardly have caught Obama by surprise. Yet the administration was oddly resistant to any meaningful involvement in the Poles' September 1, 2009, ceremony, despite the presence of Vladimir Putin, Angela Merkel, Gordon Brown, Nicolas Sarkozy, and many other heads of state. The United States initially planned to send a very former secretary of defense, William Perry, who had served from 1994 to 1997. The Poles pressed for a currently serving official, and finally, days before the ceremony, the administration announced it would send National Security Advisor General James Jones.

This tiny tempest had overtones that were not only symbolic but cumulative, seen by some observers as one in a series of actions in which the Obama administration and the Clinton State Department were devaluing Central and Eastern Europe. The Polish commemoration came amid a succession of diplomatic dustups in the administration's approach to the region, encapsulated by the Russian "reset," a policy initiative that seemed to demand ever more concessions to Russia from the United States. One of those friction points involved the missile defense program.

Missile defense, revived under the George W. Bush administration, called for the placement of Patriot missiles in Poland and a radar tracking station in the Czech Republic. A relatively modest proposal, the Patriots would be limited to ten, and the X-band radar station, looking like a gigantic white golf ball, was to be moved from its site on an atoll in the Marshall Islands and rebuilt in a village outside of Prague. The two installations would work in tandem to defend against missile threats from Iran.

Russia cried foul, insisting that any defensive system was a red line and a violation of prior arms control treaties, destabilizing the carefully negotiated nuclear balance of power. Each step of progress on missile defense brought new and hostile declarations from Putin and Medvedev, including threats to place offensive missiles in Kaliningrad, a Russian enclave sandwiched between Poland and Lithuania, that would target missile defense installations. The rhetorical escalation alarmed many Europeans. When a Russian general warned Poland, "This will not go unpunished," NATO Secretary General Jaap de Hoop Scheffer dismissed it as a "pathetic remark," but others were less sanguine.

Installation of the system deeply divided many Poles and Czechs, too. The Atlanticists among them loved the idea of a security guarantee that would pull them ever farther westward and provide an added layer of security on top of NATO. Opponents—and there were many—attacked the idea of foreign troops—even NATO allies—stationed on their soil, becoming a potential target, militarizing their countries, and despoiling the environment. In Poland, after tough negotiations, Secretary Rice and Foreign Minister Radoslaw Sikorski signed an agreement in late summer of 2008. It took considerable political capital from Czech politicians to push the agreement through the upper house of parliament, which was signed in July 2008 by Rice and Czech foreign minister Karel Schwarzenberg. An agreement in the Czech lower house proved more elusive, as Obama's election and his administration's subsequent announcement of a missile defense policy review took the wind from the sails.

Days after his inauguration, President Obama sent a secret letter to Russian president Dmitri Medvedev offering to scrap plans for missile defense in Poland and the Czech Republic if the Russians would agree to stop Iran from developing long-range nuclear weapons.[27] Three weeks later Obama's letter leaked, causing upset in Poland and the Czech Republic, as much for the lack of consultation as for the content. And on February 7, 2009, mere weeks after the inauguration, Vice President Joe Biden used the now infamous "reset" word at the Munich Security Conference, the Wehrkunde. "The last few years have seen a dangerous drift in relations between Russia and our alliance. It's time to press the reset button and to revisit the many areas where we can and should work together."[28]

Secretary of Defense Gates echoed that idea in a speech on February 20, 2009, at a NATO meeting in Krakow, Poland. "I told the Russians a year ago that if there were no Iranian missile program, there would be no need for the missile sites." Obama's inauguration, he said, offered the chance to start again. "My hope is that now, with the new administration, the prospects for that kind of cooperation might have improved."[29]

Gates, of all people, should have been aware of Central European sensibilities on the issue of Russian involvement. In a visit to Prague while still in the Bush administration, Gates had let slip that a possible "Russian presence" at the radar site might assuage Russian sensitivities to the program. The thought of any sort of Russian military or inspection workers on Czech soil, coupled with the tacit admission that the Czech government had not been consulted before the offer was made, produced a firestorm in Czech media and weakened an already teetering coalition government in Prague.[30]

The embassy was straightforward in describing the damage. "Foreign Minister Schwarzenberg told the Ambassador he was 'surprised and disappointed.' . . . He was even stronger with a visiting American that same weekend, complaining that the U.S. 'announcement' about the Russian invitation to the radar site 'had been made with no prior warning' to the [government of the Czech Republic], which was 'an embarrassment to him.'"[31] In unusually pointed language, the embassy relayed that both the deputy prime minister and deputy foreign minister complained of "continued USG inability to consult and coordinate fully with the Czechs and Poles in advance of important USG negotiations (e.g., with Russia) or announcements (e.g., the NIE [National Intelligence Estimate])."[32]

Against this backdrop of a potential policy shift in an uneasy region, Clinton met her counterpart, Russian foreign minister Sergei Lavrov, for the first time as secretary of state in Geneva on March 6. She and her staff had embraced the idea of a gag gift—a big red button bearing the word RESET. Clinton's instinct to inject a bit of humor in a frosty relationship might have worked save for two factors. Despite a wealth of Russian-speaking advisors, the word for *reset* was mangled in the translation as "overcharged." Lavrov was ungentlemanly enough to point this out publicly, embarrassing Clinton and her team. He then took the innocent gesture to draconian lengths, suggesting the red button was less reminiscent of a computer keyboard than a nuclear hot button. "It is a very, very large red button," he said. "I do hope that Russia and the United States and other countries would never ever push any other buttons associated with initiation of destructive hostilities."[33]

Awkward moments have a way of sticking and the reset became burdened with all the subsequent policy steps, missteps, and reversals. Poles and Czechs were notified of the Obama administration policy review on missile defense but were never an active part of it. The pass over rankled in a region that had witnessed Munich and Yalta, potent symbols of the habits of great powers deciding "about us without us," a phrase that has become something of an unofficial national motto. The Czech government had its own problems, and the coalition collapsed in disarray midway through its European Union presidency in winter of 2009, leaving the Czechs to be governed by a caretaker regime. The coalition, already hanging by a thread, was undone by a few parliamentary defections in a no-confidence vote that came March 24, 2009, a dozen days before hosting the Obama visit and U.S.–EU Summit April 4–5.

By summer 2009, the sense of nervousness in Central and Eastern Europe had grown. Obama's speech at the New Economic School in Moscow had done nothing to reassure skittish officials in Prague and Warsaw. "As I've made it clear this system is directed at preventing a potential attack from Iran. It has nothing to do with Russia . . . But if the threat from Iran's nuclear and ballistic missile program is eliminated, the driving force for missile defense in Europe will be eliminated, and that is in our mutual interests."[34]

The speech rattled the region, and twenty-two Central and Eastern European leaders wrote an unprecedented open letter on July 16 to the Obama administration.[35] Seen as a desperate action by leaders of friendly nations who couldn't seem to get a hearing or find a foothold in the still-new Obama administration, the letter was also read as a sign that something was amiss within the administration to have set off friendly nations so badly. The *New York Times* called it "a remarkable breach of convention" that "boiled down to a public expression of mistrust."[36] The underlying assumption was that such a letter should never have been necessary, and that its public nature was a shot across the bow, with observers noting "open letters are not the typical means by which close partners and allies voice their concerns to one another, and though one could argue with the validity of their arguments, the Obama administration clearly did not receive either the message or the method of delivery very well at all."[37]

Speaking as Atlanticist voices, the writers worried that "all was not well" in the relationship, that "NATO seems weaker," and that Washington didn't understand the threat from Russia. "It uses overt and covert means of economic warfare, ranging from energy blockades and politically motivated investments to bribery and media manipulation in order to advance its interests and to challenge the transatlantic orientation of Central and Eastern Europe." While the writers ostensibly welcomed the reset, they quickly warned, "The danger is that Russia's creeping intimidations and influence peddling in the region could over time lead to a de facto neutralization of the region."

U.S. embassies across Central Europe scrambled to provide context for the letter and sent cables warning about the timing of any announced decision on canceling the missile defense program, along with concerns about its impact on internal politics. In Bratislava, the embassy warned Assistant Secretary Alexander Vershbow of the testy mood within a normally friendly forum, the Slovak Atlantic Council, the country's leading transatlantic-oriented security and defense NGO, where he was scheduled to speak. "You should be aware, however, that there is a good deal of skepticism among this group (which includes several signatories of the CEE open letter) about the direction of U.S. policy. They believe we do not have a strategy toward Russia other than appeasement and they are worried.[38]

The coup de grace arrived on September 17, when the Obama administration abandoned missile defense. It was done in rapid-fire one-hour meetings—just long enough to deliver the blow in person— first with the Poles, then the Czechs, and then at NATO headquarters. The three-member delegation consisting of Under Secretary of Defense for Policy Michèle Flournoy, Lieutenant General Patrick O'Reilly of the Missile Defense Agency, and the State Department's Under Secretary for Arms Control and International Security Affairs Ellen Tauscher delivered the news behind closed doors, answered a few questions, and left what can only be called a mess behind.

Obama's reticence to engage the leaders directly was best symbolized, at least in the Czech case, with a perfunctory midnight phone call to Prime Minister Jan Fischer—a fact Fischer was quick to let the Czech media know. In Poland, the September 17 announcement came on the anniversary of the day the Soviet Union had invaded Poland. Thus World War II–related anniversaries came full circle, managing to haunt the United States twice in one season.

From any political vantage point in Central Europe, it had been a terrible summer. A departing ambassador, Victor Ashe in Warsaw, wrote an end-of-tour cable lecturing Washington on how to put relations "back on track"—a startling tone, even for an official soon to depart. The disappointed Polish reaction to the president's missile defense policy shift did not occur in a vacuum, he argued, nor was it mainly about missile defense. Rather, he wrote, Poles felt their military (and economic) contributions in Europe, Iraq, and Afghanistan were consistently underappreciated.[39]

A week later, thirty-one American officials, some of whom were former ambassadors, wrote their own open letter to Obama, echoing the concerns of the original open letter writers. "Though the signatories of this bipartisan letter have varying views on the merits of your administration's proposed missile defense architecture for Europe, we are united in our concern about the effect that even the perception of U.S. disengagement from Central Europe could have on our allies in the region.[40] In response to the outcry, the administration dispatched Vice President Biden to the region in November 2009 to soothe wounded feelings and put relationships back on track.

As a final symbolic slap to the Czech Atlanticists, the signing of the new START treaty between the United States and Russia on April 8, 2010, which reduced the number of nuclear missile launchers by half and instituted a new inspection and verification process, was held in Prague, a location that resonated with Obama as a bookend to his speech on nuclear nonproliferation a year earlier. The successful conclusion to the treaty negotiations was tightly linked to the administration's willingness to abandon missile defense, and the choice of Prague for the signing sent a discouraging message to those Czechs who continued to see Russia as a security threat.

The Obama administration insisted it had not abandoned missile defense but rather exchanged it for what it called a "European Phased Adaptive Approach," which envisioned a network of radar facilities and interceptor sites in Europe, all focused on threats from Iran. This, too, met with huge opposition from the Kremlin, and in March 2013 Obama would capitulate and drop the most controversial fourth phase of the program, citing budgetary limitations and a need to shift resources to protect against a growing missile threat from North Korea.

Secretary of State Clinton left office in February 2013. Events in Ukraine did not begin until November of that year, and the Russians did not illegally annex Crimea until March 2014. Nonetheless, as secretary of state during the now-infamous Russian reset, she must at least share responsibility for a U.S.–Russia policy that largely failed. The cables leave a damning trail of evidence, not only from Poland and the Czech Republic, but from Ukraine, Georgia, and the Baltics, showing that American diplomats on the ground were sending her plenty of information about Russian destabilization and aggression.

As the Czech politician Alexandr Vondra had warned, the demise of missile defense left the region a different place. Atlanticists were hard to find. "Some statements from the new generation of politicians who incline to realpolitik in Prague, Bratislava, Budapest or even Warsaw have shown that even in those parts of Europe, a pro-Atlantic stance should not be taken for granted."[41] After the Ukraine crisis in 2014, both Czech and Slovak government leaders had a tepid response, dismissing the notion of sanctions and stating that they had no desire for NATO troops on their soil (despite being NATO members) and that Obama's belated initiative to bolster defense in Central and Eastern Europe would have to take place elsewhere.

It's hard to find Clinton's footprints in anything concerning missile defense. The topic is almost absent from her memoirs. She makes the briefest of appearances in the fall of 2010 when the Obama administration turned to the ratification process of the new START accord, a treaty that was negotiated by her State Department. Her contribution centered on finding the necessary votes in the Senate, work for a skilled politician but not necessarily a diplomat.

In some ways, Clinton's absence as a key player in missile defense—and in the Russian reset—might burnish her credentials with Russia skeptics. Her treatment by Lavrov—not only with the reset button but in other encounters—makes her an unlikely champion for any new forays into Russian rapprochement. Her admiration for Walesa and Havel seems genuine and suggests a rapport with the region's Atlanticists that Obama lacked. But as the embassies reported, the heyday of dissidents has waned. A new generation of European politicians has risen with no memories of pre-1989 conditions. Former secretary Albright's iconic statement of the United States as "the indispensable nation," first stated in 1998 as justification for military intervention in Iraq and repeated frequently since, might be contested or puzzling to a younger audience that has neither lived through World War II nor the Communist divide that separated Europe. As pro-democracy dissidents like Havel and Walesa leave the scene, Clinton might find forging partnerships with a new and younger Europe more difficult, thanks to the painful lessons the region learned on missile defense.

A GREAT COMMUNICATOR
FOR A NEW ERA

Forty years ago, no one asked if Henry Kissinger was a great communicator. His job was to think strategically and to propose and carry out global initiatives. If he had something important to announce, he could simply call a press conference. No secretary of state in today's world could replicate his secret trip to China. The public scrutiny he was able to avoid is now a critical part of the job.

Clinton's tenure coincided with an unprecedented era of social media, and new formats for conversation seemed to pop up every week. She proved to be an adept practitioner of all kinds of public diplomacy to reach foreign audiences—often at the end of what must have been exhausting days. The foreign policy establishment has not given nearly enough weight to this job requirement, nor enough credit to her successes. The embassy reporting cables, by contrast, come alive with an enthusiasm that would be hard to fake. Officers from around the world praised her willingness to engage and her knack for outreach.

On a March 2009 visit to Ramallah, Clinton agreed to an interview for a Palestinian youth television show, *Ali Soutik*. According to the consulate, the director of the NGO that produced the program said feedback was overwhelmingly positive. "You cannot believe the phone calls we received, the emails . . . everyone is talking about the [opportunity] Mrs. Clinton has given to Palestinian youth," the director said. The program, which normally attracts half a million viewers, was watched by 1.2 million people, including both President Abbas and Prime Minister Fayyad.[42]

Embassies deployed a new format, called a "townterview," in which Clinton would be interviewed onstage in front of a live, town hall–type audience, usually a mix of civil society leaders, students, NGOs, business professionals, and others. The success of the format requires that the interviewer—as well as the interviewee—engage in a conversational style that plays to the audience. For a while, these hybrid media events were new enough to create news stories of their own, producing an additional publicity bounce.

Clinton tried the format in Bangkok, going onstage with two of Thailand's leading broadcast journalists before an audience of about 250 and a television audience of some 2.4 million. "The event received overwhelmingly positive media coverage, not only for its substantive policy discussions but also due to the witty banter between Secretary Clinton and the co-hosts that created a comfortable, at-ease atmosphere that had the audience erupting in laughter throughout the Townterview."[43]

Clinton used a variation on this theme in her first visit as secretary of state to Turkey in March 2009, agreeing to appear on Turkey's most popular talk show *Come and Join Us,* hosted by four Turkish women and filmed in front of a small studio audience of students and NGO members. She won points for openness and honesty from the cohosts, and the broadcast was hailed in major Turkish newspapers as "the perfect way of practicing public diplomacy to improve the U.S. image in Turkey." She published an article for the Turkish daily *Zaman* in connection with International Women's Day, noting, "Problems today are too big and too complex to be solved without the full participation of women."[44]

Clinton also included one of the first bloggers to join the more traditional traveling press corps on her Asian trip in 2009. Japanese blogger Nozomu Nakaoka wrote an engaging account of how he was invited.

> Last weekend, I received a telephone call from someone at the U.S. Embassy who asked me: "There has been an instruction from the Department of State to include a Japanese blogger in the press corps traveling with Secretary Clinton. You, Mr. Nakaoka, are a blogger, aren't you? Can you join them?" I said in response, "I am a journalist and have my own blog," and I accepted the offer, seeing it as the chance of a lifetime. I heard later on from a U.S. Embassy employee that including a Japanese blogger in the traveling press corps was the Secretary's personal desire.[45]

The cables also reveal some imperfect coordination between Clinton's Washington staff and the embassies. On any given day, the secretary is deluged with media requests from all over the world, and deciding which, if any, interviews to grant is a strategic process. In countries where media outlets are divided strictly along government and opposition lines, such decisions inevitably are an act of taking sides.

One day in 2009, Clinton's State Department staffers decided she should grant an exclusive interview to Venezuela's embattled opposition television Globovision, in which she would announce the role of Costa Rica's Óscar Arias as mediator in the Honduran coup and call for better relations between the United States and Venezuela. However, relations between the United States and Venezuela were at such a low point that no such interview would be seen as innocent or neutral. Even before the interview hit the airwaves, the U.S. embassy in Caracas was fielding complaints. The embassy noted, with some asperity, that it had not been consulted about the interview and had just learned of it before the phones started ringing—an awkward position to be in. They nonetheless tried to soothe Venezuelan feelings without great results.

> The DCM [told the foreign minister] that Chávez had publicly expressed doubts about the true intentions of the U.S. government in Honduras, accused the United States of being behind the coup, and that Clinton was responding to a request for an interview by Globovision that allowed her to speak directly to the Venezuelan people on the issue of Honduras and our hopes for an improved dialogue with Venezuela. The foreign minister protested . . . saying that the Globovision principals were nothing more than coup plotters.[46]

The interview would cause the embassy headaches for months afterward.

THINKING SMALL

One of the themes of Clinton's tenure was the dilemma she articulated in her memoirs, and one that is occasionally posed in diplomatic cables: What happens when U.S. interests conflict with U.S. values?

This question played out in Egypt's Tahrir Square, where an impetuous Obama wanted to be on the right side of history and a clearly torn Clinton counseled caution. It played out in Syria, where Clinton's instinct to arm the rebels fighting the Assad regime clashed with the White House's hesitation. Clinton was forthright in expressing her views but loyal in supporting the president's. A more fundamental question might be: What is the proper role for a modern secretary of state and what can be learned from Clinton's relationship with her embassies?

There are too many places where Clinton was either inactive or sidelined. Clinton has said little about global corruption, despite copious reporting from the embassies. Disarmament was President Obama's initiative. The ongoing problem of Iraq was given to Vice President Biden. Afghanistan and Pakistan belonged, until his death, to Special Envoy Richard Holbrooke. George Mitchell was named special envoy for the Middle East. In fact, the Obama administration named an unprecedented twenty-four special envoys, special representatives, special advisors, and special coordinators for a host of global hotspots. None required Senate confirmation. They operated with staffs ranging from one to thirty, and only eleven of them reported to the secretary of state. Clinton dismissed the notion that she risked becoming marginalized by so many special envoys. "That's not the way I saw it. Appointing people who were qualified to serve as Secretary themselves [she was thinking of Holbrook and Mitchell] enhanced my reach and the administration's credibility."[47]

But that assessment is too facile for State Department hands with long experience of the special envoy problem—and it is a problem. There has been extensive debate over the utility of special envoys. While they can elevate the profile of an issue and secure meetings with high-level counterparts, they come at a high price. They have trouble moving policy papers through a turf-driven bureaucracy, their mandate is often too vague, and there can be nasty disputes over confused lines of authority.[48]

A 2014 U.S. Institute of Peace study on the role of special envoys, with many examples drawn from the Clinton State Department, illustrates how these individuals—especially those who are White House–appointed—can marginalize not only the secretary, but embassies. The first U.S. special envoy for Sudan and South Sudan

> made poor use of the embassies, cutting them out of both the policy and negotiating process and Washington policy debates. They were asked, in effect, to serve simply as travel and logistics support for the [office] and were often not included in meetings in the country. This lowered morale in the embassies and bifurcated reporting and analysis channels. . . . [The office] was not structured well to oversee all the projects it initiated, some of which were ill-conceived and poorly supervised.[49]

The report also mentioned the stormy stints of Richard Holbrooke, whom Clinton refused to fire despite strong White House pressure, and George Mitchell, who reportedly resigned over differences on Middle East policy within the Obama administration. By failing to challenge the insertion of twenty-four special envoys into her State Department, Clinton lost chances to influence foreign policy processes or to impose her own overarching worldview across countries and issues, tacitly agreeing to the compartmentalization of foreign policy. It is hard to imagine some of her predecessors meekly agreeing to so many oft-called baronies.

Being secretary of state is a once-in-a-lifetime opportunity, which leads to the second observation: Clinton tended to settle for too little and squandered her influence on the small stuff. She fought the Obama White House to get the right chief of protocol—why? She wrote in her memoir that she learned from her time as first lady that protocol is important to diplomacy. This is a misreading. Protocol chiefs work on guest lists, table seating, and VIP gifts. What's far more important to diplomacy is policy, and she might have traded the chit for her favorite protocol officer for something more substantive.

She found time to promote a clean cookstoves initiative, an issue she said was at the crossroads of energy, environment, economics, and public health, and certainly benefited people who used inefficient and dangerous stoves.[50] Bravo, but was this the best and highest value use of her time? She stated that her key foreign policy goals were food security, global health policy, LGBT rights, and Haiti.[51] That's an interesting list but one better suited to USAID than to the State Department. She mentioned other priorities, too, such as engaging activists on social media, helping determine energy pipeline routes, limiting carbon emissions, encouraging marginalized groups to participate in politics, standing up for universal human rights, and defending common economic rules of the road, a list that speaks for itself.[52]

Perhaps James Dobbins said it most diplomatically: "Circumstances have denied her opportunities for the transformative accomplishments of Dean Acheson," secretary of state to President Truman from 1949 to 1953 and one of the architects of the postwar world.[53] The Berlin Wall did not fall on her watch nor was the World Trade Center attacked. She did not bring peace to the Middle East, although she did manage to broker a ceasefire in November 2012 in Gaza between the Israelis and Hamas. Unlike Henry Kissinger, she did not orchestrate an opening to China, but she was largely responsible for the opening to Burma, which she began at the start of her tenure in early 2009. In general, she stayed within the lines and played the hand that history dealt her.

Clinton believes firmly in the power of public-private partnerships, and therein lies both the strengths and weaknesses of her approach. Her list of foreign policy priorities, logically enough, frequently coincides with the work of the Clinton Global Initiative, established by Bill Clinton as a policy platform for an activist approach to scores of global issues, and her earlier work with Vital Voices. The proliferation of NGOs—some of which are well funded and powerful—means outside voices can influence foreign policy without the scrutiny of the electorate or the mandate of the ballot box. Unlike NGOs, the State Department is uniquely able to speak for the U.S. government, yet it will increasingly have to speak more loudly as it navigates a global landscape littered with private organizations—some of which will have agendas decidedly at odds with the policies of a U.S. administration. As vested interests clash, future secretaries of state may find their speeches pay less homage to starting more public-private partnerships and instead delineate where those partnerships end.

Clinton, always a practitioner rather than a theoretician, searched for a phrase that would accurately encompass her worldview. She chose the term *idealistic realist* to emphasize the duality of both the idealistic and the realistic aspects of the issues she confronted. She also believed in smart power, a term she has continued to use following her tenure as secretary, which encapsulates the crossroads of what she called the three Ds—diplomacy, development, and defense. Clinton defined smart power as an ever-expanding toolkit in which diplomats might work on unconventional issues using new technology and skills. It echoes the theme of what she hopes will be her lasting contribution to the State Department itself—the Quadrennial Diplomacy and Development Review.

The QDDR, conducted in 2010, is probably the best reflection of Clinton's worldview from within the State Department looking out. Through it, she attempted to tackle the single most debilitating problem for the department, year after year: erratic funding from Congress. The QDDR focuses on four areas:

+ Building America's civilian power by bringing together the unique contributions of civilians across the federal government to advance U.S. interests
+ Elevating and transforming development to deliver results by focusing investments, supporting innovation, and measuring results

+ Building a civilian capacity to prevent and respond to crisis and conflict and give the U.S. military the partner it needs and deserves
+ Changing the way America does business by working smarter to save money, planning and budgeting to accomplish priorities, and measuring the results of investments[54]

Here is Clinton the CEO at her best. Not the first to try to impose managerial order on the inherently unmanageable State Department, she tried throughout the document (clearly prepared with Congress in mind) to link initiatives, resources, and measurable outcomes. She reached out to the field multiple times, seeking input, ideas, and reactions.[55] The field responded in kind, and she heard in rapid succession from posts as varied as Tel Aviv, Mexico, Ankara, Dhaka, Abuja, Brussels, and Maputo. No doubt the dialogue continued beyond the last date of the leaked cables on February 28, 2010.

Unsurprisingly, Clinton used the QDDR to recapitulate her call for women to play larger roles. She continued to think about her working definition of smart power, suggesting in a controversial Georgetown University speech in December 2014 that it might even include empathizing and showing respect for one's enemies. She offered the example of two women in the Philippines who became agents for peace in a decades-long conflict. "This is what we call smart power—using every possible tool . . . leaving no one on the sidelines, showing respect, even for one's enemies, trying to understand and insofar as is psychologically possible, empathize with their perspective and point of view, helping to define the problems, determine a solution."[56]

Clinton's perseverance in the areas she valued most and her insistence on defining her own role as secretary of state may have clashed with State Department traditionalists looking for a Henry Kissinger, George Shultz, or Colin Powell, but in areas where she had a free hand she demonstrated consultative engagement, managerial prowess, and an instinct for outreach. And, depending on the State Department's ability to institutionalize the QDDR architecture, she may be one of the few modern secretaries of state to have left the institution financially stronger than she found it.

There is no "Hillary doctrine," and no true diplomatic breakthroughs, perhaps reflecting the fact that in today's era even powerful people have less freedom of action. There are too many problems and too many stakeholders. Should Clinton become president, she would do well to reconsider the many cables from embassies describing anti-Americanism, corruption, and threats to security and democracy. These enduring issues resist once-and-for-all resolution. They will continue to delimit America's place in an uneasy world. Her determination as a future president to chart a new course may well be circumscribed by the nuances of what the embassies were telling her all along.

EPILOGUE

MORE THAN FIVE YEARS HAVE PASSED SINCE THAT late November day when I stood in front of a group of students wondering how to answer their questions on WikiLeaks. Some have stayed in touch, sharing the delightful news that they have become new foreign service officers. Each term I meet new students, all equally enthusiastic, anxious to know how to master the selection process. A few are daring enough to contemplate openly what many are secretly wondering: How long will it take to become an ambassador?

The students' questions are a constant reminder that Americans know too little about the work of foreign service officers. This book attempted to use the officers' own writing to tell at least some of their stories and demystify their work. Having heard too many people confuse the foreign service with the foreign legion, I found the opportunity to draw on officers' cables to illustrate the innovative skills with which they practice twenty-first century diplomacy irresistible. While that would be reason enough to write this book, it is not the only reason.

A thoughtful perusal of the cables illustrates almost instantly the many divergences between the impressions of those in the field and the beliefs of policymakers in Washington. Such a revelation is unlikely to surface so starkly ever again, because the usual slow pace of the declassification process shields the data behind the lens of distant decades.

The leaked cables give us the work of today's diplomats in real time, and it is also the first opportunity to examine the conduct of American foreign policy solely from the perspective of U.S. embassies and consulates. The opportunity to read the cables transports the reader in a way that secondhand accounts never could. One can make much or little of the disconnect, which ranges from perceptual gulfs to minor nuances, but there are points worth underscoring.

The dynamic tension between the field and Washington will inevitably swing toward Washington. Many of the best and most descriptive WikiLeaks cables were enterprise work—the products of instinct rather than a response to any request, speaking perhaps to the age-old desire of travelers to write home. It seems reasonable to assume that as the load for mandated reporting continues to rise, along with support for increasing numbers of embassy visitors, the time an officer might have for writing a leisurely but informative cable will diminish.

If there is an agenda here, it involves three pleas. The first is that the foreign policy establishment include embassy voices in the decision-making process. Officers have more than earned their seat at the policymaking table. Too often they are crowded out by ideology or perceived urgencies. Their writing eloquently testifies to their ability to ask the right questions and bring perspective, reality checks, and seasoned experience. Ignoring them or dismissing them as "the field" has impoverished the policymaking process.

The second plea is that the secretary of state give public diplomacy officers the same professional leadership that is frequently granted to their colleagues in other career tracks—an under secretary who comes from their own ranks. Public diplomacy has produced many capable senior officers who are the intellectual equivalents of some of the more legendary under secretaries—people such as William Burns and Nicholas Burns, who served as under secretaries for Political Affairs, and

Patrick Kennedy, who continues to serve as under secretary for Management. The current roster of senior public diplomacy positions in Washington is weighted with too many political appointees—some of them drawn from the partisan ranks of congressional offices. Naming career officers to the top spots would professionalize a division that has succeeded in spite of poor leadership. It would also encourage the movement of experienced public diplomacy officers from the field back to Washington to take part in the policymaking process, a step toward closing the disconnect between the field and home.

The third plea is that the State Department not wait twenty-five to thirty years to declassify the leaked cables. It's a safe bet that embassy cables will never again surface as they did during the WikiLeaks scandal. It's an equally safe bet that this won't be the last time that the U.S. government deals with leaked documents, intercepted conversations, and other waylaid communications. Those charged with protecting confidential data have an unenviable task. But the WikiLeaks cables have now been on a number of Internet sites for five years. As education in political science and international relations increasingly draws its professoriate from the professional ranks—and as students increasingly come from mid-career jobs in government—it seems pointless to argue that the WikiLeaks cables, widely available to the world at large—should be off limits to those carrying security clearances. This unfairly disadvantages those who are the most knowledgeable and have the most to contribute. International relations and related fields are among the most internationalized parts of most campuses, attracting professors and students from many countries, all of whom could easily use the cables in their research. American students and scholars should have the same access.

*　*　*　*

IT SEEMS REASONABLE to wonder whether cable writing will maintain its relevance in an age of instantaneous communication. Diplomats originally wrote telegrams because they represented the cutting-edge technology of the time. It would be silly to cling to an old technology when there are so many better means available. Just as the digital age has changed the way we read books, it will continue to change the way diplomats report home. Policymakers will turn to other, faster means to get a quick read-out, for example, on what was said after a démarche was delivered.

But gains rarely come without losses. Cable writing is thoughtful and reflective—a cross between reporting and essay writing. One's understanding and perspective on what just happened in a meeting can change over time. Anger felt upon leaving a foreign ministry might ultimately fade to something closer to understanding. A reaction that seemed explosive in the heat of the moment might, in a larger context, be more forgivable. Cables provide context.

It would be a shame, too, if all the details that make the cables worth reading—what was worn, how many drinks were consumed, the number of hunting trophies on the wall behind the president— are scrapped for the sake of speed. Diplomacy is still an art, as is good writing. The act of thoughtful and reflective writing about diplomacy surely ought to endure.

ACKNOWLEDGMENTS

- - - - - - - - - - - -

MY THANKS GO to my literary agent, Andy Ross, for seeing the value in my first attempt at formulating a book proposal. His expansive definition of being an agent meant staying in touch throughout the writing process, offering encouragement and insightful comments. My editors, Brendan Curry and Sophie Duvernoy, along with many others at Norton, did a fine job in all the many aspects involved in the art of book publishing.

The unique circumstances of writing a book that relied heavily on information that is clearly in the public domain but has not been declassified became an intriguing problem. I owe a debt to Jessica Friedman, who first raised the issue. Boston attorney Paul Johnson, a friend, connected me to lawyer/writer/film producer Thomas Herman who understood the complexities of writing a book based on leaked documents. Tom, in turn, led me to John B. Bellinger III, the former State Department legal advisor, whose intimate knowledge of the pre-publication review process proved invaluable. I am grateful to all of them for grappling with the unusual issues that arose from working with WikiLeaks cables.

My family endured far too much dinner table talk about cables, bearing with me as I exclaimed over yet another great find. My parents, to whom this book is dedicated, checked in regularly, and my late husband, Harold, who always liked to say he was "worldwide available," was a sounding board for my ideas. My children Andie, Gareth, and Gwyneth shared my overseas assignments and are proud of being third-culture kids. They all read parts of the manuscript and identified the boring bits, and if I have failed to remove them it is not their fault. Son-in-law Sean offered encouragement, and my brothers Chet and Colin had such exciting thoughts about how to market the book that I couldn't help but finish it. I am lucky to have an uncle, William Irwin Thompson, who is the literary giant of the family and who offered a thoughtful critique on every chapter.

Because the leaked cables are still considered classified, I was unable to get input from my foreign service colleagues who are still serving, but my academic colleagues were willing and able to help. Dr. Marissa Lombardi read the chapter on corruption, and Dr. Leslie Hitch and Dr. Micky Cokely were constant sources of wise counsel. Four graduate students—Dana Stranz, Lin Feng, Ruth Garcia, and Jingshu Zhu—all took on research work, and Dana Stranz also did enormous additional editing.

I believe higher education is critical to our nation's place in the world, and I was privileged to attend three fine schools that gave me the analytic skills to succeed in my profession. California State University Northridge taught me to be a journalist and a lifelong writer. Tufts University's Fletcher School helped me achieve my ambition to become a diplomat, and the University of Pennsylvania's Graduate School of Education gave me the chance to think critically and analytically about the role of educational exchanges, which were central to my work as a public diplomacy officer. At Fletcher I was blessed with phenomenal professors such as the late ambassador Hewson Ryan, former ambassador William Rugh, diplomatic historian Alan Henrikson, security studies expert Richard Shultz, and many more. At Penn I was exposed to the minds of professors Robert Zemsky, Matt Hartley, and Mary-Linda Armacost, along with the fine members of Cohort 10.

Writing a book turns out to be a great way to find out who your friends are. Many people offered encouragement and helpful insights. Dean John LaBrie of the College of Professional Studies at Northeastern nudged me along, as did Jo Ann Gammel and Mary Huegel at Endicott College. Imogen Sieveking is one of the best interpreters of Latin America I have ever met. My many students inspire me.

My former boss, Ambassador Richard Graber, led by example and ran a great embassy. Ambassador John Hamilton personified for many of us the meaning of the word *integrity*. As I wrote, I had images in my mind of incidents and scenes from embassies and consulates led by extraordinary people such as Eric Edelman, Bruce Wharton, Deborah McCarthy, John Ordway, Adrian Basora, and Steve McFarland. I enjoyed a special relationship that comes from a shared career interest with public diplomacy officers such as Susan Domowitz, Jeff Sexton, Dan Whitman, Kay Mayfield, Ryan Rowlands, Ida Heckenbach, Paula Wikle, John Vance, John Law, and David Gainer. I learned a great deal from other FSOs with different skills, such as Stuart Hatcher, Marty Melzow, David Lindwall, Mike Foster, Kevin Rubesh, Michael Rinker, Charles Blaha, Kenneth Meyer, Tom Nave, Joanne Ingalls, Martina Strong, Judy Pruitt, Michael Dodman, Amy Carnie, Greg O'Connor, and many more. These people run embassies. They give their all, every day.

All of us worked alongside locally employed staff—the people who serve as the continuity for U.S. foreign policy abroad. They serve as windows into their countries, and the best of them tirelessly educate each new crop of American officers, transforming us from raw beginners to people who can interpret events with a practiced eye. They contributed content and editorial value to many of the cables. Helena Markusová was such a person for me. Others include Markéta Kolářová, Jana Kernerová, Jana Ruckerová, Helena Vágnerová, Marie Bártová, Zuzana Kučerová, Karel Sedlák, Miroslav Černik, Petr Doležal, Jakub Hornek, Louis Quintal, Paloma Herrera, Asunción Sanz, Geraldine Melby, Carmen Fonseca, and many, many more.

My husband was a member of one last group of great importance— the spouses of foreign service officers, such as Stephanie Rowlands,

Gerry Andrianopoulis, Irene Mills, Richard Gilbert, Collette Rinker, Jean O'Connor, and many more. These talented and devoted people don't often get credit for their enormous contribution to the foreign service. They make it possible for officers to be sent to unaccompanied posts in Iraq, Afghanistan, and Pakistan, and they handle the pack-outs and move-ins, schools, medical issues, and so much more.

NOTES

- - - - - - - - - - -

A Note on WikiLeaks Citations

The WikiLeaks cables are accessible from a variety of public websites, including newspapers involved in the original release in 2010. The author accessed the cables through cablegatesearch.net. The cables have since been reorganized by WikiLeaks to wikileaks.org, which features Plus D, The Public Library of U.S. Diplomacy. The searchable database allows researchers to look by country, topic, date, or combinations of all three. The name "Cablegate" is the WikiLeaks term for the release of the 251,287 State Department cables. The WikiLeaks site contains many documents in addition to the Cablegate tranche from other U.S. government agencies and the private sector.

Unsurprisingly given their provenance, there is no consensus on how authors should cite WikiLeaks cables. This book includes the city of the originating embassy or consulate, the date, and the subject line (or title). The subject line offers valuable additional information. FSOs are trained to compose titles designed to catch the attention of busy State Department readers, as their cable will compete with hundreds of others each day. The titles often convey humor, wit, nuance, or additional headline-style information, such as "Foreign Minister Rejects Initiative." An overburdened desk officer can read further to find out why, but the subject line, much like a headline, conveys the essence. In the case of situation reports, or sitreps, the subject lines often offer sequential numbering in addition to the date, so it is clear where the cable fits in the course of the crisis.

Prologue

1. See Alan Rusbridger, *Play It Again: An Amateur Against the Impossible* (New York: Farrar, Straus and Giroux, 2013), for his diary account of the drama behind the collaboration with the *New York Times*.

Chapter 1. 251, 287 LEAKED CABLES

1. Abba Eban, *Diplomacy for the Next Century* (New Haven, CT: Yale University Press, 1998), 92.
2. See David Paull Nickles, *Under the Wire: How the Telegraph Changed Diplomacy* (Cambridge, MA: Harvard University Press, 2003), for an excellent discussion on the concept of time and its impact on the work of governments and diplomats.
3. Gary J. Bass, *The Blood Telegram: Nixon, Kissinger, and a Forgotten Genocide* (New York: Alfred A. Knopf, 2013).
4. Ibid.
5. Hannah Gurman, *The Dissent Papers: The Voices of Diplomats in the Cold War and Beyond* (New York: Columbia University Press, 2012).
6. Alexander Star, ed., *Open Secrets: WikiLeaks, War, and American Diplomacy* (New York: Grove Press, 2011).
7. Christopher Beam, "Dispatches: The WikiLeaks Cables as Literature," *Slate*, December 1, 2010, http://www.slate.com/articles/news_and_politics/politics/2010/12/dispatches.htm.
8. Fareed Zakaria, "WikiLeaks Shows the Skills of U.S. Diplomats," *Time*, December 2, 2010; and Timothy Garton Ash, "U.S. Embassy Cables: A Banquet of Secrets," *Guardian*, November 28, 2010.
9. Numbers published by the American Foreign Service Association, reflecting full-time permanent employees as of December 30, 2012, as prepared by the State Department's HR/RMA/WPA office and cleared for public release.
10. Bushnell's accounts have been widely published in the media, but for a highly compelling first-person account, see her entry in Moments in U.S. Diplomatic History on the Association for Diplomatic Studies and Training website, http://adst.org/2012/08/prudence-bushnell-on-the-us-embassy-nairobi-bombings/.
11. U.S. Department of State Office of Inspector General, *Compliance Followup Review of Embassy Islamabad and Constituent Posts, Pakistan*, Report # ISP-C-12-28A, Washington, DC, May 2012.
12. Alasdair Roberts, "The WikiLeaks Illusion," *Wilson Quarterly*, Summer 2011, http://wilsonquarterly.com/stories/the-wikileaks-illusion/.
13. David E. Sanger "How Our Diplomats Think," in *Open Secrets: WikiLeaks*,

War, and American Diplomacy, ed. Alexander Star (New York: Grove Press, 2011), 331.

14. Timothy Garton Ash, "Historian Relishes WikiLeaks Cable Dump," interview by Renee Montagne, *NPR Morning Edition*, Washington, DC, December 1, 2010, http://www.npr.org/2010/12/01/131719047/historian -relishes-wikileaks-cable-dump.

15. Steven Alan Honley, ed., "AFSA Members Speak Out on the WikiLeaks Mess," *Foreign Service Journal* 88, no. 3 (March 2011): 15–22.

16. Michele Keleman, "Ex-Diplomats Fear Leak Will Lead to Cautious Cables," *NPR Morning Edition*, Washington, DC, November 30, 2010, http:// www.npr.org/2010/11/30/131686336/ex-diplomats-fear-leak-will-lead -to-cautious-cables.

17. Michael A. Lindenberger, "The U.S.'s Weak Legal Case Against WikiLeaks," *Time*, December 9, 2010.

18. Stephen Hadley, "How Will New Wikileaks Revelations Affect Diplomatic Candor?," interview by Judy Woodruff, PBS *NewsHour*, November 29, 2010, http://www.pbs.org/newshour/bb/government_programs-july -dec10-weakileaks2_11-29/.

19. John Campbell, "Expert Roundup: Will WikiLeaks Hobble U.S. Diplomacy?," interview by Deborah Jerome, December 1, 2010, http://www.cfr .org/diplomacy-and-statecraft/wikileaks-hobble-us-diplomacy/p23526.

20. Elisabeth Bumiller, "Gates on Leaks, Wiki and Other," *New York Times*, November 30, 2010.

21. Frederick Hitz, "Are WikiLeaks Leaks Good for America?" interview by Jim Zirin, *Digital Age*, December 14, 2010, http://www.digitalage.org/ video/are-wikileaks-leaks-good-for-america/.

22. Ibid.

Chapter 2. ANTI-AMERICANISM

1. U.S. Embassy Oslo, "Muslim American Congressman in Norway on Faith, Peace, and Combatting U.S. Stereotypes," January 18, 2008.

2. Steven R. Weisman, "Saudi Women Have Message for U.S. Envoy," *New York Times*, September 28, 2005.

3. Glenn Kessler, "Turks Challenge Hughes on Iraq," *Washington Post*, September 29, 2005.

4. Fred Kaplan, "Karen Hughes, Stay Home!," *Slate*, September 29, 2005.

5. U.S. Embassy Cairo, "U/S Hughes Meeting with Egyptian Prime Minister Nazif," September 29, 2005.

6. U.S. Embassy Riyadh, "A Public Diplomacy Strategy for Saudi Arabia," September 29, 2005.

7. U.S. Embassy Ankara, "Turkish Media Coverage—Visit of Under Secretary of State for Public Diplomacy and Public Affairs," October 3, 2005.

8. "Global Public Opinion in the Bush Years (2001–2008)," Pew Research Center, Washington, DC, December 18, 2008. Pew found that the United States remained broadly disliked in the countries surveyed, and attitudes toward the United States were unsurprisingly negative in the Muslim world. What was surprising was the degree of disparity in Western countries and traditional allies, especially on security issues. "Indeed, opinion of the U.S. continues to be mostly unfavorable among the publics of America's traditional allies. In Turkey, hostility toward the U.S. and the American people has intensified." Many allies faulted the United States for conducting a unilateral foreign policy.

9. U.S. Embassy Athens, "The Case for Increasing Greece's IMET Funding," February 8, 2010.

10. "Global Public Opinion in the Bush Years (2001–2008)," Pew Research Center, Washington, DC, December 18, 2008.

11. Andrew Kohut, "Obama Unlikely to Find a Quick Fix for U.S. Global Image," Pew Research Center Global Attitudes Project, Washington, DC, March 31, 2009.

12. Ibid.

13. "America's Image in the World: Findings from the Pew Global Attitudes Project," Pew Research Center, Washington, DC, March 14, 2007.

14. U.S. Consulate Jeddah, "Jeddah Journal 17," August 7, 2006.

15. U.S. Embassy Manama, "Shia Commemorate Ashura with Large, Orderly Crowds and Processions," February 1, 2007.

16. U.S. Consulate Jeddah, "From the Eastern Province: An Anti-American Sermon," March 22, 2006.

17. U.S. Embassy Nouakchott, "Spies Like Us: The Media's Tendency to See U.S. Agents Everywhere," December 21, 2008.

18. U.S. Embassy Harare, "Zanu-PF Peacefully Protests Sanctions in Front of the U.S. Embassy," February 24, 2010.

19. U.S. Embassy Dushanbe, "Interior Minister—That's Not My Anti-American Screed," February 3, 2010.

20. Jon Kelly, "Hugo Chávez and the Era of the Anti-American Bogeymen," *BBC News Magazine*, March 7, 2013.

21. U.S. Embassy Brasilia, "Understanding Brazil's Foreign Ministry: Part 1 Ideological Forces," February 11, 2009.

22. U.S. Embassy Cairo, "Egyptian Media Themes Sept. 26 to Oct. 2: Six More Years! Mubarak Inaugurated for Fifth Term; Simpsons Coming to Town," October 3, 2005.

23. U.S. Embassy Riyadh, "Ideological and Ownership Trends in the Saudi Media," May 11, 2009.

24. U.S. Embassy Ottawa, "Primetime Images of U.S.–Canada Border Paint U.S. in Increasingly Negative Light," January 25, 2008.

25. U.S. Consulate Istanbul, "Turkish Media Figures Discuss Headscarf, Politics, and U.S. Image in Turkey," February 27, 2008.

26. U.S. Embassy Moscow, "Local Pundits on Russia's Escalating Rhetoric," June 5, 2007.

27. U.S. Embassy Moscow, "Russian Analysts Tell A/S Gordon Anti-Americanism Pillar of Russian Foreign Policy," September 16, 2009.

28. U.S. Embassy Paris, "Responding to Russian Threats Against Missile Defense in Poland and the Czech Republic," February 22, 2007.

29. U.S. Embassy Paris, "Codel Tanner: Meeting with French Political Director Araud," February 27, 2007.

30. U.S. Consulate Toronto, "Ignatieff's COS Donolo on Elections, U.S., IPR," February 2, 2010.

31. U.S. Embassy Bishkek, "Kyrgyz Officials Offended by Cross on Swiss Flag," April 25, 2009.

32. Richard T. Arndt, "Rebuilding America's Cultural Diplomacy," *Foreign Service Journal* 83, no. 10 (October 2006): 39.

33. Walter Douglas with Jeanne Neal, *Engaging the Muslim World: Public Diplomacy after 9/11 in the Arab Middle East, Afghanistan, and Pakistan* (Washington, DC: Center for Strategic and International Studies, 2013).

34. William A. Rugh, ed., *The Practice of Public Diplomacy: Confronting Challenges Abroad* (New York: Palgrave Macmillan, 2011).

35. William A. Rugh, *American Encounters with Arabs: The "Soft Power" of U.S. Public Diplomacy in the Middle East* (New York: Praeger Security International, 2005).

36. "State Department: Staffing and Foreign Language Shortfalls Persist Despite Initiatives to Address Gaps," Government Accountability Office, Washington, DC, GAO-07-1154T, August 1, 2007.

37. U.S. Embassy Riyadh, "A Public Diplomacy Strategy for Saudi Arabia," December 12, 2005.

38. "Comprehensive Plan Needed to Address Persistent Foreign Language Shortfalls," Government Accountability Office, Washington, DC, GAO-09-955, September 17, 2009.

39. Edward P. Djerejian, *Danger and Opportunity: An American Ambassador's Journey through the Middle East* (New York: Threshold Editions, 2009).

40. Joe Johnson, "How Does Public Diplomacy Measure Up?," *Foreign Service Journal* 83, no. 12 (October 2006): 44–52.

41. Ibid.

42. Robert J. Callahan, "Neither Madison Avenue nor Hollywood," *Foreign Service Journal* 83, no. 10 (October 2006): 33–38.

43. U.S. Embassy Moscow, "IRF Reactions: MFA Gets Nasty, ROC Nice," October 29, 2009.

44. U.S. Embassy Beijing, "Media Reaction: Human Rights, Gary Locke, U.S.–China Military Relations," February 27, 2009.

45. Rosie Johnston, "Topolanek Lashes Out at U.S. over Human Rights Report," Český rozhlas/Radio Prague, March 13, 2008.

46. U.S. Embassy Buenos Aires, "Public Diplomacy Best Practices; Countering Anti-Americanism in Argentina," November 21, 2008.

47. "Staff Report on the Office of the Under Secretary for Public Diplomacy and Public Affairs," Advisory Commission on Public Diplomacy, Washington, DC, December 12, 2011.

48. See "Ambassadors Call for a Public Diplomacy Professional at State Department, Public Diplomacy Council, May 24, 2013, http://publicdiplomacycouncil.org/commentaries/05-24-13/ambassadors-call-public-diplomacy-professional-state-department

49. Philip Giraldi, "Clueless in Gaza: Karen Hughes and the Collapse of American Public Diplomacy," Antiwar.com, March 7, 2007, http://antiwar.com/orig/giraldi.php?articleid=10632.

50. Elizabeth Williamson, "Karen's Rules on Diplomacy: Talk to the Media—If You Dare," *Washington Post*, November 8, 2006.

51. Shawn Zeller, "Damage Control: Karen Hughes Does PD," *Foreign Service Journal* 83, no. 10 (October 2006): 19–26.

52. Thomas L. McPhail, *Global Communication: Theories, Stakeholders, and Trends.* (Hoboken, NJ: Wiley-Blackwell, 2010), 85.

53. James K. Glassman, "U.S. Leadership Rating Rises. Huh?," *The American*, American Enterprise Institute, April 16, 2014.

54. Al Kamen, "A Lovely Consolation Prize for Ms. Kennedy?," In the Loop, *Washington Post,* January 23, 2009.

55. Marc Lynch, "Why Judith McHale Would Be a Bad Public Diplomacy Choice," *Foreign Policy,* January 23, 2009.

56. U.S. Embassy Asunción, "Ambassador Showcases Asunción's Biodiversity, Promotes Eco-Tourism," October 21, 2005.

57. U.S. Embassy Rome, "'Hunger Banquets' and Public Diplomacy: A Proposal," June 28, 2005.

58. U.S. Interests Section Havana, "In Havana, a (Mostly) Happy Fourth of July," July 5, 2006.

59. U.S. Embassy Athens, "Muslim Engagement in Greece," January 19, 2010.

60. U.S. Embassy London, "Engagement with Muslim Communities in the UK," February 5, 2010.

61. U.S. Consulate Jeddah, "American Culture and Commerce Festival in Abha," January 9, 2008.

62. U.S. Embassy Cotonou, "Benin: Blood Drive Muslim Community Project," October 27, 2009.

63. U.S. Embassy Nouakchott, "First Ever Muslim American Couple Visit Cements New Relationship with Mauritania," September 28, 2009.

64. U.S. Embassy Asmara, "GSE Shuts Down Embassy Asmara Iftar," August 27, 2009.

65. U.S. Embassy Buenos Aires, "Public Diplomacy Best Practices; Countering Anti-Americanism in Argentina," November 21, 2008.

66. U.S. Embassy Paramaribo, "Suriname: Request $13,350 in Additional Public Diplomacy Funding," April 29, 2008.

67. Remarks by President Obama at Strasbourg Town Hall, April 3, 2009, https://www.whitehouse.gov/the-press-office/remarks-president-obama-strasbourg-town-hall.

68. A. M. Sperber, *Murrow: His Life and Times* (New York: Bantam Books, 1986), 624, citing the author's interview with Henry Loomis, April 4, 1985.

69. Zeller, "Damage Control."

Chapter 3. CRISES

1. Peter Kolshorn, "U.S. Embassy Port-au-Prince Officer Recalls Memories of Haiti Quake," DipNote, U.S. Department of State Official Blog, July 13, 2010, http://blogs.state.gov/stories/2010/07/13/us-embassy-port-au-prince-officer-recalls-memories-of-haiti-quake.

2. In 2014 the UN Development Programme's Human Development Report ranked Haiti first in the Western Hemisphere on its list of countries with low human development; globally, it ranked Haiti 166 out of 187.

3. According to the UN's World Health Organization website, the World Food Summit in 1996 defined food security as existing "when all people at all times have access to sufficient, safe, nutritious food to maintain a healthy and active life." Obstacles to food security include both physical and economic access, conflicts, and natural disasters.

4. U.S. Embassy Port-au-Prince, "Haiti Earthquake Sitrep 2 as of 1900," January 14, 2010.

5. U.S. Embassy Port-au-Prince, "Embassy Port au Prince Earthquake Sitrep as of 1200, Day 4," January 15, 2010.

6. U.S. Embassy Port-au-Prince, "Embassy Port-au-Prince Sitrep as of 1800 Day 4," Janaury 16, 2010.

7. U.S. Embassy Port-au-Prince, "Embassy Port au Prince Sitrep as of 1200, Day 4," January 15, 2010.

8. U.S. Embassy Port-au-Prince, "Embassy Port-au-Prince Sitrep as of 1800 Day 4," January 16, 2010.

9. U.S. Embassy Port-au-Prince, "Port-au-Prince: Read Out on Secstate Visit," January 19, 2010.

10. Ibid.

11. U.S. Embassy Port-au-Prince, "Haiti Earthquake One Week Later, January 21, 2010.

12. U.S. Embassy Port-au-Prince, "USAID/DART Overview of Search and Rescue Operations in Haiti," January 25, 2010.

13. U.S. Embassy Port-au-Prince, "Embassy Port Au Prince Earthquake Sitrep as of 1800, Day 12," January 26, 2010.

14. Hillary R. Clinton, *Hard Choices* (New York: Simon & Schuster, 2014), 527. Clinton uses the larger death toll of 230,000, plus another 300,000 injured. USAID became skeptical of that number and commissioned a consultancy report, which put the figure between 46,000 and 85,000. Some news sources, such as the BBC, also disputed the 230,000 figure, and the *Columbia Journalism Review* noted that the Haitian government raised the death toll on the first anniversary of the quake from 230,000 to 316,000, with no explanation.

15. The U.S. State Department continues to call the country Burma, in deference to the wishes of political dissidents who reject the military regime's use of the name Myanmar. Regional experts argue that the name Burma favors one ethnicity in a multiethnic society, and most countries now favor using Myanmar. This book uses the name Burma, which provides consistency for readers, since it draws heavily on cables that refer to the country by that name.

16. U.S. Embassy Rangoon, "Burma: Preparations for Cyclone Nargis," May 2, 2008.

17. U.S. Embassy Rangoon, "Burma: Cyclone Nargis Disaster Alert," May 5, 2008.

18. U.S. Embassy Rangoon, "Burma: Cyclone Nargis Declaration of Disaster," May 5, 2008.

19. Ibid.

20. U.S. Embassy Rangoon, "Burma: Cyclone Nargis Sitrep No. 1," May 5, 2008.

21. U.S. Embassy Rangoon, "Burma: Political Implications of Cyclone Nargis," May 6, 2008.

22. Ibid.

23. U.S. Embassy Rangoon, "Burma: Cyclone Nargis Sitrep No. 2," May 6, 2008.

24. U.S. Embassy Rangoon, "Burma: Fuel Shortage Imminent," May 6, 2008.

25. U.S. Embassy Rangoon, "Burma: The Politics of Cyclone Nargis Assistance," May 7, 2008.

26. U.S. Embassy Rangoon, "Burma: Update on Humanitarian Assistance," May 16, 2008.

27. U.S. Embassy Rangoon, "Burma: Than Shwe Is the Problem," May 8, 2008.

28. U.S. Embassy Rangoon, "Burma: Prying Open the Door for Humanitarian Aid," May 9, 2008.

29. U.S. Embassy Rangoon, "Burma: Cyclone Nargis Sitrep No. 6," May 12, 2008.

30. U.S. Embassy Rangoon, "Crouching Tiger, Hidden Economy: Burma-China Economic Relations," February 24, 2010.

31. U.S. Embassy Rangoon, "First Tranche of USG Cyclone Assistance Arrives in Burma," May 13, 2008.

32. U.S. Embassy Rangoon, "Media Reaction: Burmese Highlight Delivery of U.S. Humanitarian Aid Post Cyclone Nargis," May 15, 2008.

33. U.S. Embassy Rangoon, "Burma: A General Willing to Meet," August 8, 2008.

34. U.S. Embassy Rangoon, "Burma: NLD Supports Policy Review, Cautions Against Any Deal That Would Cut Out the Party," September 28, 2009.

35. U.S. Embassy Rangoon, "Burma: Regime Backtracking on Its Cyclone Relief Commitments," June 17, 2008.

36. U.S. Embassy Rangoon, "Burma: Donors Focus on Access at Cyclone Nargis Conference," May 27, 2008.

37. U.S. Embassy Rangoon, "Burma: Including ICRC on the Dialogue Agenda," October 14, 2009.

38. U.S. Embassy Rangoon, "Burma: Some Political Prisoners Released in Amnesty," September 18, 2009.

39. U.S. Embassy Rangoon, "Burma: Assistance Organizations Feeling the Pre-Election Squeeze," October 22, 2009.

40. U.S. Embassy Rangoon, "Burma's Keystone Cops," July 25, 2008.

41. U.S. Embassy Oslo, "Norwegian Opinions on the Suu Kyi Verdict and Burma," August 14, 2009.

42. U.S. Embassy Rangoon, "Burma: Promoting Democratic Change through Cyclone Nargis Relief," June 27, 2008.

43. Clinton, *Hard Choices*, 126.

44. Ibid., 266–67.

45. U.S. Embassy Tegucigalpa, "Honduran Coup: Sitrep #11," July 6, 2009.

46. U.S. Embassy Tegucigalpa, "Honduran Coup Sitrep #12," July 7, 2009.

47. Clinton, *Hard Choices,* 266–68. Clinton gives a firsthand account of seeking out President Arias as the ideal older statesman for this crisis and reports his statement to her that he agreed to take on the task because of his belief in democratic principles, "not because I like these people. . . . If we allow the de facto government to stay, the domino effect goes all around Latin America."

48. Ibid., 257.

49. U.S. Embassy Tegucigalpa, "Worst Case Scenario for Weekend Violence," July 17, 2009.

50. U.S. Embassy Tegucigalpa, "Honduras Coup: Sitrep #11," July 6, 2009.

51. U.S. Embassy Tegucigalpa, "Honduran Coup: Sitrep #4," June 29, 2009.

52. "The Wages of Chavismo," Review and Outlook, *Wall Street Journal*, July 2, 2009.

53. Mary Beth Sheridan, "U.S. Condemns Honduran Coup but Makes No Firm Demands," *Washington Post,* June 30, 2009.

54. Mary Anastasia O'Grady, "Honduras Defends Its Democracy; Fidel Castro and Hillary Clinton Object," *Wall Street Journal,* June 29, 2009.

55. James Kirchick, "Ousting Zelaya," *New Republic,* October 3, 2009.

56. Mark Weisbrot, "More of the Same in Latin America," *New York Times,* August 11, 2009.

57. Arshad Mohammed and Anthony Boadle, "U.S. Limits Visas in Honduras, Stepping Up Pressure," Reuters, August 25, 2009.

58. U.S. Embassy Tegucigalpa, "Honduran Coup: Sitrep #4," June 29, 2009.

59. "Coup, Uninterrupted," *New York Times,* editorial, November 6, 2009.

60. U.S. Embassy Tegucigalpa, "President Arias Discusses His Mediation Efforts," July 28, 2009.

61. U.S. Embassy Tegucigalpa, "Honduras Coup: Sitrep #1," June 28, 2009.

62. U.S. Embassy Tegucigalpa, "Honduras Coup: Sitrep #4," June 29, 2009.

63. U.S. Embassy Tegucigalpa, "Honduras Coup Sitrep #15," July 9, 2009.

64. U.S. Embassy Tegucigalpa, "Ambassador and President Arias Discuss Honduran Crisis," October 22, 2009.

65. Jim DeMint, "What I Heard in Honduras," *Wall Street Journal,* October 10, 2009.

66. U.S. Embassy Tegucigalpa, "Honduran Coup: Sitrep #7," July 2, 2009.

67. U.S. Embassy Tegucigalpa, "Honduran Coup Timeline," July 2, 2009.

68. U.S. Embassy Tegucigalpa, "Open and Shut: The Case of the Honduran Coup," July 24, 2009.

69. U.S. Embassy Tegucigalpa, "President Arias on Mediation," July 13, 2009.

70. U.S. Embassy Tegucigalpa, "Full Court Press to Bring Micheletti Around," July 18, 2009.

71. U.S. Embassy Tegucigalpa, "Ambassador's July 30 Conversation with President Arias," July 31, 2009.

72. U.S. Embassy Tegucigalpa, "President Arias' Call to Ambassador Llorens," August 17, 2009.

73. U.S. Embassy Tegucigalpa, "Zelaya's New Control Center; The Situation at the Brazilian Embassy," September 24, 2009.

74. U.S. Embassy Tegucigalpa, "TFH01: Tegucigalpa/San Jose Agreement Signed," November 2, 2009.

75. U.S.Embassy Tegucigalpa, "TFH01: WHA PDAS Kelly's Meeting with President Zelaya," November 13, 2009.

76. U.S. Embassy Tegucigalpa, "TF101: Elections Sitrep—Final," November 30, 2009.

77. Ibid.

78. Timothy F. Geithner, *Stress Test: Reflections on Financial Crises* (New York: Crown Publishers, 2014), 222.

79. Ibid., 394–95.

80. U.S. Embassy Reykjavik, "Reykjavik CIWG Annual Meeting," December 24, 2009.

81. Ian Parker, "Lost: Letter from Reykjavik, *New Yorker*, March 9, 2009.

82. U.S. Embassy Reykjavik, "International Media Continues to Dissect Icelandic Economy, Though Analysts Not Agreed on Whether Imbalances Represent Serious Threat to Economic Stability," April 12, 2006.

83. U.S. Embassy Reykjavik, "Iceland Scenesetter for Under Secretary Nicholas Burns," June 13, 2007.

84. Parker, "Lost: Letter from Reykjavik."

85. "Address by Prime Minister Mr Sigmundur Davíð Gunnlaugsson, at Austurvöllur, 17 June 2013," Prime Minister's Office, Iceland, http://eng.forsaetisraduneyti.is/minister/sdg-speeches/nr/7626.

86. U.S. Embassy Reykjavik, "Is Icelandic Government Doing Enough to Halt Economy's Sudden Downfall?," April 7, 2008.

87. U.S. Embassy Reykjavik, "Iceland: Govt Buys 75 Percent Share in Third-Largest Bank," September 30, 2008.

88. U.S. Embassy Reykjavik, "Icelandic Government Takes Control of Banking Sector Amid Crisis," October 7, 2008.

89. U.S. Embassy Reykjavik, "Icelandic Financial Crisis: As Emergency Powers Go into Effect, Russians Offer Loan," October 7, 2008.

90. U.S. Embassy Reykjavik, "Icelandic Economic Crisis: Time for the USG to Get Involved?," October 8, 2008.

91. U.S. Embassy Reykjavik, "Icelandic Central Bank Asserts Russian Loan is 95 Percent Sure," October 8, 2008.

92. U.S. Embassy Reykjavik, "Icelandic Economic Crisis: Third Bank Goes Down as Mass Firings Start," October 9, 2008.

93. U.S. Embassy Reykjavik, "Icelandic Economic Crisis: Time for the USG to Get Involved?," October 8, 2008.

94. U.S. Embassy Reykjavik, "Icelandic Economic Crisis: GOI-UK Negotiations on IceSave Accounts Go Badly," October 23, 2008.

95. U.S. Embassy Reykjavik, "Icelandic Economic Crisis: GOI Officials Cautiously Optimistic in Meetings with USG," October 28, 2008.

96. U.S. Embassy Reykjavik, "Icelandic Central Bank Asked NY Fed for One Billion USD Loan or Currency Swap," October 29, 2008.

97. U.S. Embassy Reykjavik, "Iceland's Financial Crisis: The Russia Angle," November 3, 2008.

98. U.S. Embassy Reykjavik, "Iceland's Request for a Loan: What's in It for Us," October 31, 2008.

Chapter 4. TRAVEL

1. U.S. Consulate Lagos, "Tourism in Nigeria: For the Birds," November 5, 2003.

2. U.S. Consulate Guangzhou, "Where Lonely Planet Does Not Go: A Visit to Xilin," June 23, 2006.

3. U.S. Embassy Paramaribo, "Informal Gold Rush in Southeastern Suriname," January 11, 2010.

4. U.S. Embassy La Paz, "Get This Monkey Off My Back: Bolivian Ecotourism," December 30, 2008.

5. Ibid.

6. U.S. Embassy Bogotá, "Into the Jungle: Ambassador Visits Amazonas," December 22, 2009.

7. U.S. Embassy Tbilisi, "Georgia: Life on the Brink in Gali," September 21, 2009.

8. Ibid.

9. U.S. Embassy Dushanbe, "Beware of Garm! Winter in Central Tajikistan," January 31, 2007.

10. U.S. Embassy Dushanbe, "The Road to Khorog: The Tajik/Afghan Border," November 7, 2007.

11. U.S. Consulate Calcutta, "Arunachal Pradesh: Isolated Tribal State," January 18, 2005.

12. Ibid.

13. U.S. Consulate Chiang Mai, "Long Neck Minority Group Caught in Refugee and Citizenship Limbo," April 24, 2007.

14. U.S. Embassy Baku, "Lords of the Mountains Will Fight No More Forever," September 18, 2009.

15. U.S. Embassy Ashgabat, "Turkmenistan/Uzbekistan Border: On the Road with Iranian Truckers," April 2, 2009.

16. U.S. Embassy Ashgabat, "Iran/Turkmenistan: President's Cairo Speech Sparks Brawl," December 4, 2009.

17. U.S. Embassy Jakarta, "Papua—Continued Problems, and Possible New Hope, for Indonesia's Troubled East," September 30, 2009.

18. Simon Montlake, "Cave In: Freeport-McMoRan Digs a Heap of Trouble in Indonesia," *Forbes*, January 26, 2012.

19. U.S. Embassy Jakarta, "Papuan Separatist Leader Kelly Kwalik Reported Killed in Shootout with Police," December 17, 2009.

20. U.S. Embassy Jakarta, "Papua—Shootings Continue Near U.S. Mining Operation," August 24, 2009.

21. Montlake, "Cave In."

22. U.S. Consulate Jeddah, "I Left My Heart in Freedom and Came Home," November 24, 2007.

23. U.S. Consulate Istanbul, "Iran/Culture: So You Want to Be a Rock and Roll Star," December 16, 2009.

24. David Browne, "The Yellow Dogs Open Up About Their Nightmare in Brooklyn," *Rolling Stone,* November 15, 2013.

25. U.S. Embassy Vatican, "New Media, Eternal Message: The Holy See and the Web," January 26, 2009; and "Pope Issues Forceful Environmental Message for World Peace Day," December 16, 2009.

26. U.S. Embassy Vatican, "Sex Abuse Scandal Strains Irish-Vatican Relations, Shakes Up Irish Church, and Poses Challenges for the Holy See," February 26, 2010.

27. U.S. Embassy Berlin, "Berlin Senate Administration Defends Decision to Deny Residence Permits to Amcit Scientologists," January 12, 2010.

28. U.S. Consulate Yekaterinburg, "Minority Religions in the Urals—Walk Softly and You Will Not Be Harassed," August 10, 2009.

29. U.S. Consulate Shanghai, "Shanghai Authorizes Expat Mormons to Hold Weekly Religious Services," January 20, 2010.

30. U.S. Embassy Dakar, "Animism in Senegal," July 14, 2009.

31. U.S. Embassy Vientiane, "IRF Visits Provincial Laos to Gauge Religious Freedom," June 17, 2009.

32. U.S. Consulate Chiang Mai, "CNS Leaders Look to the Stars for Hope and Good Luck," April 10, 2007.

33. U.S. Embassy Rangoon, "Burma's Generals; Starting the Conversation," April 2, 2009.

34. U.S. Consulate Jeddah, "Hajj 2009/1430—An American's Inside View of the Pilgrimage," December 8, 2009.

Chapter 5. FRENEMIES

1. U.S. Embassy Brussels, "EU President Van Rompuy's Plans Following Copenhagen and for Afghanistan," January 4, 2010.

2. U.S. Mission to the EU Brussels, "New EU Leadership: Van Rompuy and Ashton Emerge to Join Barroso," November 20, 2009.

3. U.S. Embassy Berlin, "Media Reaction: U.S., India-Pakistan, Syria-Iran, Cuba, EU, Falklands, Turkey, EU-Greece," February 26, 2010.

4. "Ukip's Nigel Farage tells Van Rompuy: You Have the Charisma of a Damp Rag," *Guardian,* February 25, 2010.

5. *Sois Belge et Tais-Toi*—Bruxelles-Strasbourg, édition 2011 [television broadcast], n.d., seen on YouTube, https://www.youtube.com/watch?v=LteanfFylxE.

6. U.S. Embassy Pretoria, "Calls for Health Minister's Dismissal Intensify," August 23, 2007.

7. U.S. Embassy Pretoria, "Death of Former Health Minister Shows How Far South Africa Has Moved from Former AIDS Denialist Policies," December 21, 2009.

8. U.S. Embassy Banjul, "The Gambia: President Jammeh as Traditional Healer," January 19, 2007.

9. U.S. Embassy Banjul, "Ambassador Meets with President Jammeh," February 26, 2010.

10. Ibid.

11. Michelle Nichols, "Gambian President Says Gays a Threat to Human Existence," Reuters, September 27, 2013.

12. U.S. Embassy Riga, "Peoples Party's Junkyard Dog: Gundars Berzins," June 16, 2008.

13. U.S. Embassy New Dehli, "Mayawati: Portrait of a Lady," October 23, 2008.

14. U.S. Embassy New Dehli, "Mayawati Cancels Birthday Party, Cash Gifts Still Welcome," January 16, 2009.

15. U.S. Embassy Dushanbe, "President Rahmonov Celebrates Third Term with Precious Jewels and a New Bentley," November 22, 2006.

16. U.S. Embassy Oslo, "Jagland's Candidacy for Next COE Secretary General," March 26, 2009.

17. U.S. Embassy Berlin, "SPD Chancellor-Candidate Steinmeier Expresses Confidence Germans Will Reject CDU/CSU-FDP Coalition," September 11, 2009.

18. U.S. Embassy Managua, "Sandinistas Attack U.S. Embassy," October 30, 2009.

19. U.S. Embassy Managua, "Death to the Yanqui—Ortega Lambastes U.S. at Nicaraguan Army's 30th Anniversary Celebrations," September 17, 2009.

20. U.S. Embassy Managua, "Ortega Calls U.S. Relief Effort in Haiti a Military Invasion," January 20, 2010.

21. U.S. Embassy Managua, "Ortega and the U.S.: New-found True Love or Another Still-Born Charm Offensive?" February 25, 2010.

22. U.S. Embassy Managua, "Atmospherics of Ortega Inauguration: Chaos and Populism Trumps Security and Protocol," January 25, 2007.

23. U.S. Department of State, International Women of Courage Award, posted at http://www.state.gov/s/gwi/programs/iwoc/.

24. U.S. Embassy Kabul, "2010 Afghan International Women of Courage Nominees," December 1, 2009.

25. U.S. Embassy Kabul, "Nominations for Women of Courage," February 8, 2007.

26. U.S. Embassy Buenos Aires, "Argentina: Nomination for International Women of Courage," February 15, 2007.

27. U.S. Embassy Baghdad, "Nominations for 2009 Secretary's Women of Courage Award," October 28, 2008.

28. U.S. Embassy Harare, "Nomination for the Secretary of State's Award for International Women of Courage," November 27, 2009.

29. Dan Moshenberg, "Zimbabwean Activist 'Released,'" *Guardian,* March 12, 2013.

30. U.S. Embassy Colombo, "IWOC: Proposed Revisions to Announcement of 2010 Sri Lankan Recipient," February 3, 2010.

31. U.S. Embassy Tashkent, "MFA Drubbing over Tadjibayeva Award," March 13, 2009.

32. U.S. Embassy Tashkent, "Uzbekistan: Nomination for International Women of Courage Award," October 27, 2008.

33. "Kyrgyzstan President Roza Otunbayeva Given U.S. Honour," BBC News, March 8, 2011.

34. U.S. Embassy Bishkek, "Opposition Believes Government Reforms Will Lead to Maksim Bakiyev as President," December 18, 2009.

35. U.S. Embassy Seoul, "Seoul: Press Bulletin," February 5, 2010.

36. U.S. Embassy Damascus, "Syria Nominates Sister Clauda Isaiah Naddaf for the Secretary's International Women of Courage Award," December 3, 2009.

37. U.S. Embassy Niamey, "Niger: Woman of Courage Nominee Hadizatou Mani," October 30, 2008.

38. U.S. Embassy Berlin, "Merkel vs. Steinmeier? What Do the German Elections Really Mean for U.S. Interests?" September 22, 2009.

39. U.S. Embassy Berlin, "Germany's Next Foreign Minister?: The World According to FDP Chairman Guido Westerwelle," September 18, 2009.

40. U.S. Embassy Berlin, "FDP Dizzy from Identity Crisis and Coalition Animosity," February 16, 2010.

41. "Norm Naimark, Orhan Pamuk on Armenian Genocide," The Book Haven: Cynthia Haven's Blog for the Written Word, March 11, 2011, bookhaven.stanford.edu.

42. U.S. Embassy Ankara, "Dink Assassination Leads to National Soul-Searching," January 24, 2007.

43. U.S. Embassy Ankara, "Nationalism Turning Nasty in Turkey," February 9, 2007.

44. U.S. Embassy Ankara, "Media Reaction," August 27, 2009.

45. U.S. Embassy Ankara, "Turkish Parliament (Finally) Amends Article 301," April 30, 2008.

46. U.S. Embassy Ankara, "Turkey's Plans to Amend Controversial 'Article 301' Hung Up for Now," January 11, 2008.

47. U.S. Embassy The Hague, "Tension and Debate in Holland," November 12, 2004.

48. U.S. Embassy The Hague, "Netherlands: Overview for the President's July 14 Meeting with Dutch Prime Minister Balkenende," July 6, 2009.

49. Ibid.

50. Rachel Donadio, "Provocateur's Death Haunts the Dutch," *New York Times,* October 30, 2014.

51. U.S. Embassy Singapore, "Singapore Allows First Political Film Since 1998," September 24, 2009.

52. U.S. Embassy Abuja, "Nigeria: Scenesetter for USCIRF Visit," March 19, 2009.

53. U.S. Embassy Baku, "President Ilham Aliyev—Michael (Corleone) on the Outside, Sonny on the Inside," September 18, 2009.

54. U.S. Consulate Jeddah, "Saudi Actress Stirs Mixed Gender Audience in Jeddah," March 5, 2009.

55. Neil Slaven, *Electric Don Quixote: The Definitive Story of Frank Zappa* (London: Omnibus Press, 2009 Edition).

Chapter 6. WILD ANIMALS

1. U.S. Consulate Guangzhou, "Devouring Dragon, Disappearing Tigers: A Look at South China's Tiger Farms and Reserves," July 12, 2007.

2. See U.S. Department of State, OES Overseas, Regional Environmental Hubs at http://www.state.gov/e/oes/hub/. Robert Hormats, Under Secretary of State for Economic Growth, Energy, and the Environment, was a trendsetter in this new field of diplomacy. Having spent his graduate school days in East Africa, he developed a passion for wildlife and occasionally served as a game guide for photo safaris. During his tenure from 2009 to 2013, he took numerous opportunities to speak out on wildlife issues and wrote extensively on the topic, all the while serving in a key leadership position during the global economic crisis. See, for example, "Wildlife and Foreign Policy: What's the Connection?," http://www.huffingtonpost.com/bob-hormats/wildlife-and-foreign-poli_b_2093161.html; or "The Illegal Wildlife Trade: A Survey of Greed, Tragedy, and Ignorance," http://www.huffingtonpost.com/bob-hormats/elephants-africa_b_1514758.html.

3. U.S. Embassy Brasilia, "The Atlantic Rainforest Wildlife Trafficking Assessment," May 7, 2007.

4. See the CITES website: What is CITES? https://cites.org/eng/disc/what.php.

5. U.S. Embassy Lusaka, "Zambia Sets its 'CITES' on Exporting Ivory," February 16, 2010.

6. U.S. Embassy Dar es Salaam, "CITES: Tanzania Pushes for Ivory Sales," February 2, 2010.

7. U.S. Department of State, "Wildlife Under Siege: A U.S. Government Perspective," speech by Robert D. Hormats, Under Secretary for Economic Growth, Energy, and the Environment, Central Park Zoo, New York City, July 15, 2013.

8. U.S. Embassy Harare, "Ambassador Hall Surveys Empty Breadbasket," August 19, 2005.

9. U.S. Embassy Harare, "Poaching of Wildlife Is Rampant in Zimbabwe," May 21, 2002.

10. U.S. Embassy Harare, "Environment Suffering as Poaching Increases," September 22, 2008.

11. U.S. Embassy Harare, "Resettlement in the Farms: The Reality on the Ground," May 31, 2002.

12. U.S. Embassy Windhoek, "Ambassador Delivers Démarche: Export Permit for Cheetahs," February 9, 2009.

13. Brendan Borrell, "Saving the Rhino Through Sacrifice," *Bloomberg Businessweek*, December 6, 2010.

14. John R. Platt, "Hunter Allowed to Import Rhino Trophy in U.S. for First Time in 33 Years," *Scientific American,* April 25, 2013.

15. Michael Graczyk, "Texas Club Auction Right to Hunt Endangered Rhino," *Bloomberg Businessweek*, October 31, 2013.

16. U.S. Embassy Harare, "Zimbabwe at the Epicenter of Rhino Poaching," December 14, 2009.

17. U.S. Embassy Harare, " SAVE Valley: Struggling to Hold On," December 17, 2004.

18. U.S. Embassy Harare, "ZANA-PF Governor Forcing Himself on Amcit-Owned Conservancy," May 29, 2009.

19. U.S. Embassy Kathmandu, "Maoist Ambush Mars Annual Rhino Relocation," March 11, 2002.

20. Ibid.

21. Dan Levin, "From Elephants' Mouths: An Illicit Trade to China," *New York Times,* March 1, 2013.

22. U.S. Embassy Rangoon, "Burma Timber Industry Threatens Elephant Population," June 16, 2009.

23. U.S. Embassy Bamako, "Efforts Continue to Save Mali's Elephants," April 24, 2008.

24. U.S. Embassy Bamako, "Drought Threatens Mali's Migratory Elephant Herd," April 22, 2009.

25. U.S. Embassy Abuja, "Nigeria's Mbe Mountains Function as Important Wildlife Corridor for the Endangered Cross River Gorilla," January 26, 2010.

26. U.S. Embassy Abuja, "Great Apes, Ecotourism in Cross River, Nigeria," January 26, 2010.

27. U.S. Embassy Abuja, "Nigeria: A Glance at the State of Wildlife and Forestry in Nigeria," January 2, 2009.

28. U.S. Embassy Yaounde, "Cameroon's Lom Pangur Is World Bank's Dam Problem," June 9, 2009.

29. U.S. Embassy New Dehli, "Wildlife Conservation in India's Gujarat State Yields Impressive Dividends but Pride Leaves Lions Exposed," May 5, 2008.

30. U.S. Consulate Mumbai, "Mumbai Masala: Consul General Visits Kutch, Mundra Sez and Gir Forest in Gujarat," January 27, 2009.

31. Kumar Sambhav Shrivastava, "Gir Lions Get a Second Home," Down to Earth, April 15, 2013, http://www.downtoearth.org.in/news/gir-lions-get -a-second-home—40813.

32. U.S. Embassy Kathmandu, "Momentum Builds for the Global Tiger Initiative," April 23, 2009.

33. U.S. Embassy Kathmandu, "Kathmandu Meeting Agrees on Plans to Help Tigers Avoid Extinction," November 4, 2009.

34. U.S. Embassy Bangkok, "Asian Ministerial Continues Effort to Prevent Extinction of Wild Tigers," February 24, 2010.

35. U.S. Consulate Vladivostok, "Highway Threatens Endangered Leopard Habitat," November 16, 2008.

36. U.S. Consulate Vladivostok, "Amur Leopard: World's Rarest Big Cat at the Crossroads," November 16, 2007.

37. U.S. Consulate Vladivostok, "Forest Mafia Adapts to the Economic Crisis," January 29, 2009.

38. U.S. Embassy Zagreb, "Croatian Storks Turn Up Dead in Somalia," December 11, 2006.

39. U.S. Embassy Rangoon, "Burma's Pro-American Kachin State," January 20, 2006.

40. U.S. Consulate Rio de Janeiro, "Brazilian Police Arrest Suspect in Environmentalist's Death," March 3, 2005.

41. U.S. Embassy Yaounde, "Cameroon Forestry and Wildlife Minister Discusses CITES, Forests," February 9, 2010.

42. U.S. Embassy Abuja, "Nigeria: A Glance at the State of Wildlife and Forestry in Nigeria," January 2, 2009.

43. U.S. Embassy Hanoi, "We Eat Everything on Four Legs Except the Table," October 9, 2007.

44. U.S. Consulate Ho Chi Minh City, "Vietnam's Caged Bears: HCMC's Small Steps at Protection Aren't Up to the Challenge," February 20, 2008.

45. Charles Homans, "Zoopolitics: How Caged Animals Became a Tool of Statecraft," Foreign Policy, May 26, 2010.

46. U.S. Consulate Chengdu, "Many Panda Twins Flourish at New Ya'an Breeding Center," December 9, 2009.

47. U.S. Embassy Tirana, "Obama Mania Hits Tirana," January 26, 2009.

48. U.S. Embassy Baghdad, "Baghdad Zoo—Respite from the Urban Jungle," February 21, 2008.

49. U.S. Embassy Bangkok, "Half-Baked Idea for Zoo Increases Doubt About Thai Commitment to Wildlife," December 13, 2005.

50. See the Night Safari, Chiang Mai website, http://www.visitchiangmai.com
.au/night_safari.html.

51. U.S. Embassy Bangkok, "Half-Baked Idea for Zoo Increases Doubt About
Thai Commitment to Wildlife," December 13, 2005.

52. U.S. Consulate Chiang Mai, "Night Safari Provides Touchstone for Attack-
ing Thaksin," August 17, 2006.

53. U.S. Embassy Bangkok, "Orangutan Odysseys in Southeast Asia," November 29, 2006.

54. U.S. Embassy Ashgabat, "Turkmenistan: Only Basic Veterinary Services,"
January 8, 2010.

55. U.S. Embassy Moscow, "Gimme Shelter: Strays Find New Home in Moscow," May 15, 2007.

56. U.S. Embassy Beijing, "New Dog Rules Unleash Emotional Debate in Beijing," December 4, 2006.

57. U.S. Consulate Guangzhou, "Who Let the Dogs Out? Canine Ownership
in Guangdong on the Rise," April 11, 2006.

58. U.S. Embassy Riyadh, "Saudi Pet Ban Raises Hackles," August 12, 2008.

59. U.S. Embassy Riyadh, "Must Love Dogs," September 12, 2006.

Chapter 7. CORRUPTION

1. U.S. Embassy Sofia, "Sofia's Mean Streets," April 2, 2009.

2. U.S. Embassy Sofia, "Bulgarian Media: Lacking Money and Morals," June
18, 2009.

3. U.S. Embassy Sofia, "Bulgarian Soccer Receives a Red Card for Corruption," January 15, 2010.

4. U.S. Embassy Sofia, "Bulgaria's Most Wanted: The Skull, the Beret, the
Chicken, and the Billy Goat," September 11, 2009.

5. U.S. Embassy Sofia, "Bulgarian Government Makes Historic OC Bust,"
February 12, 2010.

6. Stephen Castle, "Law and Order, Bulgarian Style," *New York Times,* July
20, 2011.

7. Transparency International, Corruptions Perceptions Index, 2015, http://
cpi.transparency.org/cpi2015/results/.

8. Timothy Frye, "The Culture of Corruption: Russians Pay, but They Don't
Like It," *Washington Post,* February 17, 2014.

9. Joshua Yaffa, "The Waste and Corruption of Vladimir Putin's 2014 Olympics," *Bloomberg Businessweek*, January 2, 2014.

10. U.S. Embassy Kyiv, "Ukrainian Presidential Elections—On the Road to
Happiness and Other Vignettes," February 11, 2010.

11. Ibid.

12. U.S. Embassy Tbilisi, "DAS Bryza Meets Election Task Force Members," February 5, 2008.

13. U.S. Embassy Tashkent, "Parliamentary Elections in Uzbekistan: Nothing Wrong but the Big Picture," December 30, 2009.

14. U.S. Embassy Bratislava, "Regional Elections: Playing Rough in Bratislava," November 13, 2009.

15. U.S. Embassy Moscow, "Ryazan Regional Elections: Yabloko Quits, Lashes Out at Rigged System," February 19, 2010.

16. U.S. Consulate Yekaterinburg, "Bashkortostan—Waiting for Change," July 15, 2009.

17. U.S. Embassy Brasilia, "Brazil 'Monitors' Zimbabwe Elections," April 23, 2008.

18. U.S. Embassy Managua, "Nicaraguan Electoral Authority Continue Manipulation of Regional Elections," February 2, 2010.

19. U.S. Embassy Yaounde, "Cameroon: USG Sends Message on Election Agency," February 2, 2009.

20. U.S. Embassy Nassau, "Pre-Election Roundup: Momentum to FNM as Parties Hit Issues," April 30, 2007.

21. U.S. Embassy Luanda, "Samakuva Discusses Unita's Defeat and Next Steps," September 22, 2008.

22. U.S. Embassy Sofia, "Bulgaria: From Prison to Parliament," June 18, 2009.

23. U.S. Department of Justice, Foreign Corrupt Practices Act, http://www.justice.gov/criminal/fraud/fcpa/.

24. Organization for Economic Cooperation and Development. OECD Convention on Combating Bribery of Foreign Public Officials in International Business Transactions, http://www.oecd.org/corruption/oecdantibriberyconvention.htm

25. U.S. Embassy Bratislava, "Fico Fires Environment Minister, but It's No Cleanup," August 21, 2009.

26. Much of the information from this section contains cables that were written while the author served as deputy chief of mission (2007–2008) and as chargé d'affaires (2009–2010), and that bear her signature. She also attended many meetings with key figures mentioned in the cables.

27. U.S. Embassy Prague, "Defense Procurement in the Czech Republic: Shady Deals and Big Dollars," March 16, 2009.

28. Ibid.

29. U.S. Embassy Prague, "Pandura's Box: Corruption Scandal Lifts the Lid on Czech Defense Procurement," February 24, 2010.

30. U.S. Embassy Prague, "Defense Procurement in the Czech Republic: Shady Deals and Big Dollars," March 16, 2009.

31. Jan Richter, "Ex–U.S. Ambassador Accuses High-Ranking Czech Government Official of Corruption," Czech Radio 7, November 12, 2010.

32. Czech News Agency, "Former U.S. Ambassador Speaks Before Czech Court," *Prague Post,* March 17, 2014.
33. Daniel Bardsley, "Former Tatra Boss Cleared over Bribery Allegations," *Prague Post,* October 3, 2013.
34. U.S. Embassy Prague, "Corruptionism in the Czech Republic," February 3, 2010.
35. U.S. Consulate Naples, "Can Calabria Be Saved?," December 2, 2008.
36. U.S. Consulate Naples, "Report Shows Alarming Increase in Organized Crime in Naples," October 1, 2009.
37. U.S. Consulate Naples, "Organized Crime in Italy I: The Political Dimension," June 4, 2008.
38. Ibid.
39. U.S. Consulate Naples, "Organized Crime III: Confronting Organized Crime in Southern Italy," June 6, 2008.
40. U.S. Consulate Naples, "Organized Crime in Italy I: The Political Dimension," June 4, 2008.
41. U.S. Consulate Naples, "Organized Crime III: Confronting Organized Crime in Southern Italy," June 6, 2008.
42. U.S. Consulate Naples, "Organized Crime in Italy II: How Organized Crime Distorts Markets and Limits Italy's Growth," June 6, 2008.
43. Ibid.
44. U.S. Consulate Naples, "The Naples Garbage Crisis: A Case Study in Southern Italian Paralysis, with Some Signs of Hope," November 20, 2007.
45. Ibid.
46. U.S. Consulate Naples, "Organized Crime in Italy II: How Organized Crime Distorts Markets and Limits Italy's Growth," June 6, 2008.
47. U.S. Consulate Naples, "Organized Crime in Italy I: The Political Dimension," June 4, 2008.
48. U.S. Consulate Naples, "Reaching Out to Calabria," April 22, 2009.
49. U.S. Consulate Naples, "Can Calabria Be Saved?" December 2, 2008.
50. U.S. Consulate Naples, "Organized Crime III: Confronting Organized Crime in Southern Italy," June 6, 2008.
51. Ibid.
52. U.S. Consulate Naples, "Reaching Out to Calabria, April 22, 2009.
53. U.S. Embassy Dushanbe, "Dam If You Do, Damned If You Don't: Roghun Pressure Mounts," January 13, 2010.
54. Ibid.
55. U.S. Embassy Prague, "How to Succeed in Law School without Really Trying," November 6, 2009.
56. U.S. Embassy Ashgabat, "Turkmenistan: Bribery Is Pervasive in Government Services," February 23, 2010.

57. U.S. Embassy Ashgabat, "Turkmen Doctors Pay Bribes to Avoid Penalties," February 2, 2010.

58. U.S. Embassy Ashgabat, "The Translucent State of Turkmenistan," February 1, 2010.

59. U.S. Embassy Moscow, "The Luzhkov Dilemma," February 12, 2010.

60. Ibid.

61. Ibid.

62. U.S. Embassy Moscow, "Medvedev Using MVD Reform to Increase Standing," December 30, 2009.

63. U.S. Consulate Guangzhou, "China: Amcit Business Dispute Shakedowns Increasing as Economic Conditions Worsen," March 15, 2009.

64. Ibid.

65. U.S. Embassy Bratislava, "One Down, One Dirty: Corruption and Incompetence Taint Slovak Border Police," February 19, 2010.

66. U.S. Embassy Banjul, "The Gambia: Embassy Cable About Bogus Congressman in Public Domain," January 9, 2007.

67. U.S. Consulate Jeddah, "Conversations with Saudi Education Official and Journalist Describing Widespread Discontent and Anti-Americanism in the Kingdom," September 27, 2009.

Chapter 8. IRAQ

1. Christopher R. Hill, *Outpost: Life on the Frontlines of American Diplomacy* (New York: Simon & Schuster, 2014), 321.

2. Ibid. 296.

3. Karen DeYoung, "Envoys Resist Forced Iraq Duty," *Washington Post,* November 1, 2007.

4. Helene Cooper, "Foreign Service Officers Resist Mandatory Iraq Postings," *New York Times,* November 1, 2007.

5. Hill, *Outpost,* 296.

6. U.S. Embassy Baghdad, "Surge Staffing II: Ministerial Capacity Development," October 6, 2007.

7. U.S. Embassy Baghdad, "Surge Staffing I: PRT Staffing," October 6, 2007.

8. U.S. Embassy Baghdad, "Recommendation for Future U.S. Civilian Presence in Iraq," January 29, 2010.

9. U.S. Embassy Baghdad, "PRT Wasit Gets a Laugh," May 9, 2008.

10. U.S. Embassy Baghdad, "Ninewa: Songs in the Key of Ain Sifni," March 19, 2009.

11. U.S. Embassy Baghdad, "Erbil RRT: Standing Room Only Audiences for U.S. Election Expert," November 9, 2008.

12. U.S. Embassy Baghdad, "Rock Chalk, Jayhawk! U Kansas Professor Wows Kurdistan Region," March 12, 2009.

13. U.S. Embassy Baghdad, "Baghdad Requests Participation in IIP's Strategic Speaker Initiative with Walter Russell Mead," November 16, 2008.

14. U.S. Embassy Baghdad. "ECA A/S Ameri from Ambassador Ereli," July 3, 2008.

15. U.S. Embassy Baghdad, "ECA A/S Goli Ameri's Meeting with Iraqi Higher Education Officials," October 29, 2008.

16. U.S. Embassy Baghdad, "Strategic Framework Agreement Landmark Met with GOI Contribution Doubling Fulbright," June 11, 2009.

17. U.S. Embassy Baghdad, "Iraqis Desperate to Learn English," September 14, 2008.

18. U.S. Embassy Baghdad, "Progress in the Cultural Cooperation of the Strategic Framework Agreement," October 7, 2009.

19. U.S. Embassy Baghdad, "Visas for Iraqis—A Strategic Vulnerability," February 7, 2009.

20. U.S. Embassy Baghdad, "RRT Erbil: The 1991 Generation on College, Jobs," March 16, 2009.

21. U.S. Embassy Baghdad, "Educating Ali—Teaching Saddam's Lost Generation to Read," November 25, 2009.

22. U.S. Embassy Baghdad, "Baghdad U.: Students Talk Politics, Offer Blunt Views About Today's Iraq—and Us," April 6, 2009.

23. U.S. Embassy Baghdad. "Expo Najaf Draws Support from Shi'a Clerics, Generates Praise for PRT," November 12, 2009.

24. U.S. Embassy Baghdad, "The Najaf Religious Establishment in Shi'a Politics and Society," June 23, 2009.

25. Aaron D. Snipe, "Iraq/U.S. Embassy Baghdad Social Media Outreach," in William P. Kiehl, ed., *The Last Three Feet: Case Studies in Public Diplomacy* (Washington, DC: The Public Diplomacy Council, 2012), 93–107.

26. U.S. Embassy Baghdad, "Need to Generate Public Discussion on Al Qaeda's Resilience and Changing Tactics," August 24, 2008.

27. U.S. Embassy Baghdad. "Encouraging Credible Voices to Counter Violent Extremism—The Case of Iraq," December 8, 2008.

28. U.S. Embassy Baghdad, "PRT Muthanna: Rental Sheiks and Lost Iranian Weekends," January 22, 2010.

29. U.S. Embassy Baghdad, "Iraq's Border Surveillance Project Takes Shape, First on Syrian Border," February 1, 2010.

30. Joseph S. Nye Jr., *Soft Power: The Means to Success in World Politics* (New York: PublicAffairs, 2004).

31. Joseph S. Nye Jr., "Get Smart: Combining Hard and Soft Power," *Foreign Affairs* 88, no. 4 (July/August 2009).

32. Hillary Clinton, Confirmation Hearing to Be Secretary of State Before the Committee on Foreign Relations, United States Senate, S-Hrg 111-249, January 13, 2009.

33. Secretary Condoleezza Rice, "Transformational Diplomacy," Georgetown University, Washington, DC, January 18, 2006.

34. Secretary Condoleezza Rice, "Remarks on Transformational Diplomacy," Georgetown University, Washington, DC, February 12, 2008.

35. Dean Acheson, *Present at the Creation: My Years in the State Department* (New York: W. W. Norton, 1969).

Chapter 9. HILLARY CLINTON

1. Susan B. Glasser, "Head of State: Hillary Clinton, the Blind Dissident, and the Art of Diplomacy in the Twitter Era, " *Foreign Policy*, June 2010.

2. Adrienne Klasa, "Debating Hillary," *Foreign Policy*, June 2012.

3. Hillary Rodham Clinton, *Hard Choices* (New York: Simon & Schuster, 2014), x.

4. Nick Gass, "10 Moments of Over-the-Top Flattery in Hillary's Inbox," *Politico*, July 2, 2015, http://www.politico.com/story/2015/07/hillary-clinton-emails-10-most-flattering-119693.

5. Peter Nicholas, "Clinton Emails Show Blumenthal No Fan of Axelrod," November 30, 2015, http://blogs.wsj.com/washwire/2015/11/30/clinton-emails-show-blumenthal-no-fan-of-axelrod/.

6. Patrick Healy, Jonathan Martin, and Maggie Haberman, "Hillary Clinton's Handling of Email Issue Frustrates Democratic Leaders," *New York Times*, August 27, 2015.

7. Stephan Dinan, "State Department Can't Find Enough Staffers to Process Hillary Clinton Emails," *Washington Times*, October 13, 2015.

8. Matthew Connelly and Richard H. Immerman, "What Hillary Clinton's Emails Really Reveal," *New York Times*, March 4, 2015.

9. Rachael Bade, "Clinton Aides Abedin and Mills Duke it out over Email," *Politico*, October 30, 2015.

10. Ibid., 585.

11. See Vital Voices Global Partnership website, "What We Do," at http://www.vitalvoices.org/what-we-do.

12. Office of Global Women's Issues, Fact Sheet, U.S. Department of State, Washington, DC, 2013, http://www.state.gov/r/pa/prs/ps/2013/03/205866.htm.

13. Clinton, *Hard Choices*, 567.

14. Ibid., 569.

15. Ayelet Waldman, "Is This Really Goodbye?" *Marie Claire*, October 2012.

16. Justin Wm. Moyer, *"Why Women Still Can't Have It All* Author 'Devastated' by Former Boss Hillary Clinton's Reaction, Emails Reveal," *Washington Post*, December 1, 2015.

17. Yochi Dreazen and John Hudson, "Michèle Flournoy Takes Herself Out of the Running for Top Pentagon Job," *Foreign Policy*, The Cable, November 25, 2014.

18. USEU Brussels, "EU: What Is 'Mainstreaming' Women's Issues and How Can We Help?" January 27, 2010.

19. U.S. Embassy London, "Engagement on U.K. Women's Issues," February 4, 2010.

20. U.S. Embassy Kabul, "Women Activists Push for Inclusion in Reintegration Planning Process," February 26, 2010.

21. U.S. Embassy New Dehli, "India: Celebrating Women in Science: Not Yet Equal," September 8, 2009.

22. U.S. Embassy Valletta, "Malta's Engagement on Women's Issues," January 8, 2010; and U.S. Embassy Kuala Lumpur, "Scenesetter for Visit to Malaysia for Ambassador for Global Women's Issues Melanne Verveer," November 30, 2009.

23. U.S. Embassy Warsaw, "Women's Issues in Poland—Scenesetter for Ambassador Verveer's June 20–22 Visit to Warsaw," June 17, 2009.

24. U.S. Consulate Shanghai, "Shanghai Women's Federation Chairwoman on Plenum Outcomes and Future of NGOs," September 25, 2009.

25. U.S. Embassy Tokyo, "Ambassador Verveer Calls for Cooperation on Women's Empowerment Issues," December 17, 2009.

26. This quote is also attributed to Marshall Brickman, the co-screenwriter for the movie *Annie Hall. New York Times* columnist William Safire investigated further and found that the percentage varies from 80 to 90, and the subject can be either life or success.

27. Peter Baker, "Obama Offered Deal to Russia in Secret Letter," *New York Times*, March 3, 2009.

28. The White House, "Remarks by Vice President Biden at 45th Munich Conference on Security Policy," February 7, 2009.

29. Baker, "Obama Offered Deal."

30. U.S. Embassy Prague, "Czech Government Faces a Firestorm of Criticism and Attempts to Calm Fears of Russia," October 26, 2007.

31. U.S. Embassy Prague, "Czech Republic and Missile Defense: Concerns About Russians Addressed; Looking Ahead to Timeline and Economic Benefits," November 13, 2007.

32. U.S. Embassy Prague, "Czechs Raise 'Alarm' on U.S. Missile Defense Site in Europe," December 11, 2007.

33. David S. Cloud, "Video: Wrong Red Button," *Politico*, March 6, 2009.

34. The White House, "Remarks by the President at the New Economic School Graduation," July 7, 2009.

35. See Radio Free Europe/Radio Liberty, "An Open Letter to the Obama Administration from Central and Eastern Europe," July 16, 2009, http://www.rferl.org/content/An_Open_Letter_To_The_Obama_ Administration_From_Central_And_Eastern_Europe/1778449.html.

36. John Vinocur, "Central and Eastern European Countries Issue Rare Warning for U.S. on Russian Policy," *New York Times,* July 21, 2009.

37. Heather A. Conley, "President Obama's Return to Prague: An Opportunity to Reset," CSIS: Center for Strategic and Inernational Studies," April 5, 2010.

38. U.S. Embassy Bratislava, "Scenesetter for Visit to Slovakia of Assistant Secretary of Defense Vershbow," October 16, 2009.

39. U.S. Embassy Warsaw, "Repairing U.S.–Polish Relations," September 24, 2009.

40. "Open Letter to President Obama on Central Europe," The Foreign Policy Initiative, October 2, 2009, http://www.foreignpolicyi.org/content/open -letter-president-obama-central-europe.

41. Alexandr Vondra, "Letter to Obama: Five Years Later," CEPA Center for European Policy Analysis, July 10, 2014.

42. U.S. Consulate Jerusalem, "Secretary Clinton Interview with Palestinian Youth TV Garners Record Number of Viewers," March 10, 2009.

43. U.S. Embassy Bangkok, "Secretary Clinton's Bangkok 'Townterview': Substantive, Funny, and Well-Received," July 24, 2009.

44. U.S. Embassy Ankara, "Ankara Media Reaction Report," March 9, 2009.

45. U.S. Embassy Tokyo, "Daily Summary of Japanese Press," March 2, 2009.

46. U.S. Embassy Caracas, "Chavistas Feeling Boxed in by the Secretary's Interview and Latest Developments Regarding Honduras," July 8, 2009.

47. Clinton, *Hard Choices,* 29.

48. John K. Naland, "U.S. Special Envoys: A Flexible Tool," U.S. Institute of Peace, 2011.

49. Princeton N. Lyman and Robert M. Beecroft, "Using Special Envoys in High-Stakes Conflict Diplomacy," U.S. Institute of Peace, 2014.

50. U.S. Embassy Kampala, "4th PCIA Forum Tackles Indoor Pollution," April 23, 2009.

51. Clinton, *Hard Choices,* 27.

52. Ibid., 33.

53. Adrienne Klasa, "Debating Hillary," *Foreign Policy,* June 20, 2012.

54. "The QDDR: Leading Through Civilian Power," U.S. Department of State, December, 2010.

55. Secretary of State, "Global Context Section of the QDDR—Seeking Input from the Field," November 20, 2009.

56. "Clinton: Including Women Essential to Peace Processes," Georgetown University, Washington, DC, December 3, 2014, http://www.georgetown .edu/news/hillary-clinton-security-inclusive-leadership.html.

INDEX

- - - - - - - - - - -